W9-BMX-013

AMERICAN BOOK-PLATES

FOUNDED·1884·   NEW·YORK·

THE

GROLIER

CLUB·

American Book-Plates

A Guide to their Study with Examples

By Charles Dexter Allen

Illustrated with many reproductions of rare and interesting book-plates
and in the finer editions with many prints from the original
coppers both old and recent

BENJAMIN BLOM
New York/London
1968

First Published Boston 1894
Reissued 1968
by Benjamin Blom, Inc., Bronx, New York 10452
and 56 Doughty Street London, W.C. 1

Library of Congress Catalog Card Number 68-20212

Printed in the United States of America

PREFACE.

IN a few years Book-plate literature will have a place in the
catalogues of the Libraries, as
it now has in those of the
dealers in books.   The works
of   the   Hon.   J.   Leicester
Warren   (Lord   de   Tabley),
Mr. Egerton Castle, and Mr.
W. J. Hardy on the English
plates, Mr. Walter Hamilton, M. Henri Bouchot,
and M. Poulet-Malassis on the French, Herr
Warnecke on the German, and M. Carlander on
the Swedish, are all the work of master hands,
and are recognized as authorities.   In our own
country the lists and essays of Mr. Richard C.
Lichtenstein and Mr. Laurence Hutton have long
been of invaluable service, and occupy a position
both at home and abroad of undisputed eminence.

A large number of articles has also been contributed to periodical literature by those well
informed upon the subject, and numerous mono-
graphs testify to the growth of interest in this
fascinating study, and by the names of their
authors, to the class of scholars and students of
antiquarian lore who deem the humble book-plate
worthy of their attention.

In view of what has been and of what will be
written, this present modest attempt to introduce

more fully than has yet been done, the book-plates of America, needs to be understood as simply a pioneer work; a great deal of information will reward the patient and painstaking investigator of the future, which is now inaccessible, and without doubt, too, much will be found even within the present to supplement these pages.

This book could not have been undertaken nor carried to completion had the writer been denied the generous assistance and hearty sympathy of our collectors, to whom he desires to express his appreciation of the kindnesses shown him.

Especially to Mr. R. C. Lichtenstein, Mr. E. N. Hewins, and Mr. Fred J. Libbie of Boston, does he feel under deep obligation for the generous loan of their splendid collections, for ready advice and counsel, for cheerful assistance whenever asked for, and for that tangible sympathy and lively interest which are worth so much to one engaged in such work. To many others also is he indebted, both for the loan of plates and for kindly words of encouragement.

To Mr. S. P. Avery, Mr. Beverly Chew, Mr. E. H. Bierstadt, Mr. Henry Blackwell, Mr. D. McN. Stauffer, Mr. Edward D. Harris, Mr. Laurence Hutton, and Mr. E. W. Nash, of New York City; to Mr. W. G. Brown of Washington and Lee University at Lexington, Va.; Mr. H. E. Deats of Flemington, N.J.; Dr. C. E. Clark of Lynn; Hon. W. A. Courtnay of Charleston, S.C.; Miss Helen E. Brainerd of the Columbia College Library; Mr. Pickering Dodge of Washington, D.C.; Mr. Charles T. Martin, Mr. Frank B. Gay,

Mr. A. C. Bates, and Mr. John C. Parsons, of Hartford; Dr. Henry C. Eno of Saugatuck; Dr. J. H. Dubbs of Lancaster, Penn., President of Franklin and Marshall College; Mr. D. V. R. Johnston of the State Library at Albany; Mr. Nathaniel Paine of Worcester; Mr. Daniel Ravenel of Charleston, S.C.; Mr. Howard Sill of Glendale, Md.; Mr. R. A. Brock of Richmond, Va.; Mr. Howard Edwards of Philadelphia; Dr. Swan M. Burnett of Washington, D.C.; Mr. Richard Wijnkoop of Brooklyn; Mr. Bisbee of Dartmouth College; Mr. William Kelby of the New York Historical Society; and to Mr. Lyon G. Tyler of Williamsburg, Va., President of William and Mary College, does he wish to make acknowledgment for the favors which have contributed so much to the value of the work. From over the sea, particularly kind assistance has come from Rev. T. W. Carson, the veteran collector and eminent authority of Dublin.

To all others who by letter, gift, or advice have assisted him, the writer wishes hereby to make suitable and hearty acknowledgment.

The writer's thanks are also extended to those who have so kindly permitted him the use of their plates for the illustrating of the book.

A word more is due to Mr. E. N. Hewins, who very kindly, at the writer's request, accepted the labor of preparing the excellent Bibliography which appears in the volume.

CHARLES DEXTER ALLEN.

HARTFORD, CONN., June, 1894.

CONTENTS

LIST OF ILLUSTRATIONS.

COPPER-PLATES.

FULL-PAGE REPRODUCTIONS.

ILLUSTRATIONS IN THE TEXT.

Jereᵇ. Wadsworth.

AMERICAN BOOK–PLATES.

INTRODUCTORY.

E cannot venture to guess which was the first book-plate made in America, nor to say with absolute certainty whence came the first plate used in our country; but undoubtedly the latter came over already pasted into some book of a Dutch or English settler.

The larger part of our books came from England, and very few plates are found with arms of other nationalities. The colonists who came from England bringing books, brought also the home ideas concerning books, and the book-plate was a natural piece of property to acquire. Their descendants, who continued the connection with the mother-country, used plates more generally, and the fashion spread naturally. It never became very general, but was confined to those of gentle birth; the clergy, the lawyers, and men of education. We shall see that it was not confined to the men alone, but that the women of literary accomplishments also used plates.

By far the greater part of the plates are cut on
copper, but there are some woodcuts as will be
seen in an examination of the list; also, there are
some which look as if cut in silver, which was

George Lee Turberville.
Virginia.

an easier metal to work, or perhaps in type-metal.
One example is known in which brass was used,
and this old plate is now in the possession of the
writer.   The steel engravings are of rather recent
date; and while there are a number of these, the

new plates are mostly on copper. The simple labels are printed from type.

The larger part of our early plates are armorial in character; and while heraldry forms so prominent and important a feature, it is left practically untouched in the present volume. The number interested in the science is small, the authorities on coats-of-arms and on blazoning differ, and the present writer had not the time to make the

J. Thomas, print.

thorough investigation necessary to a satisfactory treatment of this interesting branch. Upon consultation with other collectors, and with their advice, it was decided to leave this subject for a future volume should any call for it arise.

A decided difference is noticed between the book-plates of the Northern and the Southern Colonies. In the South, to which came men of wealth and leisure with cultivated tastes, we would expect to find the little superfluities and niceties of daily life sooner in vogue and more

generally used.   Bringing books and musical instruments with them, retaining their connection
with the far-away home by correspondence and
visits, sending their sons to the great Universities
to be educated, and to the Law Schools for a fin-
ishing course, and ordering their clothes, books,
furniture, and all of the luxuries of life from
England, they would naturally be the first to use
the book-plate.   Very few of the Southern plates
were engraved by American engravers.   They
were nearly all done in London, when some
member of the family was over, or by order from
the Colony; for this reason the Southern plates
are better in heraldry, design, and execution than
those of New England and New York.   They
were the product of men experienced in such
work; they were all armorial and in the prevail-
ing English mode.

The earliest comers to New England had
a prejudice against coats-of-arms and trinkets
of such-like character, which their descendants,
however, soon forgot.   Pride of ancestry and love
of the display of aristocratic claims developed
when the hard circumstances of the former years
had worn off, and we find the prominent families
of the North using book-plates, and having their
arms upon their coaches.   In one important feature, however, these Northern plates differ from
the Southern, — they are mostly the work of our
native engravers, very few being done in England.

The work of these native artisans, who were
mostly self-taught in this art of engraving on
copper, is confessedly inferior to that of the Lon-

don experts found upon the Southern plates, both in drawing and execution, but their work is of more value to the collector from this very fact of their being American work. They furnish examples of native skill, both in engraving and in copper-plate printing.

The ornamentation of buttons, spoons, table-ware, and other articles of silver was already

practised when the demand for the book-plate arose, so that there were skilful men ready to turn their attention to this new branch of their art.

The War of the Revolution naturally affected the native production of book-plates, but a few years after its close, when Boston, New York, and Philadelphia were active in publishing books, the engraver found work more plenty, and very many who were employed upon the plates for the illustration of books also produced book-plates.

Nathaniel Hurd was the principal engraver of book-plates in the North before the war, though Thomas Johnson, who was born before him and who also died before he did, made some plates, while Turner and Paul Revere were also working at this period.

Henry Dawkins, in Philadelphia, came over from England, and so did the elder Maverick, who made so many plates for the New Yorkers.

The literary plates are smaller in number than we could wish, and they do not show a wide range of ideas either. Very probably some of the designs were borrowed from English plates, and were produced over again for different customers, or were freely copied by other engravers who liked, or who found customers who liked, the design of others. The plate used by *George Goodwin* is one of four of this same design. The shelf of books is also seen in the plate of *G. C. M. Roberts*, *M.D.*, *Thomas Robbins*, and the

Virtus et scientia ad uſilitatem dirigunt

Elijah F. Reed, which is a direct reproduction of the *Robbins*. Piles of books, but not the regulation "Book-pile," are seen in the *Brown* and *Lewis* plates, while the only real library interiors are the *Tayloe* plate, the *Moral Library* and the *Village Library* (Farmington, Conn.). John Allan, the old-book lover of New York, used a plate with an open book against an anchor, and the plate of

Edmund Penn shows a love for books in the dainty volumes disposed about the frame.

The patriotism of our book-lovers is shown in very many designs, which use the American flag or the eagle. The thirteen stars also, the motto of the United States, and various private mottoes of a very patriotic nature, are frequently used.

It is noticeable that as compared with the Southern plates there are but few of the Northern examples which give the address or residence of the owner; that is, speaking of the armorial plates, the printed name labels give these particulars quite often.

The *Jared Ingersoll* plate gives *New Haven* as the residence of the owner, while *Rhode Island* follows the name on the plate of *Samuel Elam.*

Other Northern plates which are so engraved are the *Colonel Eustace of New York, Comptroller Elliston* also *of New York, Lenox of Philadelphia, Atlee of Lancaster, John Franklin, Boston, New England,* and *Robert Hale of Beverly.* Of the Southern plates, *Wormeley, Waller, Tuberville, Tazewell, Skelton, Randolph,* and *Ludwell*

give *Virginia* as their residence ; *Drayton* names *South Carolina,* the *Dr. Cabell* plate names *Richmond,* and the *John Walters Gibbs* names *Charleston, S.C.* The plates used in the West Indies also show the residence quite often. There, too, as well as in the Southern colonies, the profession or position of the owner, as well as the London

John Walters Gibbs &
Charleston, S° Carolina.

ihernothin Sculp.

law school in which he was educated, are often given. Thus we have *William Blanc, Middle Temple, Dominica ; Chas. Pinfold, LL.D., Governor of Barbadoes ; Peyton Randolph of the Middle Temple, London ; Francis Page of the Inner Temple Esqr. ; William Assheton of Gray's Inn.* In the Northern examples we find *John Gardiner of the Inner Temple,* and *Jonathan Belcher, E Societate Medij Templi.*

We note also in running through the List that the occupations most often noted on the bookplates are those of the medical and the legal profession. Barristers, lawyers, and attorneys are often so named, and the initials *M.D.*, or the full word *Doctor*, are seen.

The abbreviations of other degrees are found also, and the plates of clergymen are not uncommon.

Several plates remain unnoticed in the following pages, which are probably American, but which, for lack of positive information, it is thought best not to include. Among these is an early Dutch plate which, if it could be accurately traced to its original owner, might prove to be one of the earliest plates used in America.

It seems that a word is needed in defence of the perfectly legitimate and gentle pursuit of collecting book-plates. A great deal of sarcasm

and indignation have found their way into the columns of periodical literature, particularly in England, the especial purpose of which is to trouble the humble collector, and to discredit him in the eyes of the world. He is pointed out as a destroyer of valuable books, as an animal so greedy in the pursuit of his insignificant prey as to ruin elegant bindings that he may secure worthless bits of paper, and as actually so devoid of good sense as to remove such of these as are interesting — for it is reluctantly admitted that some interest does attach to the plates used by certain men of fame in historical annals — from their rightful place within the covers of the very books read and handled by these illustrious owners.

Let it be remembered that but a small part of the many books published have a permanent value, and that a book once eagerly sought may outlive its usefulness, and come to have a commercial value of so much a pound as old paper, instead of so much a copy in different styles of

binding. Surely, no one can quarrel with the collector who removes the book-plate, found within it, from such a worn-out specimen, even if the removal necessitates the ruin of the cover. But to remove a book-plate does not necessarily mean to ruin the cover; it requires some skill and considerable patience to remove a valuable plate without injury to either itself or the cover upon which it was pasted, but it is done daily. Surely no one can find fault with this — a skilful operation resulting satisfactorily to the plate-collector and to the book-owner.

Again, no intelligent book-plate collector will separate the plate of a famous man from the book which has been its home for years, and which was once handled and read by its famous owner. Even a worthless book will thus be saved by the collector, which was fit but for the fire or the ash-heap, and which would have gone

Samuel Elam
Rhode Island

thither, plate and all, save for his discriminating eye, while a valuable book no one would think of despoiling. Would an intelligent collector, having a book from the library of George Washington, with his plate upon the cover and his autograph in its accustomed place, think of soaking off the plate and cutting out the signature ? Not at all ; no matter how worthless the book might chance

to be, the fact that it was Washington's is sufficient to insure it from any harm, while the presence of the autograph and the book-plate but
adds to the value as establishing beyond perad-
venture the original ownership.

The book-plate collector is naturally a book-
lover. He must not be accused or suspected of
crimes against his own kith and kin. He is a
harmless and useful specimen of the *genus* collector, who with assiduity, perseverance, and in-
telligence seeks to preserve these memorials of
past days, which in the rage for indiscriminate
collecting were overlooked, and are but now beginning to receive the attention they are worthy of.

It is, however, to be admitted that at first
glance, the general reader who has not developed
a special liking for the things of the past in
history, art, or biography, may see no especial
interest in book-plates. But let him examine a
collection of good plates with their intelligent
owner, who can point out to him the facts worthy
of note; let him once understand that celebrated
artists like Albrecht Durer, Jost Amman, William
Hogarth, William Marshall, George Vertue,
Bewick, Bartolozzi, and even Raphael Morghen
were willing to devote time and taste to the designing or engraving of the book-plate; let him
handle some of their work, and reflect upon the
effort the master considered so small a design
worthy of; let him see the plates of some of the
noted names in history, art, letters, medicine, the
sciences, and the professions; let him take in his
hands the plates of William Penn, the friend of

the Indian and benefactor of his race, of Laurence Sterne, of David Garrick, of Horace Walpole, of Samuel Rogers, of Charles Dickens, or
of George Washington, of John Adams, and
Charles Carroll, signers of the Declaration ; let
him see a plate engraved by Paul Revere whose

John Adams.

services in the Revolution he has known of from
his schooldays ; — let him see these and scores
more of similar interest, and he cannot fail to
respond to the enthusiasm of their owner. But
indeed it is a pursuit, the delights of which are
discernible to those only who bring to it the
capacity for such pleasures.

NAME–LABELS AND MOTTOES.

F all forms of book-plates the simplest possible is the printed name of the owner, unaccompanied by either motto, device, or ornamentation of any kind. Such a plate had *Philip Hone*, one of the founders of the Mercantile Library, and in the early twenties a mayor of the city of New York. His plate is merely a bit of paper with his name in bold script printed upon it from an engraved copper-plate.

This style of plate is not chronologically the earliest, but is taken as our starting-point because of its unrelieved simplicity; this fulfils the mission of the book-plate, — it proclaims the ownership of the book in which it is seen; not in delicate language, to be sure, not with any invitation to dip into the volume in hand, not with any evidence of the owner's taste in reading, but with a directness not to be misunderstood.

The essential part of the book-plate is the name of the owner; and while this is sufficient of itself, it is found profitable and pleasant to accompany it with an apt quotation from a favorite author, with a caution against the improper hand-

TREN A LA VERITE

James Eddy Mauran.

ling of books, with a warning of the sad result of declining Wisdom's guidance, or with an invitation to enjoy the beauties of literature and to share the benefits of careful reading. In addition to these mere typographical adjuncts an opportunity is offered for the display of those more decorative garnishments which have led to the development of the handsomer styles of plates.

Alexander Stedman's : Thomas Thaxter's, 1791 : *William W. Potter's Book : Aaron Woolworth's, Ex Dono Rev. S. Buell, D.D.* These plates use the possessive case, are embellished with borders of ornamental type, and supply some further information by showing the date of their being used, or by naming the giver of the volumes. Other styles of expressing book-ownership are afforded by the following: *Nicolas Pike His*

Book 1768: *Hannah Adams, Medfield* 179–: *The Property of John Clap, Roxbury* 1791 : *Davidis Dickinson Liber, A.D.* 1796: *Lieut. E. Trench-ard, U. S. Navy: Simeon Baldwin, Owner: Ex Libris I. G. Thomas: Library T. W. Curtis, No.: Belonging to the Library of Thomas Forrest Betton, Germantown Pa.: The Property of John Weld native of Pomfret, Conn. Resident of Pom-*

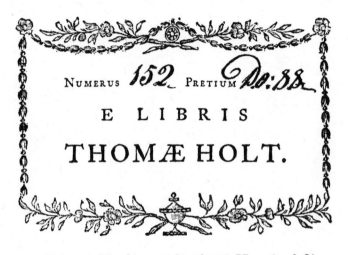

fret, Bo't of Mr. James Steele of Hartford, January 12, 1796: *W. Lewis, Ejus Liber: Johann Christoph Kunze, Prediger in Philadelphia: Emmanuel Jones e Coll; Gul; et Ma:* 1756.

These old type-set labels with their quaint borders of ornamental type, — scrolls, flourishes, stars, vines, and even grammatical signs, — are usually found to be printed on good white hand-made paper, which was seldom trimmed with care;

occasionally a tinted paper is found, — yellow more often than any other, but sometimes a blue or green; these served the less pretentious of our ancestors in lieu of the coats-of-arms and family mottoes of those of higher lineage, and are found in quantities throughout the New England and Middle States: even farther south they are not uncommon, but are not so numerous.

JOHN CAMPBELL,

Charles County.

In making up these ornamental borders the type was usually set in the form of a parallelo-gram, occasionally in a square, oval, circle, or diamond, and seldom in fanciful shapes. The most ambitious plate of this kind which has come under my observation is that which once graced the books of Mary McGinley; this is a rather large plate, and the type is set in the form of an urn, within the lines of which are given the motto and the owner's name.

A step in advance of these wholly typographi-cal examples are those which employ a woodcut

border to surround the name, and instances can
be given of such a border enclosing the name
printed from type; festoons of flowers or of cord,
and draperies of cloth, were also used as a simple
setting for the owner's name.   In this connection
mention may be made of the work of T. Sparrow,
an obscure engraver of Maryland; no heraldic
or pictorial examples of his workmanship have
been identified, and he probably confined himself

to the simple woodcut designs of which but a
small number are known.   Always using a border of floriated scrolls, he never omitted an original contrivance which is the characteristic mark
of his work, —a group of thirteen stars surrounded
often by a wreath.   This is always found in a
prominent place, and is an indication of his patriotism as well as that of the owner of the plate.

It must not be supposed that the heraldic
book-plate was an outgrowth or development of

the name-label: not at all; they were contempo-
raneous and were both used in England long
before they were here.

Coming now to the subject of mottoes, we find
a wide field to travel over, many languages to
read, many quotations to recognize, with hints
and warnings, and even threatenings, by the score,
from jealous book-lovers.   Mottoes readily fall
into two classes: those which are chosen by the
owner for some personal reason, and those which
are family mottoes, and which are used without
thought because they are a family inheritance, or
with a commendable pride in such legacies from
an honorable ancestry.   Latin is the language
most often used probably, though English is a
strong rival, while German, French, Greek, and
even Hebrew and Welsh are also found upon our
book-plates.   Sentiments opposing the habit of
book-borrowing are of frequent occurrence, and
in some instances are of such severity as to leave
no doubt of their effectiveness.   For brevity and
pointedness the following example can hardly be
exceeded : —

> *This book was bought and paid for by*
> *D. C. Colesworthy.*
> *Borrowing neighbors are recommended*
> *to supply themselves in the same manner.*
> *Price seventy-five cents.*

On the book-plate of *D. W. Jayne* the following verse from the Bible is used : —

> *Go ye rather to them that sell and buy for yourselves.*
> *Matt. Chap. xxv. ver.* 9.

Thomas O. Selfridge,

B O S T O N,

1799.

Verses from Holy Writ are quite frequently used on plates, and the style of expression found in the Psalms and Proverbs is borrowed as adding an authoritative emphasis to the words of caution and advice, —

The wicked borrow, and returneth not: do thou not like unto them.

Return what thou borroweth with the most sacred punctuality, and withhold it not.

On the plate of a book-lover in Charleston, S.C., —

And ye shall keep me until the fourteenth day. And it shall be when thou hast made an end of reading this book. Send me away unto my master. Ex. xii. 6: Jer. li. 63 : Gen. xxiv. 54.

Every one has suffered from book-borrowers,
even from school-day times, when the rude
doggerel, —

> *Steal not this book for fear of shame,*
> *For here you see the owner's name,*

or its variant,

> *Steal not this book for fear of strife,*
> *For its owner carries a huge jack-knife,*

was printed in coarse letters across the cover of
the books most likely to go astray. How irritat-
ing it is to find the very volume one needs at the
moment, missing from its accustomed place on
the shelf; if anything is lacking to complete the

(N°.   44   )

THE PROPERTY OF THE

Worcester Circulating Library Company.

First Cost, £ *05 12 7*

FINE *for detention,* 4 1/2   *per day.*

torment of the discovery, let it be impossible to find out who has taken the desired volume, or to get any clew as to when it went or where!

Private Library of J. N. Candee Cole, This book is not loaned. Matt. xxv. 9.

———

Read not books alone : but men, and be careful to read thyself. The property of John Lambert, South Reading.

———

To Borrowers of Books.
You *remember, my friend, I freely comply'd*
With the favour you asked me, and fully relied
On a favour from you, which, tho' promised, I find,
As it hasn't been granted, is out of your mind,
To return in due time what I've wanted to see,
The Book, which 'tis long since you borrow'd of me.
Another I now with reluctance implore,
'Tis only to ask that you borrow no more.

———

Stolen from J. W. Houx,

———

Book-keeping taught in three words,
Never lend them.

The would-be borrower who finds these senti-ments in the book he was about to ask for will scarcely be encouraged to do so, and for direct-ness they are exceeded by only one example, in which the owner's name is followed by the simple declaration, *He does not lend books.* The motto on the plate of the late *George Ticknor* — *Suum cuique, To every man his own* — was also calcu-lated to discourage the borrower.

But some people do lend books, and have them returned too, — in good second-hand condition. And so it comes about that the proper use of books is made the subject of another class of mottoes.

My Friend! Should you this book peruse,
Please to protect it from abuse:
Nor soil, nor stain, nor mark its page,
Nor give it premature old age:
And, when it has effected all,
Please to return it ere I call.

The following verse is common property and is found on several plates: —

If thou art borrowed by a friend,
Right welcome shall he be
To read, to study, not to lend,
And to return to me.

Not that imparted learning doth
Diminish learning's store,
But books, I find, if often lent,
Return to me no more.

Read slowly,
Pause frequently,
Think seriously,
Return duly with the corners of the leaves not turned
    down. ─────

Neither blemish this book, nor the leaves double down,
Nor lend it to each idle friend in the town:
Return it when read, — or if lost please supply
Another, as good to the mind and the eye.
With right and with reason you need but be friends
And each book in my study your pleasure attends.

─────

If through respect or love I lend
This book unto my worthy friend,
He must not soil, abuse, nor tear,
But read with diligence and care;
And when its contents you have learned,
Remember, it must be RETURNED.

On the plate of *Samuel W. Francis* appear the
following lines : —

Any one may borrow,
But a gentleman returns.

─────

The property
of
Thomas C. Cowan.

Borrower,
read, mark, and AVOID
the former part
of
Psalm xxxvii. 21.

─────

IF *you borrow, freely use it,*
Take great care and don't abuse it:
Read, but neither lose nor lend it,
Then unto the owner send it.

Never open a book farther than to bring both sides of the cover on to the same plane. Never lend a borrowed book, but return it as soon as you are through with it, so that the owner may not be deprived of its use. You may think this a strange request, but I find that although many of my friends are poor arithmeticians, they are nearly all of them good book-keepers.

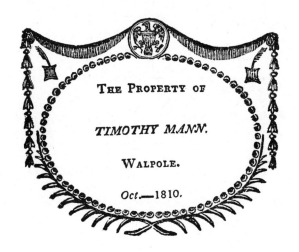

THE PROPERTY OF

TIMOTHY MANN.

WALPOLE.

Oct.—1810.

In strong contrast to all the preceding are those mottoes of generous souls who find no pleasure in withholding their treasures, but who wish to have it understood that they are for the use of all; not very many are bold enough to thus advertise their willingness to lend, but a few do so, and generally by the use of the Latin, *Sibi et amicis*, or *et amicorum*.

Sentiments in praise of books and reading are not uncommon, and quotations from classic

writers both in prose and poetry do good service
on book-plates.   Pope's well-known lines —

> *A little learning is a dangerous thing,*
> *Drink deep or taste not the Pierian Spring;*
> *Where shallow draughts intoxicate the brain,*
> *But drinking largely sobers us again.*

are found on an old American plate.
  On a recent New York plate, —

> *Far more seemly were it for thee to have thy Study*
> *full of Books than thy purse full of money.   Lilly.*

On a Maine plate, —

> *Who learns and learns but does not what he learns,*
> *Is one who plows and plows but never sows.*

> *Weigh well each thought, each sentence freely scan,*
> *In Reason's balance try the works of man.*
> *Be bias'd not by those who praise or blame,*
> *Nor, Servile, Yield opinion to a name.*

On a recent Boston plate, —

> *Un bon livre est un bon ami.*

On a recent Western plate, —

> *A jolly goode booke,*
> *Whereon to looke,*
> *Is better to me than golde.*

On a recent Washington plate, —

> *A trusty villain, sir, that very oft when I am dull*
> *with care and melancholy lightens my humour.*

UN BON LIVRE
EST UN BON
AMI

EX LIBRIS A.L.HOLLINGSWORTH.

The mottoes on the plates of those who have achieved distinction have a peculiar interest, especially when chosen by the owners themselves. The plate of *Henry W. Longfellow* bears the following line : —

Non clamor sed amor,

which is from an unknown author and is found in the following verse : —

> *Non vox sed votum,*
> *Non chordas sed cor,*
> *Non clamor sed amor,*
> *Sonat in aure Dei.*
>
> *Not voice but vow,*
> *Not harp-string, but heart-string,*
> *Not loudness but love,*
> *Sound in the ear of God.*

The motto of *George Washington*, — *Exitus acta probat*, is not given in the accepted lists as the family motto of his ancestors, but it may have been such. The meaning of it has brought out criticism recently because of its Jesuitical sound, — "*The end shows the deed.*" But this may also be taken as a patriotic utterance in view of the part of the illustrious owner of this plate in the Revolution.

On the plate of *William Penn* we see a motto most fitting for the character he sustained, *Dum clavum rectum teneam* — "*While I hold to glory, let me hold to right.*" In the plate the third word is omitted, as the engraver found the motto too long for the space reserved, and through some

George Bancroft

blunder the *r* in *clarum* is changed to a *v*, which
makes no sense at all.

On the plate of *George Bancroft*, the late historian, a chubby cherub bears a panel on which
is the motto, *Sursum corda.* Another plate was
also used by Mr. Bancroft which was in all
respects like the above, except that the motto
was changed to ΕΙΣ ΦΑΟΣ.

The plate of the late *Mr. George W. Childs*
has the following motto whose appropriateness is evident at once, — *The pen is mightier
than the sword.* Above this a second motto
of equal appropriateness is given, — *Nihil sine
labore.*

On the plate of *Dr. Oliver Wendell Holmes*,
Per ampliora ad altiora is given upon a ribbon
under a beautiful drawing of the "chambered
nautilus."

WILLIAM PRESCOTT

Instances of mottoes which are cleverly made
to carry some meaning, or some word, which will
be seen at a glance to be taken from the name
of the owner, are found often.

On the plate of *Harold Clarence Ernst* this
motto is given, *Ernst ist das leben.*

On the plate of *George Curry, D.D.,* — *Sic curre capias.*

On the plate of *Edward Spencer Dix,* — *Quod dixi id feci.*

In concluding this list of mottoes two from the Welsh can be instanced, one on the plate of a New York collector of Welshiana, which is *Cared Doeth Yr Encilic,* meaning, " *The learned love the*

things of the past."   The other is on a Washington plate, and reads thus, *A fynno Dwy y Fydd*,
meaning, "*What God wills, will be.*"

In the list of languages used on book-plates,
we must now include the Volapük, for we have
the first instance of its use already in a New
York plate ; the motto reading, *Menad bal pukbal*,
and meaning, " *One humanity, one language.*"

Edward Penington

Philadelphia.

Eugene Field.

ARMORIAL BOOK–PLATES.

OOK–PLATES admit of many
kinds of extraneous ornamen-
tation, and wholly apart from
the special function of recording the ownership of books,
they serve as expressions of
artistic taste; they lend themselves readily to many forms
of design, and have passed
through several changes or " styles " in the three
hundred years of their existence; they can be
dignified or flippant, serious or punning, of artistic
beauty or positive deformity; they can express
the owner's choice of reading and can preserve
lines from his favorite authors; can convey warning or invitation, and can, in short, be made a
very personal affair.

The first book-plates were heraldic. In those
early and, in some senses, good old days, before
the schoolmaster was abroad in the land, when
learning was the possession of the aristocrats
and the churchmen only, and consequently when
handwriting was not in use among the people,
families were distinguished by emblems which
were known of all. These heraldic devices were
painted on their shields, carved upon their walls,

engraved upon their breast-plates, woven upon their banners and their tapestries, displayed upon their own persons, upon those of their dependents, and even upon their animals and the furniture and books of their homes; even the purely

Gabriel Jones,
Attorney at Law, in Virginia.

ornamental and ephemeral luxuries came to be adorned with the family coat-of-arms.

The armorial bearings, stamped upon the back or sides of a book, or printed upon paper and pasted within the cover, were sufficient, without a name, to identify the family to which it belonged. Libraries descended from father to son, and were kept intact for generations; and the family arms and motto were the most appropriate label possible.

Warren, one of the first to study book-plates and to give to others the benefit of his researches, has divided the armorial plates into general classes, and has given them suitable names, which are accepted the world over. A considerable number of subdivisions has been made; and while they may be serviceable where book-plates are plentiful, they are but an incumbrance to the collector of the early plates of America, for our examples are few in number, and are quite sufficiently distinguished — for the purpose of the present work, at least — by the following styles: Early English, Jacobean, Chippendale, Ribbon, and Wreath. Distinctive, easily remembered characteristics pertain to each of these, and fairly accurate dates of their adoption and continuance can be given.

Adopting then the nomenclature of Warren, and following his lead, we come now to consider the meaning of the different styles and the diversity of their designs.

The very earliest class is the Early English, in which the shield of arms is present with all its accessories. In these plates the mantling is very profuse, and in large full-rounded curves surrounds three, and often all four, sides of the shield. This is the only ornamentation, nothing incidental being added as yet; the name of the owner is usually or often accompanied by a title and address, and quite frequently also by the date.

We have but few examples of this style; perhaps the most satisfactory as an example of the class will be the plate of *Joseph Dudley*, dated 1754. (This plate was really engraved much

earlier than this. Hurd erased the original name, and cut the present one with the date in its place.) In this the mantling, running out beyond the edges of the shield, curls both upward and downward, and completely envelops three sides;

the design takes on a strong resemblance to oak
leaves, and a single leaf of this is engraved upon
the helmet: the background, or space enclosed
within the scroll-work, is filled in with perpen-
dicular lines which might be taken for the tincture
gules; in the name-bracket, the oak-leaf pattern
is again made use of, forming a neat finish to the
ends.

Jer. Dummer
Anglus Americanus .

In the plate of *The Honourable Wm. Car-*
michael, Esqr., the mantling is not so completely
transformed into the oak-leaf design, although the
latter is here apparent. The plate of *Jer. Dummer,*
Anglus Americanus is peculiar in that the space
enclosed by the scroll-work is lined with the solid
brick wall of the later Jacobean style; in this the

mantling is less striking than in the *Dudley*, but it surrounds the shield well, and curves upward about the crest. In the *Minot* plate, which is very peculiar and rather difficult to classify, the

Minot

mantling is very unworthy of the name; it does not proceed from the helmet, nor indeed from anywhere in particular, but in wild and very eccentric fashion, envelops the crest and most of the shield; the field of the shield is tinctured *azure*, and it is

enclosed within a border or moulding which nearly
surrounds it, but leaves a portion at the base un-
protected; a further peculiarity of this moulding
is that it is an integral part of the helmet, for it
curves over at the top of the shield and actually
proceeds from the helmet.

A very fine example of this style is the *Francis
Page* plate.

The next style is the Jacobean, commonly
spoken of as existing from about 1700 to about
1745; the styles overlap naturally, and no hard-
and-fast period can be established within which
only one particular style of plate was used. Examples of the Jacobean plate are found in England
which would date later than 1745, and the style
which succeeded this was used somewhat before
the year which begins its accepted period: the
dates of the periods, then, are approximate. The
names by which the different styles are known
have all a good reason for their acceptance,
although each one was suggested by differing
circumstances.

The style of book-plate in vogue at the time of
the last James is designated as Jacobean; and,
while it continued in use long after the death of
the deposed monarch who gave it its name, any
change in its designation would be misleading.
The principal features of this style are its heavy,
carved appearance, the evenly balanced propor-
tions, and the exact coincidence of the two sides
of the design. The shield, always of regular outline, is usually placed upon an ornamental frame
whose background, or lining, is either filled in

with a fish-scale pattern, diapered into the lozenge form or built up solidly with a wall of brick. This lining shows at both sides of the shield, below, and, less often, above it; its sides are convoluted; they run out in foldings and scrolls resembling the carving on wood, and are often worked into

FREDERIK·PHILIPSE Esꟼ

elaborate patterns: sometimes, too, the design is surrounded by a carved moulding which makes a heavy frame of rectangular form and massive appearance. This style of plate, well-handled, is exceedingly handsome, and is capable of more repose and dignity than any other. Very forbidding indeed, and over-solemn, are some examples, but in the main the purely Jacobean plates are

very pleasing. Among the accessories usually
found are a scallop-shell with the concave side
turned towards the observer, and placed either
below the shield to support it, or above it to set
it off: this shell is always looked for in the Jacobean plates, and indeed a shelly motive is apparent
throughout very many examples. The helmet and
mantling are conspicuous, especially the latter,
as it is often enlarged and emphasized by being
drawn into the general scheme of decoration;
very full, reaching far down the sides of the
shield-frame, and indeed often curiously woven
into the convolutions of the frame itself, it at
times loses its significance: grotesque faces sometimes peer from the ornamentation, and heads of
satyrs and demons are frequently used to rest the
base of the shield upon. In some instances the
name is placed upon a bracket similar to the upper
part of the plate in decoration, or, again, it may be
seen upon a small curtain or lambrequin caught
up at the ends with string. Very often, too, no
setting is provided for the name, and it is simply
engraved beneath the design. Eagles, lions, termini, cherubs, and sometimes cornucopiæ of fruit
or flowers, angels blowing upon trumpets, and
stiff stalks of flowers are introduced into the ornamentation. But these do not succeed in enlivening
the style of the plate materially, for it is essen-
tially heavy, conservative, and formal in design
and spirit. No graceful airiness rests upon it, and
it provokes no joyous sentiment, but rather rouses
respect and enforces stateliness. The general appearance of the Jacobean plate is as if carved

from wood. We do not expect old carving to be anything but solid and immobile, and these characteristics are present in this style of book-plate. Indeed, Warren, in his chapter on the Jacobean style, says that no antiquary can fail to note the strong similarity of treatment and design between the wood-carving preserved in the churches of the time of Charles the Second and the mouldings on the monuments of the same period, and the book-plates of the style we have considered. Our finest example of the Jacobean book-plate is found in the work of Thomas Johnston, who made the plate of *William P. Smith, A.M.* This is a typical example of the later Jacobean style, and is worthy of particular study. The Elizabethan shield is set against a frame which is very elaborately carved and ornamented; the lining is covered with the fish-scale pattern, and this extends also to the arms and convolutions upon the sides. At the base of the shield the scallop-shell is in position as prescribed, and is surrounded by a little frame of its own; the mantling is very slight indeed, breaking out from the wreath and also from the lower part of the helmet, in short and simple spirals. The motto is found on a ribbon which is gracefully strung upon the scrolls at the bottom of the design.

In the *Spooner* plate, by Hurd, the shield, also of Elizabethan pattern, is set against a diapered background; beneath the shield, within a little frame, the head of a sphinx is seen; term-figures are placed in the scroll-work at either side, and from their hands depend bouquets of flowers;

DEUS NOBIS HÆC OTIA FECIT

Thomas Johnston Sculp.

William P Smith AM

the crest is overarched with a bit of old scallop-shell, and the motto is given on a plain ribbon which, wholly unsupported, maintains a curved position under the whole design.　In the *Andrew*

Andrew Tyler.

Tyler plate, also by Hurd, a grotesque face supports the shield, the lining is elaborately diapered, and a festoon of cloth depends from the lower scrolls of the frame.　In the small-sized plate of *John Allen*, the lining is embellished with the simple lattice-work, in two patterns.

CITO PEDE AETAS

PRÆTERIT

Jacob Sargeant.

Closely succeeding the Jacobean, and indeed coming into use before the latter was wholly discarded, the Chippendale style of book-plate may

John Durand Esq.

be regarded as in a way an evolution from the Jacobean. If the parent was dignified and conservative, the offspring was dainty and progressive; the Jacobean style maintained its dignity and decorous nicety to the end, but the Chippendale, which started in with a taking air of modest and light gracefulness, in strong and pleasing contrast to the solidity of its predecessor, rapidly assumed a most elaborate and ornate manner, and finally

sank into a wild, riotous, and well-nigh sensuous profusion of decorative expression, which being too heavy for it to sustain, bore it down to its end. The character of the Chippendale plate, while attractive and beautiful in its pure form, had essential elements of weakness, which, hardly able to resist development, were certain to cause its downfall.

As is natural to suppose, the name was bestowed upon this style because of its assimilation of the ornate and flowery spirit which the famous T. Chippendale at this period introduced into wood-carving and upholstery. As compared with its immediate predecessor, the differences in this style of plate are seen to be principally the

Myles Cooper *LLD* Coll·Regis Nov·Ebor·in America,Præfes,et Coll·Reginæ de Oxon·Socius·&c

liberating of the decorative features from the stiffness which thralled them in the Jacobean. Not now resembling ponderous carvings in oak and mahogany, but rising free and unrestrained, the rose branches and sprigs seem to be copied from Nature herself; not arranged with careful nicety and labored uniformity as formerly, but springing from any convenient niche, they add grace and delicacy to the whole design. The helmet is seldom

seen in this style of plate, the mantling is consequently absent, and the bracket supporting the
shield of arms undergoes a transformation; the
convolutions and scrolls on the sides become finer,

freer, and less imposing; the shield is never found
of any set rectangular pattern, but often is pear-
shaped, shell-like in form, or indeed not unlike the
oyster or the human ear in general outline; the
scallop shell which formerly served as a base for
the shield to rest on, is now broken into dainty

fragments with the pectinated edges disposed about the shield itself; the name-frame is no longer a cloth curtain, but is a scroll with indented edges and curling outlines.

In its highest development the Chippendale plate is a beautiful piece of work; the richness of its curves, its plentitude of graceful scrolls, its profusion of roses in garlands or on the stem, and the elaborate detail noticeable in all its parts,

combine to make a plate of delightful airiness and
dainty nicety; but in the hands of weak designers,
as pointed out by Warren, its possibilities of over-
ornamentation were seized upon, and we find the
most unexpected and incongruous assortment of
figures from life, architectural fragments, allegorical subjects and other features not to be
included in any particular class, occupying convenient places about the escutcheon; we find
sleek shepherds clad in the fashionable clothes of
the day, — knee-breeches, ruffled shirt with Byron
collar, large felt hats, and buckled shoes; we see
would-be shepherdesses in big hooped-skirts, very
low-necked bodices and slight waists, wearing
frizzly hair and Gainsborough hats, and carrying
dainty crooks; scantily draped figures recline
under the trees, while attendant cupids make
music or hasten up with books. Turning from
these pastoral scenes, we come across plates which
have a most frightful dragon with scaly body,
forked tail, and fiery, bulging eyes, who spits fire
as he crouches among the roses; in others we
find cornices, columns, arches, and urns; fountains,
hand-glasses, ships, nautical instruments, lambs,
dogs, — in short, it is useless to name the great
number of irrelevant articles which were made use
of. The plate was made to carry any amount of
heterogeneous ornamentation which the designer
fancied; it seems in some cases as if the details
were employed with rightful reference to the
tastes or pursuits of the owner, but in the greater
number the fancy was allowed free play.

Hurd's work furnishes us with the best examples

PROSPICERE
Jean Fecit

ULCISCI
Royal Exchange

QUAM

Peter Manigault
of the Inner Temple, Barister at Law
South Carolina.

of the pure Chippendale style; the *Chandler* plate, the *Wentworth*, and the *Dumeresque* are good examples; Dawkins gives us the later and debased Chippendale with all its profusion of

CHRISTI SERVITUS VERA LIBERTAS

Samuel Vaughan Esq.

extrinsic ornamentation. The *Samuel Vaughan* plate is a very fine example of good Chippendaleism, and may be taken as a standard by which to recognize the features of this style. The *Robt. Dinwiddie* plate is a fine example of this style, though the heraldry may be questioned: this, according to Hardy, is of Scotch make.

In the Ribbon and Wreath style, which came into vogue in England about 1770, and in the

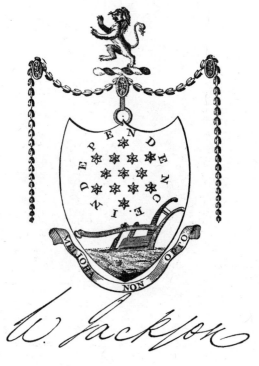

United States not much before 1790, we note a return to simplicity. The later Chippendale plates, with their over-burdened frames, now yield to this quiet style, which is unassuming and very pleasing. In this the shield is usually heart-

FLORIFERIS UT APES IN SALTIBUS
OMNIA LIBANT, OMNIA NOS
JOHN WILLIAMS *Esq*

FLORIFERIS UT APES IN SALTIBUS
OMNIA LIBANT OMNIA NOS

John Williams

shaped, is not set against a background, and has absolutely no carved work about it; the shield is often unsupported, but is sometimes hung by ribbons or festoons from wall-pins above; the decoration, as the name suggests, consists princi-

DeWitt Clinton.

pally of ribbons, and wreathing in various forms. At the present day we use in our wall-paper, upholstery, and wood-carving on furniture and mantels, and even on outside cornices, a certain form of garland or festoon tied with ribbon which we call "Colonial"; in a general way this resembles the decoration features of the Ribbon and Wreath book-plate. From wall-pins with fancy oval or round heads, festoons of flowers depend above the shield; branches of holly and palm, often tied with a ribbon whose fluttering ends bear a motto or the name, are crossed beneath the shield, and their graceful sprays extend up either side. Some of the festoons are rich with blossoms, others, more slender, are of leaves only, while a few are made of cloth; the full garlands are usually hung from above the shield, while the thinner style is draped in any place and manner acceptable to the designer, and with more or less of gracefulness, as his skill permitted. This style of plate calls for nothing more than its legitimate features to render it effective and satisfactory, and in general the plates are in the pure style; but in some of the New York plates, there are books, writing materials, and bits of landscape introduced under the shield.

The *Thomas Johnston* plate by Maverick is a fine example of this style. Maverick was the most prolific worker in the Ribbon and Wreath, while Callender and Rollinson also used it very largely. The *Prosper Wetmore* plate by Maverick, the *John Sullivan* by Callender, and the *Horatio Shepherd Moat* by Rollinson, are all excellent examples.

VIRTUTEM HILARITATE COLERE

Richard Wynkoop

PICTORIAL AND ALLEGORICAL BOOK-PLATES, AND PLATES OF COLLEGES, LIBRARIES, AND SOCIETIES.

ESIGNS which are wholly pictorial or which are meant to convey meaning by their symbolism are not very numerous with us. This style of design is no better suited to the plates of public libraries, schools, and societies, than to those of individuals, but nearly all of our early examples of this style are found to belong to the former class.

One of the early personal plates of this kind is that of *James Parker*, who was a collector of curios, medals, and books. He was a conductor on the old Western Railroad, and ran the first train between Worcester and Springfield. This plate is fully described in the List.

Of an entirely different style is the plate engraved by Harris for *Henry Andrews*. This is pictorial, introducing classical features, but hardly rising to the height of allegory. The plate of *Bloomfield McIlvaine* is also pictorial, and probably allegorical, as the figure seems to represent History. In the *Samuel Parker* plate we have

No. 161. *Anthul...*

allegory with a label to identify it; for the bank on which the muse of History reclines is labelled *Clio*. A very peculiar pictorial plate is that of *Edward Pennington*, which seems to represent an overflowing reservoir.

The plates of *McMurtrie, Kip, Mann, Russell, Swett* and *Hooper* are good examples of the class. Examples could be given at greater length, but as all are carefully described in the List, the reader is referred to it.

The most interesting of the old society and

EMOLLIT MORES.

N.º

NEW-YORK *Society* LIBRARY.

Engᵈ by P. R. Maverick 65 Liberty-Street.

1572

MOLLIT·MORES

NEW·YORK·SOCIETY
LIBRARY.
1789

P Maverick Sc. Crown Street

library plates are the three of the *New York
Society Library*, the two of the libraries in Farmington, Conn., and that of the *Society for Propagating the Gospel in Foreign Parts*.

In the plates of the *Society Library* allegory
is rampant. Minerva appears in all of them, and
in the two by Maverick is the principal figure.
In both of these she appears to an American
Indian, whose attitude shows his deep appreciation of the benefits of education as offered by the
resplendent goddess. In one case she is represented as having just arrived from Olympus, and
is still encircled by clouds; in the other, she
seems quite at home in the alcove of the library,
and has taken a suitable volume from the shelf
for the use of the savage. In the plate by Gallaudet for this library the allegory is extended,
and other prominent inhabitants of the abode of
the celestials are present. The arts and sciences
which the books of the library treat of are represented by implements and symbols easily
recognized.

The plate of the *Monthly Library in Farmington* also uses allegory. The designer and
engraver of this plate was Martin Bull, an old
deacon in the village, who was quite an interesting man. He was a goldsmith, a maker of
silver buttons, and spoons; a manufacturer of salt-
petre when needed by the army, a conductor of
church music, town treasurer for eight years,
clerk of probate for thirty-nine years, a strong
patriot, and a writer of long and appallingly
solemn letters to the youth of the village when

This Book belongs To the

Monthly Library

IN FARMINGTON
N.º 131.

LAWS

1 Twopence p.r day for retaining
A Book more than one Month.
2 One penny for folding down a Leaf
3 3/ for lending a book to a Nonproprietor.
Other Damages appprais'd by a Committee.
5 No Person allowed a Book while indebted
for a Fine.

The Youth, who, Led by WISDOM's guiding Hand,
Seeks VIRTUE's Temple, and her Law Reveres:
He, he alone, in HONOUR's Dome shall Stand,
Crown'd with Rewards, & rais'd above his Peers.

M. Bull J.ᵗ T. Lee's Sculp

63

at college. The library was founded in 1795, — about as soon as our soldier-citizens could settle down into reading stay-at-homes, — and was conducted upon the plan of monthly exchanges. On the first Sabbath of the month all members would assemble in the evening and pass in their books and receive others, the choice being auctioned off. Two dollars and a half a month was thus realized, and the meeting was the event of the month to the sturdy inhabitants of the quiet town, to say nothing of the younger folk, to whom it must have afforded coveted opportunities for pleasant meetings, and quiet walks along the lanes. On the first day of the new century, January, 1801, the library changed its name to that which appears upon the book-plate, and on which the good deacon exhibited a specimen of his highest art. Previously to this date it had gone under the name of " The Library in the First Society in Farmington," and its first book-plate, probably engraved by the good deacon, had the simple name with no pictorial accessories.

Contemporaneously with this, another library called the *Village Library*, was in operation, and continued until 1826, when it was merged with a third. This library also had a book-plate, but it was undoubtedly beyond the powers of the engraver of its forerunners. In this we see the interior of a room, in which a young lady patron of the library is storing her mind with those choice axioms which, if put in practice, far exceed the attractiveness of mere personal beauty; so says the couplet beneath the picture.

No. 254

VILLAGE LIBRARY.

Beauties in vain their pretty eyes may roll:
Charms strike the sense, but merit wins the soul.

The plate of the *Society for Propagating the Gospel in Foreign Parts* is also pictorial, and represents a ship of the Society, with its missionary, approaching the shore of savage America: this plate is dated 1704, and is very curious and interesting. The society grew from the efforts of one Rev. Thomas Bray, who established thirty-nine parochial libraries in the American Colonies for the purpose of propagating the doctrines of the Church.   In 1698, King's Chapel, Boston, received some two hundred books from this society, which were described as "an arsenal of

sound theological, ecclesiastical, and political doctrines for the Ministers of His Majesty's Chapel."   For the prevention of loss or embezzlement, and that they might be known wherever

VESTRA CURA ALITUR

1804.

SOCIAL LAW LIBRARY
Boston

found, " in every book, on the inside cover shall be these words, ' Sub auspiciis Wilhelmi III,' and also the Library to which they belong, thus ' E Bibliotheca Bostoniana.' " This must have been in addition to the plate we are considering, as no words descriptive of particular ownership are given : possibly this plate was used in all the books belonging to the society, and the supplementary one was for use in each individual library.

College plates are as a general thing very plain, but the plates used by the societies supported by the students and the alumni, are often very elaborate. The early societies in Harvard and in Yale had curious and very interesting examples of the allegorical and symbolic plate.

The *Hasty Pudding Society* and the *Porcellian Club* of Harvard College, the *Linonian Society* and the *Brothers in Unity* of Yale College, are examples. In Dartmouth College, the *Social Friends Society*, and in the smaller colleges numerous other fraternities and societies, used plates of simpler style.

The books of the Library of Harvard College were marked with plates by Hurd and Bowen, as noted in the list ; on these plates, the gifts of various benefactors are recorded, with the class to which they belonged, conditions regarding the gift of the books, or a statement of the fund from whose income the money for the books is derived.

The plate of the *Library of Congress* is an engraved label having the name and spaces for

RESPONDET · SEGES · VOTIS

1808.

HASTY PUDDING LIBRARY.

Fox

1$33

5712

LINONIAN LIBRARY YALE COLLEGE

entries surrounded by a border of oak leaves and acorns: the design is very neat, and is old in appearance.

A very beautiful plate is used by some *Orphan Asylum*, which does not give its full name upon its plate. In this a beautiful picture of the Christ blessing the little ones is given; the line " For-

asmuch as ye did it unto one of the least of these, ye did it unto Me," is given under the vignette.

In the plate of the *Library of the New York State Agricultural Society*, which was incorporated in 1832, Ceres is seen in the field; behind her the sheaves of wheat extend in rows; one arm clasps a cornucopia, and with the hand of the other she extends a wreath.

In a great many instances the plates of libra-

ries had no pictorial features, or indeed anything
at all ornamental, being but the printed rules governing the users of the books.   Two examples of
this kind of plate are given below.

This VOLUME
belongs to
PRICHARD'S
Circulating Library,
Containing nearly Two Thousand Volumes,
In Market Street, Baltimore,
where
LADIES OR GENTLEMEN
may become
READERS
By subscribing for one Month, three Months or by
Agreement for a single Book. Said Prichard has also a
very great Variety of NEW and OLD BOOKS for Sale.
He, likewise,
Gives Ready Money for New and Old Books.

Union Circulating Library,
201 *Chestnut Street, Philadelphia.*

Subscribers to pay in advance, six dollars for a year:
three dollars and fifty cents for six months: two dollars
for three months: one dollar for one month: each sub-
scriber to have three Duodecimo volumes, or one Octavo
and one Duodecimo at a time. A subscriber detaining
an Octavo longer than four weeks or a Duodecimo longer
than two weeks to pay as a non-subscriber. For each
Octavo one eighth of a dollar per week until the end of
the fourth week when the rate was doubled. For a Duo-
decimo one sixteenth of a dollar per week until the end
of the second week.

Constant attendance at the Library from Sunrise till
8 *o'clock in the evening.*

In mentioning a few examples of the plates recently made for societies and libraries, no attempt is made to furnish a complete list, nor even tc mention all the attractive plates, but to speak of a few which seem of especial interest.

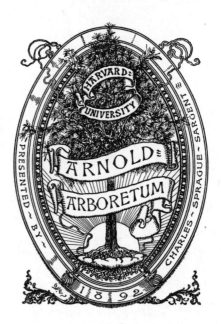

A pleasing architectural plate is used in Columbia College Library to mark the books of the *Avery Architectural Library.* This was designed by Russell Sturgis, and is in the form of a memorial window or mortuary mural tablet. The central panel bears the inscription, and the date MDCCCXC is given below.

The plate of the *Arnold Arboretum*, designed by George Wharton Edwards, is very attractive; the just-rising sun shines upon a white pine which stands within an elliptical frame; the names of the Institution and of the University appear upon ribbons which float from the pine. The plate is dated 1892, and is signed, *G. W. E.*

The same artist designed the first book-plate of the *Grolier Club* of New York City. In this, Atlas is seen supporting the arms of the club within a circular frame which bears the name, and the date of the founding of the club, 1884; rich foliations with a pounced background surround this central design. The plate is signed *G. W. E.*

The *Public Library* of the old whaling town of *New London* has a plate which is wholly nautical in construction; the name is given on a wheel which is held by a seaman, while the captain stands by in pea-jacket and rough-weather helmet, giving orders; the sail, which rises behind them, affords space for the number of the book; below the deck on which the mariners stand, are seen harpoons and spears of various sizes and kinds; two dolphins are disporting in the waves. This plate is signed by the name of the artist in full. It is by Mr. Edwards.

The *Sutro Library* of San Francisco uses a plate which gives a large and interesting picture of the natural resources of the locality, and the enterprises carried on in its vicinity; the motto, *Labor omnia vincit*, appears on the ribbon which floats in the air.

NEW-YORK SOCIETY LIBRARY

Aθηναι

Nosce teipsum

E. Gallaudet. Sc.

1754

The *Watkinson Library* of Hartford uses one of the very few portrait plates in the country; just why this style of plate should not be common is not easy to understand. They are used in Boston and Worcester, as mentioned below, but these instances are all that occur in public libraries. In this plate the portrait of David Watkinson, the founder of the library, is enclosed within an oval frame which bears the name and the date of incorporation, 1858. The plate is signed by the American Bank Note Company, New York, and is an excellent piece of steel engraving.

Almost all of the historical societies use plates in which the arms of the state or city in which they are located, are used. The *Pennsylvania*, *Connecticut*, and *Maine Historical Societies* have plates of this kind. In the last-named plate an inescutcheon bears four important dates in the history of the state of Maine.

1605, *First voyage along the Coast by Waymouth.*
1649, *Election of Godfrey as Governor.*
1678, *Usurpation of Maine by Massachusetts.*
1820, *Separation from Massachusetts.*

The *Rowfant Club* of Cleveland uses a small plate representing the corner of a library; the open window admits the fading light of the sun, which is sinking into the sea; the lattice swings idly, and the pile of books on the table proclaim a busy day.

A very striking plate is used by the *University Club of Washington*. A wall of rough-faced stone is pierced by a small quatrefoil window in which

a book is laid; the date 1891 is stamped upon the side of the book. Below this, Ionic columns support the wall; between them, in a smooth

space, is carved the name and city of the club. The plate is signed *Hy. Sandham.*

In the *Boston Public Library* a large number of different plates is used for the volumes coming from different legacies or funds, and in very many

cases these plates give a portrait of the donor.
Thus we find these portraits on the plate used in
the books from the Ticknor Fund, the Phillips
Fund, and the Franklin Club Fund. The books
remaining from the library of Thomas Prince are
also marked with a plate which gives his portrait
and a picture of the old meeting-house, in which
he preached, and in which the books were stored
at one time.

Portraits also appear upon the book-plates of
the *American Antiquarian Society*, which gives
that of Ginery Twichell; and the *Massachusetts
Historical Society*, which has a plate giving a
portrait of James Savage.

The public libraries of to-day do not usually
use elaborate plates in their book-covers; simple
labels, with perhaps a city or corporation seal, are
the common kind.

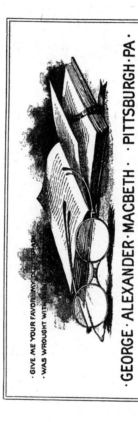

· GIVE ME YOUR FAVOR: MY DULL BRAIN

· WAS WROUGHT WITH

·GEORGE·ALEXANDER·MACBETH· ·PITTSBURGH·PA·

BOOK–PLATES OF SPECIAL INTEREST.

EVERAL reasons can be given for the fact that collectors regard some book-plates as of more value than others. With book-plates, as in other lines of collecting, rarity is a desirable feature, and is a prominent element in deciding values.

All of our early American plates can fairly be called scarce when compared with the foreign examples of the same period, for they outnumber ours, fifty to one; but many among ours are rarer than others. The *John Franklin*, brother of Benjamin, signed by Turner, is an exceeding rare plate; the *Thomas Dering*, signed by Hurd, is very rare. The plates of *Stephen Cleveland, Samuel Chase, Francis Kinloch, Edward Augustus Holyoke, John Vassal, Lewis De Blois, Lenthal, Apthorp*, the *John Pintard*, by Anderson, and many others are not seen in many collections. The plate of *George Washington* is the most valuable probably of our plates; and while we know the location of a good many of his books that have the plate within the covers, they are in no way obtainable: this plate is not very common, but more copies of it are owned than of some others.

The libraries of our early days, while of respectable size, were not so large as to require the

Stephen Cleveland

printing of thousands of book-plates; fire and mob violence have destroyed many books of those old collections and their plates with them. Harvard, Yale, William and Mary, and Princeton have all suffered the loss of books by fire, while many smaller private libraries have been thus devastated. Mr. John Pintard used to say that he had seen the British soldiers carrying away books from the library of Columbia College to

barter for grog, and a similar fate from similar hands overtook many of the books stored in the belfry-chamber of the Old South Church, Boston, while later in our history, worse depredations were committed in the Southern cities by soldiers, who took the liberty which war accords to con-testants, to despoil many a building, both public and private, ruining books, records, paintings, and other property of antiquarian and historical value. So that the early American plates, at the first not so very numerous, have been reduced at times by wholesale measures.

A second item of interest to the collector is the signature of the engraver of the plate. Signed plates have a value over those which are not signed. The identification of a plate, or the determination of its age, may be considerably strengthened if the engraver's name appears upon the copper. Then, too, the name of a famous engraver lends much additional interest to a plate. A book-plate signed by Paul Revere arrests the attention of any observer at once, and establishes a value to the same. Likewise a plate signed by Hurd, Doolittle, Dawkins, Anderson, Maverick, Callender, or Turner is worth much more to the collector than one of equal age but of unknown workmanship.

Dated plates also rank among the more valuable examples. A glance at the chronological list will show how small a number of these we can boast: many of those appearing in the list, too, are simply printed name-labels, which do not rank as high as the more pretentious specimens. Our very earliest dated example is the label of the *Rev. John Williams*, 1679, the first minister in Deerfield, Mass., and who with his wife and children was carried into captivity by the Indians in 1704. Coming next are the plates of *Francis Page*, 1703, and *William Penn*, 1703, but they are both of English make. The plate of *Thomas*

[ ]

Isaiah Thomas

Prince, who was for forty years the pastor of the Old South Society in Boston, is a simple label dated 1704. The plate of *Thomas Dering*, signed by Hurd, and dated 1749, is the first American plate by an American engraver that is both

signed and dated. The *John Burnet*, by Dawkins, dated 1754, is next in order; then comes the *Greene* plate, by Hurd, 1757, the *Albany Society Library*, 1759, concerning which very little is known, and every few years an example until we come to the opening of the century.

Naturally the artistic quality of a book-plate influences its value; the more elaborate designs are preferred to the plain armorials or the printed labels. Pictorial plates, introducing bits of landscape, interiors of libraries, or allegorical subjects, are sought for, as are plates which are accepted as particularly good types of the different styles. In addition to these technical reasons for valuing one plate more highly than another may be given others which will appear more reasonable perhaps to the general reader. All articles belonging to the noted men of the past have a certain antiquarian value greater than attaches to the kindred belongings of their contemporaries of lesser or no fame. So with book-plates.

A glance at the list will show a goodly number of names which we remember with pride and interest; the names of patriots, orators, lawyers, statesmen, officers of the army, officers of the state and nation, members of Congress, signers of the Declaration, governors, old-time merchants, authors, divines, physicians, and not a few of that plucky number who stood by the King in trying times — the American Loyalists. Quakers, too, as well as royal office-holders, and titled Americans are among those whose book-plates have come down to us.

Of our early Presidents, the plates of George Washington, John Adams, John Quincy Adams, and John Tyler are known to us. All of these except the last, which is a plain printed label, are armorial.

Members of the Boston Tea Party, of the

Constitutional Convention, and of the early Assemblies are among those whose plates we know.

Of royal officers we have: Craven, one of the Lords Proprietors of South Carolina; Elliston, Collector of His Majesty's Customs at New York;

John Quincy Adams.

Sir William Keith, Governor of Pennsylvania; John Tabor Kempe, Attorney-General under the Crown at New York; and William Penn, Proprietor and Governor of the colony which bore his name.

Owners of large estates, employers of numbers of slaves, merchants whose vessels carried on a trade with remote and prosperous shores, and who established names that have endured, used book-plates which are still known to us. Among these are the plates from the following families, well-known in New England: Ames, Bowdoin, Cabot, Chandler, Chauncey, Coffin, Lodge, Lowell,

Minot, Quincy, Sears, Winthrop, Barrell, Greene, Perkins, Swan, Vassall, and Vaughan.

Of those well-known in and about New York may be mentioned, Clinton, Colden, Constable, Cutting, De Peyster, Duer, Ellery, Goelet, Hoffman, Ogden, Paulding, Phillipse, Pintard, Van Cortlandt, and Van Rensselaer. To these should be added the Livingstons, which family had the largest number of book-plates of any we know.

In Philadelphia were the Logans, Morgans, Powels, Banckers, and Hamiltons; while further South, the Lees, Lightfoots, Tayloes, Wormeleys, Pages, Cabels, Tubervilles, Armisteads, Byrds, Blands, Bollings, Dinwiddies, Fitzhughs, Hubards,

Livius.

Magills, and Randolphs used plates and were families of prominence and distinction.

Among the prominent Loyalists are Chalmers, Cooper, Hallowell, Hamilton, Livius, Lloyd, Oliver, and Robinson. Of titled Americans the following used book-plates: Fairfax, Gardiner, Murray of Dunmore, and the Pepperrell families.

Of the early authors we can mention Alsop, Antill, Bozman, Byrd, Dana, Key, Stith, and Abercrombie; of physicians, Assheton, Bond, Beatty, Holyoke, Middleton, and Jeffries; of the statesmen, Bayard, Carmichael, Dana, Duane, Gal-

latin, Jay, Lewis, Marshall, Norris, and Randolph.

Among the early clergymen can be named Apthorp, Boucher, Williams, Jarvis, and Provoost.

Allen and Thomas, early printers; Aitkin, who made the first American edition of the Holy Bible; and Bartram, the great botanist, used plates, which are described in the list.

Bloomfield, Brearly, Banister, Chester, Eustace, Hale, Mercer, Schuyler, Sullivan, and Varick are among the soldiers of the Revolutionary army; and of the orators we have Otis and Randolph.

Coming now to the signers of the Declaration, we find that we know thus far the plates of eleven of them: John Adams, Charles Carroll, Samuel Chase, Thomas Hayward, William Hooper, Francis Hopkinson, Benjamin Rush, Richard Stockton, George Taylor, Oliver Wolcott, and George Wythe.

Surely the book-plates of all these men whose mention stirs patriotic feeling, are of exceeding interest, and worthy to rank with any in point of value and appreciation.

No book-plate, however, is of greater interest to the American collector than that of *George Washington*, not alone by reason of the prominence of that eminent man, but because of the scarcity of the plate, the high price it brings, and the interesting fact that it is the only American plate which has been deemed worthy of counterfeiting.

A genuine contemporary print of this plate is readily recognized by the connoisseur. The plate has no striking features, but is a regular design in the pure Chippendale style. The arms are displayed upon a shield of the usual shell-like form, and the sprays and rose branches of this style are used in the ornamentation of the sides of the escutcheon. The motto, *Exitus acta probat*, is given upon its ribbon at the base of the shield, and the name is engraved in script on

EX LIBRIS
EDWARD HALE BIERSTADT

NVNC MIHI

MOX ALIIS.

the bracket at the bottom of the design. In general appearance the plate is like scores of Chippendale plates of the period.

The interesting question of the probable engraver of the plate has arisen, and in a most

readable article from the pen of Mr. R. C. Lichtenstein, in the "Curio," on the Library of Washington, the following opinion is advanced: "It was his [Washington's] habit as a general rule to write his name on the right-hand corner of the title-page and place inside his book-plate. It has been a matter of uncertainty as to whether that

book-plate was engraved in England or in this
country.   Washington, like other Virginia gentlemen before the Revolution, was in the habit of
ordering goods every year from London; but we
have searched the various orders to his agents in
London, and examined as far as practicable the
items of his household expenses, without finding
any such item.   The strongest argument that can
be said in its favor proving it to be American
work is the poor heraldry displayed in its coat-of-
arms, general make-up, and drawing.   It will be
noticed that the engraver has placed a wreath
under the crown (an absolute heresy), and this,
with the faulty drawing of the raven, makes the
whole plate a very slovenly piece of work.   No
engraver with any knowledge of the fundamental
laws of heraldry would be guilty of drawing such
a coat-of-arms as this.   The arms of Washington
engraved on his seal and ring, undoubtedly cut in
England, are correctly done.   It seems more than
probable, if the plate had been done in England
that the engraver would not have been guilty of
making such blunders.   We have seen a great
many English plates, but have never noticed one
bearing these peculiarities.   From its general appearance we should say that the plate was made
in America somewhere between the years 1777
and 1781."

Collectors are divided in their opinions upon
this question, and although not ready to hazard a
guess at the engraver, the present writer believes
the plate was engraved in England, and would
place the date nearly a decade earlier.   As the

friend of the Fairfax family, Washington might have had the plate made upon the occasion of their ordering work of the same kind from England, or, indeed, it might have been a gift to him from them, or from some admiring friend. As he was a methodical man, the fact that no entry of an expense for such an article is found in his records may lend color to the presentation theory. As to the errors in heraldry, there is a plate of one Richard Washington, which has all the peculiarities of this plate, and this is signed by Bickham, who was an English engraver of some note. He was a trifle early perhaps to have been the engraver of the *George Washington* plate, but he may have made the plate which served as a copy for it. But whether the plate was of domestic or foreign make, we know that the copper was in this country, and that impressions were made from it not so very many years ago. The late Mr. Mauran of Newport knew the man who owned this, and it seems that having printed what he deemed a sufficient number of re-strikes from it, this man, fearing lest others would in time get it and make more prints, cut the copper into pieces and going out on a bridge over the Schuylkill River, threw them in! There they may be looked for by any who choose.

The counterfeit of this plate appeared in an auction sale of books, in the city of Washington, about the year 1863. The late Dr. W. F. Poole with Dr. J. M. Toner was present at the sale. The plate was placed in these books for the purpose of getting a higher price for them than could otherwise have been obtained. These gentlemen detected the fraudulent plate, and denounced it as such in the auction-room, and the books brought only their actual value as books. Copies of this plate turn up now and then, and the unsuspect-

ing are still deceived by it. It is readily detected if one is forewarned. The work is manifestly inferior to the good plate, the alignment of the name is poor, the quality and appearance of the paper belie its professed age, and the printing is of decidedly different appearance, being bold and strong in the genuine, and weak and thin in the forgery. A further difference is noted in the crest, which is tinctured *gules* in the forgery and *sable* in the genuine. These plates are sometimes claimed to be genuine and to be an early and unsatisfactory piece of work, which Washington rejected, and which was replaced with the other and accepted plate. This idea is plausible perhaps to some, but to any who had information from Dr. Poole it is an impossible theory. Another source of confusion is in the reproductions of the plate which have been made from time to time to illustrate works on the life of Washington, some of these being quite faithful duplicates of the genuine plate with its trifling flaws; but the paper and the printing are usually conclusive proof of the age of the print. It is safe to say that there is but one genuine Washington plate. It is true that the re-strikes of the original copper are about, but these, too, are readily distinguishable by the printing and paper.

The plate of *Bushrod Washington*, nephew of George, is also of much interest, and the manifest similarity of its design to some of the plates by Dawkins has led to the suggestion that he made this plate. But to the mind of the writer, Dawkins was not a man of originality, and was a regular copyist when it came to book-plates; the similarity of the plate of *James Samuels* to this plate is rather to his mind a further evidence of the clever adoption of a reasonably good design by Dawkins, than of his having been chosen by Judge Washington to engrave his book-plate. The design of this plate is more spirited than any of the authenticated work of Dawkins; indeed, it surpasses the plate of the General in that respect.

The arms are the same in these two Washington plates. In his "Barons of the Potomac and the

Rappahannock" (published by the Grolier Club, 1892), Mr. Moncure Daniel Conway has referred to the older form of the arms as used by earlier members of the family. The earliest shields held "*Gules on a barre argent 3 Cinquefoiles of ye first.*" The second step was made by changing to the

following, " *Gules on a fesse sable* 3 *mullets.*" The last and present form is, "*Argent, two bars gules: in chief three mullets of the second.*" These last, it is claimed, suggested our national flag.

The plate of *Elizabeth Graeme* of Philadelphia should be noted here, as it is the only example of

an heraldic plate used by a lady of colonial times. It is fully described in the list.

Leaving now these older plates of special interest to be discovered in the Lists, we turn to a few modern plates which are worthy of particular attention.

The plate of *Daniel Webster* is a plain armorial

with the motto, *Vera pro gratis*, on the ribbon below the shield.

The etched plate of the late *James Eddy Mauran*, the early collector of American and other book-plates, was an armorial of very handsome appearance. The shield is surrounded with the style of decoration used on the Chippendale examples, oak leaves being used in lieu of mantling.

An earlier plate in two sizes shows some differences in the design.

The plate of the late *George W. Childs* seems wholly in keeping with the career of its distinguished owner. The sword, broken into pieces by the quill, is depicted within an oval garter which bears the motto, *Nihil sine labore*. The words from Lytton's Richelieu, *The pen is mightier than the sword*, are also given just within the frame.

Coming now to mention a few plates of our well-known men of letters, we naturally accept the plate of *Oliver Wendell Holmes* as worthy of the chiefest place. In this the motto, *Per ampliora ad altiora*, is given on a ribbon beneath a beautiful representation of the " Chambered Nautilus," the

> Ship of pearl, which, poets feign,
> Sails the unshadowed main, —
> The venturous bark that flings
> On the sweet summer wind its purple wings
> In gulfs enchanted, where the Siren sings,
> And coral reefs lie bare,
> Where the cold sea-maids rise to sun their streaming hair.

" If you will look into Roget's ' Bridgewater Treatise,' " said the Autocrat one morning, " you

PER AMPLIORA AD ALTIORA

Oliver Wendell Holmes.

will find a figure of one of these shells and a section of it. The last will show you the series of enlarging compartments successively dwelt in by the animal that inhabits the shell, which is built in a widening spiral. Can you find no lesson in this?

> " ' Build thee more stately mansions, O my soul,
>   As the swift seasons roll !
>   Leave thy low-vaulted past !
>   Let each new temple nobler than the last,
> Shut thee from heaven with a dome more vast,
>   Till thou at length art free,
>   Leaving thine outgrown shell by life's unresting sea.' "

A plain armorial plate with the motto, *Vitam impendere vero*, and the name in fac-simile of his autograph, was used by *J. G. Holland*.

The plate of *Brander Matthews*, designed by Edwin A. Abbey, represents the discovery of a mask of the old Greek comedy, by an American

Indian. With feathers stuck in his scanty hair, and his tomahawk laid on the ground beside him, he appears to deliberate upon the possible use of the enormous face which grins at him from his knee. On a circular frame surrounding this picture the following words from Molière are given, *Que pensez vous de cette comedie*. The appropriateness of the design is apparent for one who is a collector of the literature of the French drama, and

the author of several books relating to the stage both in America and France.

In the plate of *Edmund Clarence Stedman*, the author of " The Poets of America," we see Pan piping in the sylvan glades; the shepherd and the nymph are charmed by the music, and the god is apparently at the height of his effort. The frame surrounding the design bears the words, *Le Cœur au Metier*, which were suggested by the address of Matthew Arnold to the Authors' Club in 1883. This plate is made in three sizes.

The plate of *Thomas Bailey Aldrich* presents within a square frame a picture of a black bird resting upon a comic mask; the heavy panelled frame bears the owner's name and the words, *His Mark.* In his essay on American Book-plates, Mr. Laurence Hutton questions whether this black bird is representative of the Daw, and symbolic of Margery of that name.

In the plate of *Eugene Field* we have a beautiful example of the plain armorial, unaccompanied by motto or ornamentation of any kind.

Of similar character is the plate of *Richard Grant White.* This is armorial, but the motto, *The right and sleep*, is given, and the shield is decorated in a conventional manner, with mantling and scrolls.

A pleasing library interior is used by *Arlo Bates.* This represents an Oriental interior; a youth in scull-cap and flowing hair is reading a large book; a lily stem rises from a vase of striped Tyrian glass at his side; rows of books are seen at his back; and out of the arched window the distant fields are seen, with the palm and cypress trees on the hillside. This plate is produced in a new manner, being a gelatine print or half-tone direct from the pencil sketch. It preserves a very soft and pleasant effect; indeed, one feels sure it will smirch if rubbed.

Laurence Hutton in his plate places a full-length statue of Thackeray within a canopy, which seems to be a niche within a bookcase. Volumes flank both sides, and the amiable face of the drastic writer looks directly at the beholder.

The name of the owner is given on a ribbon at the bottom of the design.

The books of the lamented actors, *Edwin Booth* and *Lawrence Barrett*, were marked with book-plates, the former using a plain armorial with no name engraved upon it, and the latter showing the mask of Tragedy upon an open volume, with the motto, *Esto quod esse videris.*

The reading monk, with the nimbus and star over his head, is seen in the plate of *Edward Eggleston.* The sentiment, *Flie fro' the presse and dwell with sothfastnesse,* is given in old English letters.

Mr. Rossiter Johnson uses a very plain but effective label bearing the initials *R. J.* printed within a plain ruled border : all in red ink.

The patriotic motto of *General Winfield Scott* is the family motto of the Scots of Whitislaid, Scotland, and well did the character of the man who used the book-plate depicted below coincide with its meaning.

It would be interesting to extend this list of plates used by men well known throughout the length and breadth of our land, but, unfortunately, many whose names will occur to the reader do not use a book-plate.

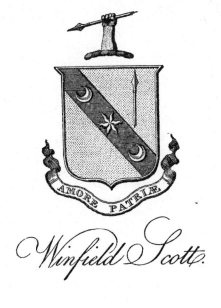

EARLY AMERICAN BOOK–PLATE ENGRAVERS.

ATHANIEL HURD, who was born in Boston, Feb. 13, 1730, and who died in 1777, was the best of our early engravers of book-plates. Very little is now known of him, the principal source of information being an article in the third volume of " The New England Magazine," published in Boston in 1832 by J. T. and E. Buckingham. The only known portrait of Hurd, which is copied from an original painting of him by Copley, and which in 1832 was owned by a descendant of Hurd in Medford, Mass., also accompanies this article, and shows him as a young man with smooth face, very pleasing and intelligent features, and wearing a cap, white neck-cloth, and clothes of a pattern which give him a decidedly clerical appearance.

The only book-plate work mentioned in this article is the large plate for Harvard College. It is said that the prints done in red ink were for use in the highly valuable books which the students were not allowed to take from the library. Several brilliant caricatures, a portrait of the Rev.

OLD BOOKS TO READ · OLD PRINTS TO SCAN

W. F. HOPSON

TO CARVE · OLD FRIENDS

EX-LIBRIS

NEW HAVEN

OLD WOOD · TO GREET

1893

No.

Dr. Sewell of the Old South Church, done in 1764, and a few other examples of his art are mentioned. He is (probably inaccurately) claimed to be the first person who undertook to engrave on copper in the United States. He was a man of natural talent and real genius, was self-instructed in his art, and was regarded as the foremost seal-cutter and die-engraver of his time, in this country.

The following advertisement from the Boston "Gazette" of April 28, 1760, is of some interest: —

"Nathaniel Hurd Informs his Customers he has remov'd his shop from Maccarty's Corner on the Exchange to the Back Part of the opposite Brick Building, where Mr. Ezekiel Price kept his Office, where he continues to do all Sorts of Gold-smiths Work. Likewise engraves in Gold, Silver, Copper, Brass, and Steel, in the neatest Manner, and at reasonable Rate."

Hurd worked principally in the Chippendale style; he made some plates in the Jacobean and a few in the Ribbon and Wreath styles, but he died before the latter was much in use, and the former was really going out when he took up the making of plates. Judging from the appearance of his work, his first attempts were in the Chippendale style, and the few Jacobeans he made were done after he had attained considerable efficiency.

One of his earliest specimens was undoubtedly the plate of *Edward Augustus Holyoke*, the famous doctor of Boston, who lived to be one hundred years old, and who was but a year or two the senior of Hurd. In this plate he used a design which he evidently believed he could improve upon, and in which he felt there were good features, for we find a number of future plates of very similar design but much better execution. In the Holyoke plate the work is very crude, the lines are stiff, the drawing is poor, and the lettering of the motto and name are not good. An ugly scroll is placed under the name, and the festoon of cloth which is draped at the bottom of the frame and around the motto ribbon is especially poor; the shell at the base of the escutcheon which figures so often in future plates is here used, and the queer little flow of water from it would not be recognized as such were this the only specimen in which it occurs; the arrangement of the rose sprays, the form of the shield, and the employment of the shelly edge show a thorough study of the elements of this style. Very likely this design was copied in great part from some foreign example which had come into his possession.

In the *Thomas Dering* plate, which is the earliest plate dated and signed by an American engraver, this same design is improved upon; it is more compact in appearance, a little freer in execution, and the drawing is improved. The name is still not very well engraved, and top-heavy flourishes weigh down the capitals.

In the *Theodore Atkinson* plate the same design is still further improved upon; the flow of water from the scallop shell is here caught in a little bowl, a little additional flowery ornamentation is added, and the heraldic drawing is better. The name is again embellished with graceless flourishes.

The design seems to reach perfection in the *Wentworth* plate; every feature is markedly better, the water still flows out of the scallop shell, the same shaped shield is used and the motto is placed upon a graceful ribbon with ends which

Robert Hale Esqr.
OF BEVERLY
N. Hurd Sc.ᵗ

run off into fancy foliations. The name is neat in appearance, but still there are too many scrolls.

In the plate of *Robert Hale of Beverly*, the old festoon of cloth noticed in the Holyoke plate is seen again, and no motto is given. The name is fairly well engraved.

Later developments of this style are seen in the plates of *Henry Marchant, Danforth, Nathaniel Tracy*, and *John Marston;* in these some of the

John Chandler Junr Esqr

N Hurd Sculp

features of the former are wanting, but they are evidently a legitimate progeny in the matter of style.

Another, and without doubt the highest type of the Chippendale plate which Hurd made, is seen in the *John Chandler, Jr.*, the *Dana*, the

Philip Dumeresque, the *Vassall*, and the *Wilson* plates. In these the shield becomes larger, the whole scheme of decoration shows more fine detail work, and the effect is lighter, more graceful, and seems at once the work of a master. The

names are engraved in large bold type, with a characteristic dash after the last period.

In the Jacobean style, the earliest of Hurd's work is undoubtedly the *Lewis De Blois*. This is crude in workmanship, not very good in drawing, but excellent in design, and faithful to the characteristics of the style; the shield is placed against a frame which is lined with the regulation fish-scale pattern; the sides are richly foliated, the

FOLLOW·REASON

Joshua Spooner.

N·H·urd *Sc.* ʹ

mantling is profuse and very well drawn, and the name is placed upon a fringed curtain which is tied up at the ends with ribbon.

The handsomest Jacobean plates by Hurd are the *Robert Jenkins*, the *Spooner*, and the *Andrew*

Tyler. In the former the lining is diapered, the scroll work at the side of the arms is very fine, and at the bottom, under the shield, a small vignette of a ship under full sail is very pretty. At the top of the scrolls on either side two turbanded female heads peer at each other across the crest.

In the *Tyler* plate the frame is very similar to the Jenkins, the lining is diapered, and the scroll at the side are the same. The little vignette at the bottom, however, is displaced by a sour face with gray hair. The two faces are replaced by urns filled with flowers, and the old cloth festoon is draped below the whole design. The *Spooner* plate bears no resemblance to the others, and is a more graceful design. The lining is latticed, the Sphinx head under the shield is enclosed within a frame of its own, and at either side are term figures from whose hands depend bouquets of flowers; the crest is overarched with a bit of the old scallop shell, and the motto is on a ribbon, which, wholly unsupported, maintains a curved position under the frame.

The Jacobean plates of *Benjamin Greene* and *Peter R. Livingston* are almost identical in design; the small frame which encloses the shield is lined with the fish-scale pattern, the mantling is handsome and profuse, and the motto ribbon is stretched in rather stiff manner below the frame.

Only two examples of the Ribbon and Wreath style are known as Hurd's work, the *John C. Williams* and the *Jonathan Jackson.* These are both signed, and are very similar in design. Garlands of roses depending from rings above follow closely the outline of the heart-shaped shield, and the ribbon for the motto is placed beneath, and is ornamented with fancy ends.

In the " detur " plate for *Harvard College* Hurd conformed to the English manner and adopted

the seal-shaped design.   The arms are displayed upon a heart-shaped shield which is enclosed within a circle which bears the name and motto, and this again is enclosed by a wreath of holly branches.

Hurd's work is the most interesting found in our early days, and a study of it shows him to have been progressive as well as painstaking. The Ribbon and Wreath style did not come into general use in England until about 1770, yet Hurd, who died in 1777, had used it. The colonies could not be expected to adopt the new styles of the old country immediately, and the condition of things from 1770 on to the time of Hurd's death was not such as to encourage the introduction of "fads" or to allow much time for the development of the fine arts.

A word must be said about the heraldry on Hurd's book-plates. This science, heraldry, was not held in such general esteem among the New Englanders as it was further south, and while many of the governors and men of high standing in the Northern colonies brought armorial seals with them, a great many who used them did so without strict heraldic authority, and when it became the fashion to use coats-of-arms in various ways, the herald painters of those days, who had but slight knowledge of heraldry and who were possessed of a copy of Guillim or some other writer on the subject, would find therein the arms of some family bearing the name of their prospective customer, and without further research would proceed to produce the coat as described. Not always were these arms so ordered correctly borne; indeed, there is much uncertainty about the arms used after about 1730 when our native engravers and painters took up the work of producing arms upon orders. Such seals as were brought by the colonists from England, and such as were used by their descendants are undoubtedly correct, but the questionable arms are those which, as mentioned above, were looked up in this country only, by means of such heraldic works as were at hand. The presence of the arms then

on some book-plates cannot be relied upon as sufficient and indisputable proof of their owners' right to them.

A list of the book-plates signed by Hurd is appended.

A LIST OF BOOK–PLATES SIGNED BY NATHANIEL
HURD.

Theodore Atkinson	Chippendale.
Thomas Brown	. . .
John Chandler, Jr.	Chippendale.
Rufus Chandler	. . .
Francis Dana	Chippendale.
Danforth	Chippendale.
Lewis De Blois	Jacobean.

Thomas Dering . . . . Chippendale.
Philip Dumeresque . . . . . . Chippendale.
Isaac Foster . . . . Jacobean.
Benjamin Greene . . . . Jacobean.
Thomas Greene, Jr. . . . . . . Jacobean.
William Greenleaf . . . .
Robert Hale, Esq., of Beverly . . . . Chippendale.
Harvard College . . . . Seal.
Harvard College . . . . Pictorial.
William Hooper . . . . Chippendale.
Jonathan Jackson . . . . Ribbon and Wreath.
Robert Jenkins . . . . Jacobean.
Peter R. Livingston . . . . . . Jacobean.
John Lowell . . . . Chippendale.
Henry Marchant . . . . Chippendale.
John Marston . . . . Chippendale.
Samuel Osborne . . . . Chippendale.
Henry Pace . . . .
Joshua Spooner . . . . Jacobean.
Nathaniel Tracy . . . . Chippendale.
Andrew Tyler . . . . Jacobean.
Wentworth . . . . Chippendale.
John C. Williams . . . . Ribbon and Wreath.

A LIST OF PLATES ATTRIBUTED TO HURD, ALTHOUGH NOT SIGNED.

Thomas Child . . . . . . Chippendale.
Henry Courtenay . . . . . Chippendale.
Edwd. Augs. Holyoke . . . . Chippendale.
By the name of Hurd . . . . Plain Armorial.
Loring . . . . Chippendale.
Lucretia E. Newton . . . . Ribbon and Wreath.
(Same copper as the John C. Williams.)
Andrew Oliver . . . . . . Chippendale.
Samuel Page . . . . Label : Chippendale frame.
Phillips Academy . . . . . Chippendale.
Ezekiel Price . . . . . . Chippendale.
John Simpson . . . . . . Chippendale.
John Vassall . . . . . . Chippendale.
David Wilson . . . . . . Chippendale. ⎫
James Wilson . . . . . . Chippendale. ⎬ One copper.

Of JAMES AKIN, who signs the *Coffin* and *Browne* plates, nothing is learned. The *Hector Coffin* book-plate is also signed by Francis Kearney, which would seem to indicate that Akin was associated with him. The *Browne* is a Philadelphia plate, and Akin may have been employed by the firm of Tanner, Vallance, Kearney and Company, which was in successful operation in Philadelphia for some years.

* * *

S. ALLARDICE was apprenticed to Robert Scott, who had been a pupil of Robert Strange, and who, coming to America, was made die-sinker to the Mint. He had previously made the architectural plates for Dobson's Encyclopædia.

Only one example of the book-plate work of Allardice is now at hand, and that is simply an engraved label for the *Library Company of Baltimore.* Ornamented with flourishes, and some fancy work, it is yet of no merit as a book-plate or an example of art.

* * *

ALEXANDER ANDERSON, who was the first American wood-engraver, was born in the city of New York, April 21, 1775, and lived to the advanced age of ninety-five years, dying, in 1870, in Jersey City, N.J., on the 17th of February.

At the age of twelve, with the spring of a pocket-knife, sharpened for the purpose, he tried

Peter A. Brown

PETER'S VILLA

Engraved by James Allen

118

to engrave on copper pennies rolled thin. In this way he made his first plate, which was a head of Paul Jones ; and his first impression from it was made in red oil paint by a rude kind of a press of his own contrivance. With tools made by a blacksmith, he went on to cut little ships and houses on type metal for the newspapers. Being in some way led to take an interest in certain medical works, he copied many of the plates, and his father, feeling that this was a true sign of his fitness for the profession of medicine, and not discerning the talent for engraving, placed him with Dr. Joseph Young, as a student of medicine.

This step was taken with great reluctance by the youth ; but he found time for both the cares of his new study, and for the pleasures of his old pastime. Various successes encouraged him, and in 1793 he cut a tobacco-stamp on wood, which appears to have been his first use of that material. Soon after this, he obtained a copy of Bewick's " Quadrupeds," and with the cuts found therein he was delighted. They had a strong influence upon his later work, and he has been well called the " American Bewick," for his small wood-cuts closely resemble those of the English master in design, and his prominence in this country was equal to Bewick's in England.

A life of Dr. Anderson has lately (1893) been issued in New York; but, to the disappointment of book-plate collectors, not a word is said of his making book-plates.

Of the seven plates by Anderson known at present, four are on wood, and three are on copper.

Only one of those on wood is signed.   The
Lot Tripp and *Josh. Russell* plates are simple
labels, and the *Typographical Society of New*

JOHN PINTARD, LL. D.

York and the *John Pintard, LL.D.*, which is
signed, are pictorial.   In the former, the emblems
and implements of the printing trade are prominent, and in the *Pintard*, which is a fine example

VIGILA

Alexr Anderson

A. Anderson Sculp

of Anderson's best work on wood, the shield of arms is shown with a landscape for background.

The plates on copper are the *Anderson*, which

is a Chippendale, the *Apprentices' Library*, and the *Columbia College*, which are allegorical.

All the above will be found described in the List.

There is a plate of the *Apprentices' Library Company of Philadelphia* which strongly resembles the wood-cut work of Anderson, but as it is not signed it is not safely attributed to him. In the plate of *A. Griggs* of Philadelphia, an even more marked resemblance to his little designs on wood is seen, but this, too, is not signed.

* * *

ANNIN AND SMITH. This firm consisted of *W. B. Annin* and *George C. Smith*, and they were established in Boston from 1820 to 1837. Annin died in 1839, in Boston, and Smith, who lived to quite an advanced age, died in 1878. They engraved a number of plates for the " Token," and for other annuals so popular sixty years ago.

The plates of *Richard Taylor Auchmuty, A. L. Peirson, William H. Prescott, John Lowell, Jr.*, and an armorial plate for the *Boylston Medical Library* are signed by them, and will be found described in the List.

* * *

ABEL BOWEN, whose name appears on one of the plates of *Harvard College*, was the first wood-engraver in Boston. He was born in New York state in 1790, and he took up engraving before he was of age. In 1812 he was a printer in Boston, probably attracted thither by his uncle, who was the proprietor of the Columbian Mu-

ASHMEAD

CHARLESTON S.C.

seum. Nathaniel Dearborn claims to be the first engraver on wood in Boston, but the honor is usually accorded to Bowen. He issued, in 1816, the " Naval Monument," and in 1817 was associated with Dearborn in engraving for Shaw's " History of Boston." In 1834 Bowen, with others, founded " The Boston Bewick Company," which was an association of engravers. In the following year they issued a map of Boston, and undertook the publishing of the " American Magazine." They were burned out in this same year. Bowen died in 1850.

* * *

JOHN BOYD, who engraved the plate of *Samuel Chase*, which is taken to be the plate of the signer of the Declaration, was a Philadelphia engraver. This is the only specimen of his work on book-plates which we have, and it is a very pretty Chippendale design, delicately engraved.

In Dunlap, a J. Boyd is simply mentioned, who was engraving in Philadelphia in 1812. This, if the engraver of the Chase plate, would make him rather young at the time of doing it, and it is very good work, and not the experiment of a novice. Whether this is the same engraver, I do not know.

* * *

JOSEPH CALLENDER was born in Boston, May 6, 1751. Very little is known about him, but he is reported to have acquired the plates of Peter

Pelham, who was presumably the first to engrave on copper in America, and to have destroyed them. Callender made most of the dies for the second Massachusetts Mint, at a cost of £1 4s. each. This was considered an exorbitant price by the superintendent, who made a contract with a Newburyport artisan, Jacob Perkins. Callender received £48 12s. for making thirty-nine dies, and repairing three others, while Perkins received but £3 18s. 10d. for his work. Callender died in Boston, Nov. 10, 1821, and was buried in the Granary Burying Ground.

The only Chippendale plate by Callender is a copy of the *Atkinson* plate by Hurd, and is for a member of the same family. As compared with its model, this plate shows very little difference, it is so close a copy, but the motto ribbon which is added is more graceful than those of Hurd usually were, the heraldic drawing is quite as good, and the lettering of the name is better. Callender, of course, would not have begun to engrave much before Hurd's death; indeed, the preponderance of the Ribbon and Wreath style in his designs goes to show that his work dated towards the close of the century.

His plates in this style are very light and graceful, with no overloading; and a faithful use of the usual features of the style is apparent.

In the *Russell* plate he was again a copyist, using for his model the *Joseph Barrell* plate. The plates for the *American Academy of Arts and Sciences*, and for the *Massachusetts Medical Society* are practically alike; the curtain, and the

Thomas Russell

Caliendos!

ribbon and festooning are very similar, while the view within the oval frame is, of course, adapted to the use of the books of the respective societies. Callender would seem by these signs to have been a lazy engraver, or to have considered his designs so perfect as to call for no further effort.

A LIST OF BOOK-PLATES SIGNED BY CALLENDER.

—— Andrews	Pictorial.
William King Atkinson	Chippendale.
Jonathan Baldwin	. . .
Luke Baldwin	. . .
Boylston Medical Library	Plain armorial.
John Callender	Pictorial.
Thomas Cary	Ribbon and Wreath.
William Erving	Ribbon and Wreath.
John Francis	Plain armorial.
Hasty Pudding Library	Pictorial.
Massachusetts Medical Society . . .	Allegorical.
Thomas Russell	Allegorical.
Daniel Sargent, Jr.	Ribbon and Wreath.
John Sullivan	Ribbon and Wreath.
James Swan	Plain armorial.
Dudley Atkins Tyng	Ribbon and Wreath.
Solomon Vose	Ribbon and Wreath.

A LIST OF PLATES ATTRIBUTED TO CALLENDER, ALTHOUGH NOT SIGNED.

American Academy of Arts and Sciences,	Allegorical.
William Emerson	Ribbon and Wreath.
Gray	Ribbon and Wreath.
Dr. John Jeffries	Plain armorial.
Porcellain Library	Allegorical.

SUB LIBERTATE FLORENT

AMERICAN ACADEMY OF ARTS & SCIENCES.

MDCCLXXX.

The GIFT of

Cephas G. Childs, who engraved the plate of *Henry D. Gilpin*, was born in Pennsylvania, in 1793. In the years 1827 to 1830, he published a set of views of the city of Philadelphia and its vicinity (Baker).

HENRY D. GILPIN.

Henry Dawkins was an engraver of but few original ideas, if we may judge him rightly by his book-plate work. In this he was very largely a copyist. Working altogether in the Chippendale style, his designs for the most part are variations of one general plan, which seems to have been borrowed from an English-made plate. In his plates we see "Chippendalism run wild." Here are introduced the love-sick swains who play upon the flute; the dandy shepherds in stiff clothes of the most fashionable cut, flowing curls, and large felt hats; the flirting young damsels in very low-cut bodices, who play at being shepherdesses for the sake of following the above-mentioned gentle keeper of sheep. Here are the music-loving Cupids, the scantily clad females who are attended by the Cupids, and who are far from home among the trees of the wood. In the *James Duane* plate we find a fountain is fixed to the side of the frame, and is spouting water from the mouth of a man's head.

But the plates of *Samuel Jones*, *Samuel Stringer*, and *Peter W. Yates* are proof that Dawkins could confine himself to the legitimate features of good Chippendale plates. In these no outside objects are introduced, and the design is good.

We do not know much about Dawkins. Dunlap says he was probably from England, and that he was first noticed in New York. Originally he was an ornamenter of buttons and other small bits of metal, but in America he worked at anything that offered, "suiting himself to the poverty of the arts at the time." Dunlap dates him about 1774, evidently on the strength of the word of Dr. Anderson, who remembered to have seen "shop-bills and coats-of-arms for books," done by him previous to 1775. However, in 1761, he engraved music for a book of Psalm Tunes published in that year in Philadelphia. His earliest dated book-plate is that of *John Burnet* (1754).

He was skilful enough to make counterfeit Continental currency, but not to avoid arrest; and in 1776 we find him suffering for this misdeed. Some time later, he forwarded the following unique petition to the Committee of Safety:—

" MAY IT PLEASE YOUR HONOURS, — The subscriber humbly relying on the known goodness and humanity of this honourable house, begs leave to lay his complaint before them, which is briefly as follows. That your petitioner was about six months past taken upon Long Island for a trespass which this house is thoroughly acquainted as by Israel Youngs he was led away to perform an action of which he has sincerely repented and your petitioner was torn away from an only son who was left among strangers without any support, or protection during the inclemency of the approaching winter, as his unhappy father hath since the first day he was taken had but one shirt and one pair of stockings to shift himself, and hath been affected during his imprisonment at White Plains with that worst of enemies hunger, and a nauseous stench of a small room where some twenty persons were confined together which hath introduced a sickness on your distressed subscriber which with the fatigue of travelling hath reduced your unhappy petitioner to a state of despondency — he therefore being weary of such a miserable life as his misconduct has thrown him into begs for a termination by death to be inflicted upon him in what manner the honourable House may see fit. The kind compliance of this honourable House will ever lay an obligation on your distressed humble servent
HENRY DAWKINS."

We do not know in what manner the honorable house received this extraordinary petition; but, as book-plates are in existence in his later style, probably it was not granted. Dawkins used three distinct varieties of the Chippendale style. The plates of *Benjamin Kissam*, the *Ludlow* and *Roome* plates, the *Whitehead Hicks* and the *James Duane* are examples of the debased

Chippendale. He had also a style which is illustrated by the *Hopkinson, Samuels,* and *Tomlinson* plates, which is closely allied to the style of the *Bushrod Washington.* The same hissing dragon,

the same tilt to the whole design, and the similarity in detail and execution have led to the question of his being the engraver of the latter plate. It is not a question easy to decide, and collectors are divided over the question. This style of plate came originally from England, we can be sure; and as Dawkins is seen to be a copyist, it is quite as likely that he copied from the *Bushrod Washington* plate, as that he designed it. He always used a squarer copper than the Washington plate is engraved upon; but this has evidences of having been cut down after engraving. The present writer does not think the plate can be safely attributed to Dawkins. 'The *Child* and *Jones* plates exemplify the third style.

The debased Chippendale plates which Dawkins made were apparently copied from an English example he had seen.

A LIST OF BOOK-PLATES SIGNED BY DAWKINS.

Gerard Bancker	Chippendale.
John Burnet, 1754	Chippendale.
Francis Child.	Chippendale.
James Duane	Chippendale.
Francis Hopkinson, ⎱ one copper	Chippendale.
Joseph Hopkinson, ⎰	
Whitehead Hicks	Chippendale.
Archibald Hunter	. . .
Samuel Jones	Chippendale.
Benjamin Kissam	Chippendale.
John Cooke Ludlow	Chippendale.
Gab. Willm. Ludlow	Chippendale.
Jacob Roome	Chippendale.
John L. C. Roome	Chippendale.
James Samuels	Chippendale.
Samuel Stringer	Chippendale.
William Sword	Chippendale.
John Tomlinson	Chippendale.
Unidentified	Chippendale.
Josias Short Vavasour	Chippendale.
W —— Whitebread	Chippendale.
Peter W. Yates	Chippendale.

The plates of *Cornelius Low* and *Lambert Moore*, although not signed, are attributed to Dawkins.

* * *

NATHANIEL DEARBORN was born in 1786, and was the son of Benjamin Dearborn, a man of attainments in science. Nathaniel was one of the first wood-engravers in Boston, and was associated with Abel Bowen for a time.

The only armorial book-plate signed by Dearborn is the *Charles Beck*, which is a peculiar design, following no particular style, but making a pretty plate.

A second plate signed by Dearborn is the simple engraved verse for *Isaac Child*.

* * *

AMOS DOOLITTLE, who was born in 1754, was one of the first engravers of historical scenes in America. In Barber's "History and Antiquities of New Haven," published in 1831, is an advertisement of "four different views of the Battle of Lexington, Concord, etc. on the 19 April 1775." A list of the plates follows, and it is remarked that they were "neatly engraved on copper from original paintings taken on the spot." In a note which follows, it is further remarked that the pictures were first drawn by Mr. Earl, who was a portrait painter, and who with Mr. Doolittle was a member of the Governor's Guard which went to Cambridge and the scene of action under the command of Arnold.

George Goodwin

Nº

As a maker of book-plates, Doolittle was fond of the allegorical style. He made two plates for the *Societies of Yale College*, and one for the village library of *Wethersfield*. The latter is an ornamental label only, but the former are quite elaborate examples of the allegorical. The plates

of *Benjamin S. Brooks*, in the Ribbon and Wreath style, and *Charles H. Wetmore*, which is a copy of one of Maverick's favorite designs, complete the number of his signed examples. The *Guilford Library* and *George Goodwin* plates, which have some features in common with the *Wethersfield Library*, are confidently attributed to him.

Benjamin S. Brooks	Ribbon and Wreath.
Brothers in Unity	Allegorical.
Linonian Library	Allegorical.
Social Library, Wethersfield	Literary.
Charles H. Wetmore	Ribbon and Wreath.

*   *   *

GIDEON FAIRMAN, whose signature is on one of the plates of *Henry McMurtrie* and one of the *Linonian Society of Yale College*, was born in Connecticut in 1774. He showed an early fondness for engraving, and made rude attempts which showed undoubted talent. In 1810, having made himself a master of his art, he went into partnership with Murray, Draper, and others, in Philadelphia. He made considerable money, and went over to England with Jacob Perkins, where, with Charles Heath for a third partner, they were successful but for a short time, the extravagance of Murray proving their ruin.

*   *   *

JOHN MASON FURNASS was the nephew of Hurd, to whom the latter left his engraving tools by will, as the young man showed so much ability in the art practised by his widely known uncle.

He was also a painter of portraits, and he had a studio in Boston, which was also used by Trumbull.

The only plate signed by this engraver, which the present writer has seen, is the *Eli Forbes*. This plate shows but few traces of the influence of Hurd. It is a Chippendale design, but

is not in either of the characteristic modes of
Hurd. It is an ambitious plate, and was meant
to be very fine, evidently. It is full of flourishes,

and the little spiral flourish at the lower right-
hand side is wholly out of place; the robin picking
rose leaves at the side is an innovation. The
scrolls under the name are somewhat in the

manner of Hurd.   The heraldic drawing is poor,
and the bunch of arrows between the shield and
the crest must be in allusion to the occupation of
the owner, who was a missionary to the Indians.

There is said to be a plate by Furnass owned
in Boston, by the name of *Foster*, but no definite
knowledge of it has been obtained.

* * *

E. GALLAUDET, who signed the plate for the
New York Society Library and the plate of *John*

Chambers, was one Elisha Gallaudet, who practised his art in New York City towards the end
of the last century.

EDWARD GALLAUDET, a relative of the above,
was superior to him as an engraver, and the
Gallaudet plate mentioned in the List is by him.
He was of the present century.

* * *

ABRAHAM GODWIN was born in New Jersey in
1763. He was intended for the profession of the
law, and was placed in the office of his brother,
at Fishkill, in New York state. Both men joined
the army, however; and when Abraham returned
to his home, it was to take up the art of engraving,
towards which he had had an inclination from
boyhood, when he made his first attempts on the
silver plate of his friends, with a graver made by
a blacksmith.

The only example of his book-plate work is a
plate fully described under the heading, " Unidentified," in the List. Most unfortunately, the
only example known has the family name torn
out. The first name is *John*. The plate is
rather rudely engraved, but is quite ambitious,
showing the interior of a large room, which might
be either a school-room or a library.

* * *

S. HARRIS, who engraved the pictorial plates
of *Henry Andrews* and the anonymous *Williams*,
was a New England engraver, who was in Boston
about 1798.

CHARLES P. HARRISON, who signed the plain armorial book-plates of *William Betts* and *David Paul Brown*, was a son of William Harrison, an English engraver, who came to New York in 1794, and was for a time an instructor of Peter Maverick the second.

* * *

SAMUEL HILL was a copper-plate engraver in Boston, about 1790, and his work consisted mostly of portraits and book work.

The following are examples of his work:—

Willm. P. & L. Blake's Circulating Library at the Boston Book Store . . .	Ornamented label.
Charles Pierpont	Ribbon and Wreath.
William Winthrop	Ribbon and Wreath.

Also the plate of *Saml. Hill*, which is of a literary flavor, is probably the engraver's own plate.

* * *

S. S. JOCELYN, of New Haven, who made a very handsome plate for the *Brothers in Unity* of Yale College, became an engraver of vignettes for bank-notes.

* * *

THOMAS JOHNSON was born in Boston in 1708. He was buried in King's Chapel Burying-ground, May 8, 1767. He engraved Psalm Tune plates

HONORATUS QUI VIRTUTEM HONORAT

EDMUND·H·GARRETT

for the Tate and Brady edition of 1760, and did some commendable work as a herald painter. In the inventory of his estate, fifteen copper plates are appraised at 40s.

Only one specimen of his book-plate work is authenticated, and that is the *Joseph Tyler*, which is signed in full, — *Johnson.*

* * *

THOMAS JOHNSTON signs the very beautiful Jacobean plate of *William P. Smith, A.M.*, and the rougher Chippendale of *Samuel Willis.* Whether this is the same engraver as the above is uncertain; the difference in the spelling of the name would not disprove the claim, as in those days such differences were frequent. The *Willis* plate bears strong resemblance to the work and designs of Hurd. If this is the same engraver as the above, these two plates are likely to be the earliest signed plates by an American, as Johnson was born some twenty years before Hurd. The *Willis* plate is quite inferior to the *Smith*, which latter is a striking example of the Jacobean style.

* * *

FRANCIS KEARNEY, who signs the plate of *Henry McMurtrie* and *Hector Coffin*, was born in 1780. He was a pupil of Peter R. Maverick, who received two hundred and fifty dollars for instructing him for three years. The advantage was all with Maverick. Soon after the opening of the century, he was engaged with Anderson, the younger Maverick, Boyd, and others, in engraving plates for a quarto Bible published by Mr. Collins, of New York.

In 1810 he removed to Philadelphia, as that city was far ahead of New York in the publishing of books, etc. He was in that city for over twenty years. His greatest work is the engraving of Leonardo da Vinci's picture of the "Last Supper."

* * *

PETER RUSHTON MAVERICK was born in England, April 11, 1755, and came to America about 1774. He was originally a silversmith, and came of a family whose members were for several generations well known as engravers, and who made the art their occupation. He was an energetic worker, getting most of his practical knowledge by his own endeavors. He was the teacher of William Dunlap and of Francis Kearney, as well as of his own son, who ultimately became a more proficient engraver than his father, and, who after instructing A. B. Durand for five years, took him into partnership.

Peter R. Maverick died in New York, about 1807, and his son Peter whose partnership with Durand resulted disastrously, died in 1831.

As a designer and engraver of book-plates, Maverick was the most prolific of all the early engravers. It is presumed that all the plates signed either P. R. Maverick, or simply Maverick, were by the same hand, as a large collection of

Weigh well each thought, each sentence freely scan,
In Reason's balance try the works of man:
Be bias'd not by those who praise or blame,
Nor, servile, Yield opinion to a Name.

proofs from his plates which furnishes examples
of both ways of signing is now in the possession
of the New York Historical Society, and the
librarian informs me that all of the plates in that
collection were done in 1789 by the elder Maverick.   This collection consists of sixty-five plates,
of which thirty-eight different ones are signed by
Maverick.   There are also others which are undoubtedly his work, although not signed, and
there are examples by Dawkins, Hutt, and Child.
Quite a number of the plates are duplicated, too.
This very interesting collection of proofs, kept by
Maverick himself, and sewed together roughly,
was in the library of his friend, John Allan.   By far
the greater part of Maverick's plates are of the
Ribbon and Wreath style, but he made a few Jacobeans, a few Chippendales, and one or two pictorial and allegorical designs.   He used the same
features over and over in his plates, and seems to
have been a rapid worker.   The plates in the following list marked * are by the younger Maverick.

A LIST OF BOOK–PLATES SIGNED BY MAVERICK.

Anonymous	Plain armorial.
Anonymous (Jacob Brown)	Pictorial.
Flamen Ball	Ribbon and Wreath.
Abraham Bancker	Pictorial.
Absalom Blackley	Ribbon and Wreath.
Philip Brasher	Ribbon and Wreath.
*Epaphroditus Champion, Jr. . . .	Plain armorial.
De Witt Clinton	Ribbon and Wreath.
William Cock	Ribbon and Wreath.
James S. Cutting	Ribbon and Wreath.
William Cutting	Ribbon and Wreath.

John I. Johnson	Pictorial.
John Johnston	Ribbon and Wreath.
Thomas Johnston	Ribbon and Wreath.
Benjamin S. Judah	Ribbon and Wreath.
John Keese	Ribbon and Wreath.
John Keese	Ornamental label.
Rufus King	Ribbon and Wreath.
Isaac L. Kip	Ribbon and Wreath.
Edward Livingston	Landscape.
Maturin Livingston	Ribbon and Wreath.
William Smith Livingston	Ribbon and Wreath.
Hugh McLean	Ribbon and Wreath.
Peter Masterton	Ribbon and Wreath.
—— Maxwell	Ribbon and Wreath.
*Nathaniel F. Moore	Ribbon and Wreath.
New York Society Library	Allegorical.
New York Society Library	Allegorical.
*Lewis Morris Ogden	Ribbon and Wreath.
Francis Panton, Jr.	Landscape.
W. Paulding.	. . . .
William L. Pierce	Ribbon and Wreath.
John Pintard	Ribbon and Wreath.
William Popham	Ribbon and Wreath.
Halcott B. Pride	Ribbon and Wreath.
Samuel Provoost	Ribbon and Wreath.
William Seton	Ribbon and Wreath.
John Sitgreaves	Ribbon and Wreath.
James Scott Smith	Ribbon and Wreath.
Thomas Smith, Jr..	Ribbon and Wreath.
Thomas J. Smith	. . . .
William Smith	Ribbon and Wreath.
William Taylor	Ribbon and Wreath.
*James Thompson	Plain armorial.
Thomas Tillotson	Ribbon and Wreath.
P. I. Van Berkel	Plain armorial.
K. K. Van Rensselaer	Ribbon and Wreath.
Prosper Wetmore	Ribbon and Wreath.
Polydore B. Wisner	Ribbon and Wreath.

A LIST OF PLATES ATTRIBUTED TO MAVERICK,
ALTHOUGH NOT SIGNED.

James Agnew, Esq.	Chippendale.
Boudinet	Ribbon and Wreath.
Charles Bridgen	Plain armorial.
Willm. Duer	Ribbon and Wreath.
John Goelet	Jacobean.
Herbert	Chippendale.
Morgan Lewis, Esq.	Ribbon and Wreath.
Rob't R. Livingston, Esq., of Cleremont,	Ribbon and Wreath.
Walter Livingston	Chippendale.
Jonathan Meredith, Jr.	Ribbon and Wreath.
Joseph Murray	Chippendale.
William Pasley	Ribbon and Wreath.
Saml. Provoost. Coll. Pet. Cant. . . .	Chippendale.
William Stephens	Jacobean.
John C. Ten Broeck	Ribbon and Wreath.
Stephen Van Rensselaer	Plain armorial.

OLIVER PELTON, who engraved a plate for the *Brothers in Unity*, at Yale College, was born in Portland, Conn., in 1799, and learned his trade with Abner Read, a bank-note engraver, of Hartford. He was an assiduous worker, and was taken into partnership after two years' work, with Mr. Read and one Samuel Stiles. Samuel G. Goodrich (Peter Parley) soon induced him to go to Boston with him, to engage in the engraving of plates for his works. This enterprise was successful, and in 1863 Pelton formed a partnership with William D. Terry, which was the foundation of the New England Bank-Note Company of Boston. The plate mentioned is the only example of his work on book-plates.

R. Rawdon, who signs the plate of *William L. Stone*, which is a very handsome steel-plate design, was born in Tolland, Conn., and was associated with his brother in Albany. The brother subsequently moved to New York.

Paul Revere, the Revolutionary patriot whose "midnight ride" is known the world over, was born in Boston, January 1, 1735, and died there on the 10th of May, 1818, after a life of great usefulness, leaving a name never to be forgotten.

He came of a Huguenot family, who spelled the name Rivoire originally.

He was self-instructed in the art of engraving on copper, although brought up by his father to the business of a goldsmith. He went on the

Crown Point expedition, 1756, and after his return, married, and settled down to the business he had already learned. He was naturally fond of mechanics, and made himself master of its general principles. One of his earliest attempts

on copper was the portrait of his friend, Dr. Mayhew. He also engraved several caricatures which were popular, and some historical pictures which are valuable now to the collector.

Paul Revere

Not many book-plates have come down to us by this celebrated patriot, and the following list comprises all that are signed.

Gardiner Chandler. . . . . Chippendale.
David Greene . . . . Chippendale.
Epes Sargent . . . . Chippendale.
William Wetmore . . . . Ribbon and Wreath.

Revere's plates do not have the compact appearance of Hurd's, and are not so well designed or so well engraved as the latter's. Presumably this branch of work was not very profitable to him, or very much cultivated.

The accompanying design was undoubtedly a book-plate, and beyond question is the work of Revere. It is a very rare plate.

* * *

WILLIAM ROLLINSON was born in England, in the year 1760. He was in youth brought up to the trade of ornamenting buttons; and, upon coming to New York, made the gilt buttons which decorated the coat worn by Washington at his inauguration as President. He did this without remuneration, so thoroughly sympathizing with the country of his adoption as to feel the honor of this service for Washington a full compensation. He was, through the friendship of Messrs. Elias Hicks and John C. Ludlow, recommended to the publishers of Brown's Family Bible, for which he made several plates. Previous to this, he found work in the shops of different silversmiths, and had taught himself the art of engraving on copper. At the beginning of the century, Archibald Robertson painted a portrait of Alexander Hamilton, which Rollinson boldly undertook to make a large engraving from. He did not understand all the processes of engraving, and invented such as he was compelled to use, as he went on. The duel in which Hamilton lost his life occurred before the portrait was fully engraved. Indeed, it had been undertaken more as an experiment than with the idea of sale; but the friends of the dead statesman urged him to complete it, which he did, and the print found a good sale. Later, Rollinson invented a machine for ruling waved lines, which was of vast importance in the manufacture of bank-notes.

As an engraver of book-plates, he adopted the Ribbon and Wreath style naturally, as it was the style in vogue when he took up the work. He made one or two plain armorials, and for the *New York College of Pharmacy* one of more ambitious design. His plates, all neat in design, are clear, skilful engraving. His work and that of Callender, in the same style, resemble each other.

The following plates are signed by Rollinson: —

Richard Harrison	Plain armorial.
Elias Hicks	Ribbon and Wreath.
George Ludlow	Ribbon and Wreath.
W. T. McCoun	Plain armorial.
Horatio Shepheard Moat	Ribbon and Wreath.
New York College of Pharmacy . . .	Ornamented label.
James Adam Smith	Plain armorial.
Thomas N. Stanforth	Ribbon and Wreath.
Teachers' Union, St. George's Church .	Engraved label.
John W. Watkins, A.M.	Ribbon and Wreath.
Charles Wilkes	Plain armorial.
Azarias Williams	Ribbon and Wreath.

J. SMITHERS, an Englishman, originally a gun-engraver employed in the Tower of London, came to Philadelphia in the year 1773.

H. C. Leeds.

He had a good name as a man and as an en-graver, and made the blocks for the Continental money. A large plan of the city of Philadelphia on three plates, which was his work, was subse-quently purchased, when copper was scarce, for thirty dollars, and cut up into smaller pieces. Among his pupils was Trenchard, of whose work we have a few examples.

The following plates are signed by Smithers: —

John Day	Plain armorial.
Fenwick	Chippendale.
Henry Hale Graham	Plain armorial.
John Magill	Chippendale.
Henry McMurtrie	Pictorial.

He sometimes signed with the final *s*, and sometimes without it. His book-plates are not especially brilliant in any way, but are good, and in the pure style. His finest attempt is the land-scape plate for *Dr. McMurtrie* of Philadelphia.

* * *

T. Sparrow was an obscure engraver on wood, who worked at his trade in Annapolis from 1765 to about 1780, and who did considerable work for " Ann Catherine Green & Son, Printers," of that town, on title-pages, tail-pieces, etc. He engraved on copper the title-page for the " Deputy Commissary's Guide of Maryland," published by the above firm in 1774, and which is a creditable piece of work. All the book-plates known at present are on wood, and they are but two in number: the *Richard Sprigg* and the *Gabriel Duvall*, both of whom were men of prominence in the colonial times, in Maryland.

* * *

WILLIAM D. TERRY, who was mentioned as the founder, with Pelton, of the Bank-Note Company, in Boston, engraved a plate for the *Redwood Library*, of Newport. This is a large representation of the library, and is a fine piece of work.

* * *

JAMES THACKARA was a partner of John Vallance, in the engraving business, and they were together for a good many years. Thackara was inferior to his partner as an engraver, according to Dunlap, and was for a long time the keeper of the Pennsylvania Academy of Fine Arts.

We know but one example of his book-plate work, and that is the *Lenthall* plate, which is a large and very interesting example of the Ribbon and Wreath style. It is an excellent piece of engraving, full of style, and graceful in design.

* * *

JAMES TRENCHARD was born in Cumberland County, New Jersey, about 1746. He was a pupil of Smithers, and engraved in Philadelphia,

ODINLENTHAL

118

about 1785. Among his pupils were Thackara, Vallance, and his nephew, Edward Trenchard, who became an officer in the United States Navy, and served in the War of 1812.

Trenchard was one of the owners of the

"Columbian Magazine," published in Philadel-phia from 1786 to 1792, and he engraved many plates for its pages.

One signed book-plate of his is known, — the *Bloomfield.* This is a Chippendale plate of no striking features. The *Luther Martin* plate is so similar to this as to leave hardly any doubt that it too was by Trenchard.

* * *

JAMES TURNER is another of the early American artists of whom very little is known now.

He was at one time in Boston, but later removed to Philadelphia. He did some portrait and some music work. Of his book-plate work we have but three signed specimens. By far the most interesting and valuable of these is the extremely rare plate of *John Franklin of Boston in New England.* This is very fully described in the List of Early American Book-plates. The other

plates are the *Sir John St. Clair*, and the plate for *Isaac Norris*, of the family of the Quaker Chief Justice of Pennsylvania.

The plate of *James Hall*, although not signed, is also attributed to him.

* * *

JOHN VALLANCE, whose name is connected with that of Thackara, engraved with him many plates

for Dobson's Encyclopædia. He made heads of Franklin and Howard, which were pronounced successful, and he had a high reputation as an engraver.

One authenticated example of his book-plate

work is known, the *Joseph Wiseman*, in the Ribbon and Wreath style; and the *David Brearly*, although not signed, is attributed to him.

* * *

Of the other engravers whose names appear on but one or two plates, no information has been obtained. There were probably many who had but a local fame, and who made but a few plates. Their names are remembered now in a way not expected at the time of signing them, undoubtedly.

* * *

In a recent article on COUNT RUMFORD, in the "New England Magazine," it is said that, when a youth, he designed book-plates. No authentic examples of his work are known, and no information can be obtained concerning any.

* * *

JACOB HURD, the father of Nathaniel, was a goldsmith of Boston, and his name is on pieces of plate in the First and Second churches in Boston, and the First Church, and Christ Church, in Dorchester. He very probably made book-plates, though no signed work is known. He died in 1758. He appears in the list of subscribers to "Prince's Chronological History of New England," as taking six copies.

In the "Boston Evening Post," for March 4, 1745, the following advertisement appears: —

"FRANCIS GARDEN, Engraver from London, engraves in the newest Manner and at the cheapest Rates, Coats-of-Arms, Crests or Cyphers on Gold, Silver, Pewter or Copper. To be heard of at Mr. Caverley's, Distiller, at the South End of Boston. N.B. He will wait on any Person in Town or Country, to do their Work at their own House, if desired : also copper-plate printing perform'd by him."

No signed example of this gentleman's work has thus far come to our knowledge. It is fair to presume, however, that he engraved book-plates.

"QUI CONTENTUS FELIX"

A LIST OF EARLY AMERICAN
BOOK-PLATES.

The following List of Early American Book-plates makes no claim to completeness : indeed it is earnestly hoped and believed that time will prove it to be quite incomplete : old plates new to collectors are continually coming to light, and there is every reason to expect their number to increase. We are persuaded that certain of the worthies of colonial times used book-plates, although no copies are now known, and that some future investigator will unearth these much-desired treasures.

Some plates will be found included which do not have a satisfactory description : this is due to their not being seen by the compiler of the List : correspondents at a distance cannot always send full details, and without them it is better to attempt little in the way of description. The aim has been to be accurate and as full as possible. There are hundreds of simple name-labels which have no place here, but all armorial examples which could be discovered are mentioned.

The plates are given in alphabetical order, and are numbered for convenience in reference. As far as possible, the first line of the description of each plate gives the exact wording of the original, with its spelling and abbreviations : the mottoes also, as well as the manner of signature, are given exactly as they appear on the original plate : wherever throughout this List *italics* are used, they denote the exact language employed upon the plate.

1. ANONYMOUS.

Armorial. A very beautiful plate with French arms : a crown above and military trophies behind the shield : French banners, cannon, quivers of arrows, anchor, horns, swords, drum, tomahawks, bugle, lances, etc. Signed, *Maingot delt. Maverick, Sct.*

EX LIBRIS

Richard C. Lichtenstein
BOSTON

Maurgot del.¹   Maverick Sc.²

2. ABERCROMBIE. *James Abercrombie.*
    Armorial. Ribbon and Wreath. Two mottoes,
    Vive ut vivas, and *Meus in arduis aequa.* Of
    Philadelphia, and mentioned in Boswell's " Life of
    Dr. Johnson."

3. ADAMS. *John Adams.*
    Armorial. The Boylston arms. The shield sur-
    rounded by a garter on which the motto is given, —
    Libertatem amicitiam retenebis et fidem. The whole
    design surrounded by thirteen stars. Second Presi-
    dent of the United States.

4. ADAMS. *John Quincy Adams.*
    Simply the name rudely engraved and surrounded
    by a narrow line. Probably the first of the J. Q. A.
    book-plates. Sixth President of the United States.

5. ADAMS.   *John Quincy Adams.*
   Armorial.   Boylston arms.   Ribbon and Wreath.
   Motto-ribbon empty.

6. ADAMS.   *John Quincy Adams.*
   Armorial.   The Boylston arms ; the shield enclosed
   within a garter, on which the motto appears, —
   Fidem — Libertatem — Amicitiam.

7. ADAMS.   *John Quincy Adams.*
   Armorial.   The shield is quartered, and bears in
   the first quarter a curious specimen of home-made
   heraldry.   The ancestors of the President bore no
   arms, and in their place appears a stag standing at
   gaze before a pine tree, while below in the water a
   fish, probably a cod, is swimming ; the whole design
   surrounded with thirteen stars.   This was his own
   invention.   The other quarters bear the Smith,
   Quincy, and Boylston arms.   The whole shield is
   surrounded by a garter bearing the motto *Fidem,
   Libertatem, Amicitiam retinebis.*   From "Tacitus."

8. AGAR.   *Property, Lydia Agar.   1806.*
   Pictorial.   An eagle bears a broad ribbon, on
   which the word *property* is given ; an oval frame
   encloses what resembles a row of eggs.

9. AGNEW.   *James Agnew, Esq.*
   Armorial.   Chippendale.   Motto, *Consilio non
   impetu.*   Attributed to Maverick.

10. AITKIN.   *Robert Aitkin.*
    Simple name label : the printer of the "Aitkin
    Bible."   Philadelphia, 1782.   The first American
    edition.

11. ALBANY.   *Albany Society Library.   1759.*
    A peculiar plate something in the shape of the fig-
    ure 8, with intertwining foliations above and at the
    sides.   The upper part of the frame is the larger,
    and contains a spirited illustration of an Indian in
    ambush aiming an arrow at a leaping fox.   On
    the frame surrounding this is the motto, *May
    concord prevail and the undertakeing prosper.*   In
    the lower and smaller part is depicted a prim

man, bewigged and ruffled, with an open book in his hand; presumably a patron of the Library. Very little can be learned concerning this early Library. It was probably interrupted by the Revolution. Some of its books are in the New York State Library.

12. ALLAN. *John Allan.*
Pictorial. An open book, across the pages of which is printed the name of the owner. Behind all an anchor. This is the plate of the old book collector of New York City.

13. ALLEN. *John Allen.*
Armorial. Jacobean. Motto, *Law & Right.* This is believed to be the plate used by John Allen, an early bookseller of Boston. He published the " News-Letter." From the general design and the crude engraving, it must be taken for early American work : circa 1720. Illustrated in " Curio," page 15.

14. ALLISON. *Joseph J. Allison.*
Armorial. Chippendale. Hour-glass, books, globe, palette, and brushes, grouped above the escutcheon. Motto, *Hinc labor et virtus.* Of Philadelphia.

15. ALSOP. *Richard Alsop.*
Armorial. Belongs to no particular style, although the ornamentation is of Chippendale tendency. Beneath the shield, at either side, stands a cupid holding out a bunch of arrows : the drawing of these figures is not above criticism : they seem to to have one arm each, and but one wing also. A Connecticut poet. Born, 1761 ; died, 1815. One of the famous " Hartford Wits."

16. AMBLER. Armorial. Of Virginia.

17. AMERICAN. *American Academy of Arts and Sciences. MDCCLXX.*
A very handsome plate, having a large curtain looped back by ribbons and cords, whereon to record the name of the giver of books to the

library, and above this an oval vignette representing Minerva with shield and spear in hand, and helmet on her head, standing upon the seashore (of Massachusetts), watching a three-master which sails far away under a glaring sun and a heavy cloud : through a corn-field and then through the woods lies the path to the distant village whose roofs can be seen : on the sand about the goddess lie scattered the scientific and agricultural implements, the uses of which it was the function of the Academy to teach. The Academy was instituted in 1779. Very good engraving but not so good drawing. The work is attributed to Callender.

18. ANDERSON. *Alexr. Anderson.*
Armorial. Chippendale. Motto, *Vigila.* Signed, *A. Anderson, Sculp.* The original plate had only the last name engraved ; the first name was added afterwards and evidently by a different hand. This plate is sometimes found with the name of his brother, John, written in before the family name, indicating perhaps that the plate was designed for the general use of the family. This is the plate of Dr. Anderson, the first engraver in wood in America.

19. ANDOVER. *Institutio Theologica Andover. Fundata MDCCCVII.*
A severely plain pediment, raised upon Doric columns, bearing on the architrave the name. A blaze of glory above has in the centre the words, יה וה. Similar rays shine over the open Bible at the foot, on which is written, Ps. cxix, 169, and Joh. xvii, 17. On the base are the words, ΑΚΟΓΩΝΙ ΣΟΥ ΧΡΙΣΤΟΥ.

20. ANDREW. *John Andrew.*
Pictorial. The implements of the engraver lie scattered upon the bench : the name is given in fac-simile of the autograph.

21. ANDREWS. Armorial. Of Virginia.

22. ANDREWS. ——— *Andrews.* (First name obliterated.)
Pictorial. The scene is out of doors and the sun rises in full strength behind a long oval frame on

which the name is engraved. A little patch of earth, two well-grown trees, and scant herbage complete the accessories. Signed, *Callender Sc.*

23. ANDREWS. *Eliza Andrews.*
Pictorial. Exactly the same as the succeeding, with the exception of the change in the name and the omission of the engraver's signature.

24. ANDREWS. *Henry Andrews.*
Pictorial: representing Minerva, crowned, with spear and shield: the owl sits upon a convenient pedestal. The name of the owner is put upon the edge of the shield which the goddess rests upon the ground. Signed, *S. Harris. Sc.*

25. ANTILL. *Edwad. Antill. Esqr., A.M.*
Armorial. Chippendale. Motto, *Probitas laudatur et alget.* A New Jersey author. Illustrated in " Art Amateur," April, 1894.

26. APTHORP. *Apthorp.*
Armorial. Chippendale. Motto-ribbon empty.

27. APTHORP. *East Apthorp, A.M. Cambridge MDCCLXI.*
Armorial. Late Jacobean. Motto, *Nemo nisi Christus.* Eminent Episcopal divine, born in Boston, 1733; educated at Cambridge, and died, 1816.

28. APTHORP. *Jno. Apthorp.*
Armorial. Chippendale. Motto, *Fari quae sentiat.* The same plate as the one mentioned above as having the motto-ribbon empty. In this example the name *Jno.* is written, and so is the motto.

29. APTHORP. *Thomas Apthorp.*
Armorial. Chippendale. Motto, *Juste rem para.* Flowers, and a huge bee in the decoration. Printed in blue ink. Born, 1741. Died in England.

30. ARCHDEACON. *S. Archdeacon.*
Armorial. Chippendale. Motto, *Esse quam videri.* Signed, *W. S.* A pretty design, with the caduceus of Mercury introduced in the ornamentation.

31. ARCHER. *William Archer.*
Armorial. Of Chesterfield County, Virginia.

32. ARCHER. *William Archer, Powhatan.*
    A plain label with the name within a type border.

33. ARMISTEAD. *William Armistead.*
    Armorial. Of Virginia. Of Revolutionary fame.

34. ASHWELL. *Charles Ashwell of Grenada.*
    Plain armorial.

35. ASSHETON. *Ralph Assheton, M.D., Philadelphia.*
    Armorial. Chippendale. Motto, *In Domino confido.* Son of the Councillor ; studied medicine in Edinburgh.

36. ASSHETON. *Willm. Assheton Esqr. of Barbadoes.*
    Armorial. Chippendale. Very ornate. No motto. Began the practice of law in Penna., and was afterwards described as " of the Parish of St. Michael's in Barbadoes, gentleman." He was Provost-Marshal of Barbadoes.

37. ASSHETON. *William Assheton Esq. of Gray's Inn, Judge of the Court of Admiralty of Penn. 1718.*
    Arms, crest, and quarterings.

38. ATKINSON. *Theodore Atkinson.*
    Armorial. Chippendale. No motto. Signed, *N. Hurd. Scp.* This is the same design that was used in the Wentworth plate, but is much better in execution. The peculiar flow of water from the shell beneath the escutcheon is caught in a bowl : the only instance. Secretary of the colony of New Hampshire, 1741 ; Chief Justice, 1754 ; Major-General of militia, 1769 ; delegate to Congress at Albany, 1754.

39. ATKINSON. *William King Atkinson.*
    Armorial. Chippendale : a copy of the preceding design. Motto, *Nil facimus non sponte Dei.* Signed, *Callender Sc.* A noted lawyer of Portsmouth, N.H. (1764–1820). Changed his name from King to Atkinson out of respect to Judge Atkinson.

40. ATLEE. *Willm. Augs. Atlee Esqr. of Lancaster PENN–SYLVANIA.*
    Armorial. Chippendale. Motto-ribbon empty ;

bears some marks of being unfinished. Judge of the Supreme Court of Pennsylvania, 1777–1791.

41. ATWOOD. *Harry Atwood.*
   Armorial. Chippendale. Very ornate; architectural and landscape effects used. No motto.

42. AUCHMUTY. *Richard Tylden Auchmuty.*
   Plain armorial. Motto, *Dum spiro spero.* Signed, *A & S.*

43. BACKHOUSE. *W. Backhouse, M.A.*
   Armorial. Chippendale. Motto, *Pax et amor.*

44. BACKUS. *Elijah Backus.*
   Armorial. Jacobean. No motto ; name on motto-ribbon. Very crude workmanship.

45. BALDWIN. *D. Baldwin, Owner.*
   An engraved label, the words being within an oval wreath.

46. BALDWIN. *Jonathan Baldwin.*
   Armorial. Signed by Callender.

47. BALDWIN. *Luke Baldwin.*
   Armorial. Signed by Callender.

48. BALL. *Flamen Ball.*
   Armorial. Ribbon and Wreath. Motto, *Semper caveto.* Signed, *P. R. Maverick. Sct.*

49. BALLORD. *Wm. Ballord's.*
   Armorial. Plain. No motto.

50. BALTIMORE. *The Library Company of Baltimore.*
   Simply the name engraved within an oval frame. Signed, *S. Allardice Phi.*

51. BANCKER. *Abraham Bancker.*
   Pictorial. An eagle bears aloft an oval frame which contains the large figure 4 always seen on the book-plates of this family. A ribbon flying from the beak of the eagle bears the motto, *Sublimiora petamus ;* beneath, a three-masted vessel, with homing pennant streaming, passes half-submerged trees and a chain of mountain peaks. Signed, *Maverick Sculp'.*

52. BANCKER.   *Charles N. Bancker.*
    Armorial in style, but showing no actual arms.
    The shield is occupied by a large figure 4, which is
    an old "merchant mark." Chippendale. Puffy
    cupids are seated on either side of the frame with
    accessories which indicate the pursuit of science.
    Motto, *Dieu defend le droit.* Signed, *Jones Sc.* Of
    Philadelphia.

53. BANCKER.   *Charles N. Bancker.*
    A Chippendale frame enclosing the figure 4, and
    showing the same motto as the above. Helmet,
    wreath and crest, the eagle's wings erect, ppr.
    Not signed.

54. BANCKER.   *Evert Bancker, Junr.*
    A smaller and older plate than the others of this
    name, and showing the same figure 4, with rather
    wild mantling, and crest.

55. BANCKER.   *Gerard Bancker.*
    Chippendale. A cupid holding a globe converses
    with a companion, perhaps about commerce and
    ocean currents ; behind them a pyramid rises, and
    two other cupids are consulting a plan. The
    figure 4 is again prominent in this plate. Signed,
    Dawkins Sculpsit.

56. BANCROFT.   *George Bancroft.*
    Pictorial. A chubby cherub approaches, with a
    panel in his hands on which the words ΕΙΣ ΦΑΟΣ
    are given. Another plate, identical in all other
    details, gives the motto, *Sursum corda.* Historian
    of the United States.

57. BANISTER.   *John Banister.*
    Plain armorial. (Arms of Banester of Easington,
    County York, according to Burke). No motto.
    Of Virginia. Revolutionary soldier. Died, 1787.

58. BARRELL.   *Joseph Barrell.*
    An allegorical plate full of detail. In the centre is
    the shield with the arms, while above the crest sits
    Hope with her anchor. As indicative of Industry, a
    very trim female figure is presented, surrounded by

signs of prosperity, such as the beehive, palette and brush, and square and dividers. In contrast to this a bare-footed, raggedly clad woman with a dead fish in her lap, snails on her shoulders, broken tools around her, and with every appearance of misery and squalor, is shown at the left. The contrast between Thrift and Indolence is continued in a second series of pictures below the shield. In these it is the begging tramp and the erect, well-clothed gentleman who depict the moral. Dilapidated shanties and well-built houses are also in contrast. Mottoes, *Not always so — Indure but hope.* A rich Boston merchant. A pioneer in the Northwest coast trade.

59. BARROLL. *William Barroll. Chestertown. 1795.*
An engraved name label, with the all-seeing eye above the oval frame which encloses the name. The palm and holly are crossed beneath.

60. BARTON. *William Barton.*
Armorial. Perhaps the plate of the capturer of Genl. Prescott (1777) in Narragansett Bay.

61. BARTRAM. *John Bartram.*
Armorial. Chippendale. Motto, *Foy en Dieu.* A second motto, *J'avance.* Celebrated botanist of Pennsylvania.

62. BATHURST. Armorial. Of Virginia. See Burke's "Extinct Baronetage."

63. BAY. *William Bay. M.D.*
Armorial. Ribbon and Wreath, Motto, *Quo fata vocant.* The heraldic drawing is poor and the charges are reversed. Born, Albany, 1773. Died, 1865.

64. BAYARD. *James A. Bayard.*
The name well engraved within an oval wreath. The Delaware statesman, leader of the Federal party, and one of the negotiators of the Treaty of Ghent. Born, 1767; died, 1815.

65. BAYARD. *Saml. Bayard.*
Armorial. Chippendale. No motto. This is a very interesting specimen of the debased Chip-

pendale. As decorative features the following are
used : a large globe, quadrant, compass, sun-dial,
beer-stein, and a little landscape. The branches
of the frame are made to support these objects
named. Jurist. Published books on law.

66. BAYLEY. Armorial. Of the Eastern Shore, Va.

67. BEATTY. *J. Beatty. M.D.*
Armorial. Pictorial. The shield rests against the
bole of an oak, and while the arms on it (Arg. a
beehive surrounded by bees) are not given in Burke,
the crest appears in Fairbairn, with some changes.
A globe, open book, scroll, caduceus, and cornucopia
of fruit complete the accessories. Not a common
type among American plates. John Beatty was
born in Pennsylvania, 1749, and died in New
Jersey in 1826. Rose to the rank of Colonel in
the Revolutionary War, and was delegate to Congress, 1783–1785. Member of Federal Convention,
and member of Congress. Illustrated in " Curio,"
page 114.

68. BECK. *Charles Beck.*
Armorial. Ribbon and Wreath. Signed, *N. D. Sc.*
(Nathaniel Dearborn). Of Cambridge, Mass.
Scholar and author.

69. BEDLOW. *William Bedlow.*
Armorial. Monogram *B L* at foot of arms.
Jacobean. Motto, *My hope on high.* Of Bedlow's
Island, New York.

70. BEETE. *Joseph Beete. Demerary.*
Plain armorial. Motto, *Fortuna perit, honestas
manet.*

71. BELCHER. (Anonymous.)
Armorial. Jacobean. Motto, *Loyal jusqu'a la
Mort.* This is the plate of the Colonial Governor
of Massachusetts and New Hampshire, 1730–1741
(Jonathan Belcher). The arms are the same as
borne on the plate of his son Jonathan, except that
this plate shows a label for difference. There is
also a shortening of the motto in the other plate.

72. BELCHER. *Jonathan Belcher E Societate Medij Templi.*
Armorial. Jacobean. Very similar to the last.
Motto, *Loyal au mort.* Son of the preceding ;
born in Boston, 1710. Graduate of Harvard,
student at the Middle Temple, one of the first
settlers of Halifax, N.S. Died there, 1776. Illustrated in " Curio," page 113.

William Belcher.

SAVANNAH.

73. BELCHER. *William Belcher, Owner.*
Literary. A shelf of books enclosed within an oval
which bears the mottoes, *With welcome use — but
use with care. The wicked borrow, — but never
return.* Of New London, Conn., circa 1790.

74. BELCHER. *William Belcher. Savannah.*
Armorial. Pictorial. A very beautiful engraving.
The shield rests upon the ground and is supported
by the oak tree which spreads over it ; willows and
pines complete the little group of trees, and beyond
a stretch of water is seen. The motto, *Loyal au
mort,* is on the ribbon which flutters along the
ground beside the shield.

75. BEL-CHIER. *J. Bel-Chier.*
      Armorial.   Jacobean.   Motto, *Loyal jusq' a la mort.*   Printed in red ink.

76. BERESFORD. *Richard Beresford, Charleston.   1772.*
      Armorial.

77. BETTS. *William Betts.*
      Armorial.   Plain.   Motto, *Malo mori quam foedari.*   Signed, *C. P. Harrison Del. Sct.*

78. BEVERLEY. *Harry Beverley.*
      Armorial.   Chippendale.   No motto.

79. BEVERLY. *Robert Beverly.*
      Armorial.   Of Virginia.   Historian.

80. BEVERLY. *William Beverly.*
      Armorial.   Signed, *J. Kirk.*

81. BLACKLEY. *Absalom Blackley.*
      Armorial.   Ribbon and wreath.   Motto, *Utere mundo.*   Signed, *Maverick Scp.*   The name supported by two quills.

82. BLAKE. *Willm. P. & L. Blake's Circulating Library at the Boston Book Store.*
      An engraved label enclosed in an ornamental oval frame.   Signed, *S. Hill. Sc.*

83. BLANC. *William Blanc.   Middle Temple.   Dominica.*
      Crest only.   Motto on a garter enclosing the crest, *Frangas non flectan.*

84. BLATCHFORD. *Thomas W. Blatchford.*
      Plain armorial.   Motto, *Providentia sumus.*   Signed, *Wm. D. Smith sc.*

85. BLEECKER. *Bleecker.*
      Plain armorial.   A festoon of cloth behind the shield.

86. BLENMAN. *Jonathan Blenman Attoray, Genl. & Judge of ye Admty. in Barbadoes.*
      A small plate, without motto, rather poorly engraved.   A little ornamentation of Jacobean manner appears at either side, and the mantling is rather profuse, but well above the shield.

Maverick Sc?

Absalom Blachly.

87. BLOOMFIELD. *Bloomfield.*
    Armorial. Chippendale. Rudely drawn books
    used in the frame. Motto, *Pro aris et focis.*
    Signed, *J. Trenchard.* Major Joseph Bloomfield
    was a soldier in the Revolution, Governor of New
    Jersey, Brigadier-General in War of 1812, member
    of Congress, 1817–21. Illustrated in the "Art
    Amateur," April, 1894.

88. BOLLING. *Robt. Bolling Esq'r.*
    Armorial. Chippendale. Figures are used as
    supporters which would appear to symbolize the
    freedom of the Garden of Eden, and the learning
    of classic Greece. Motto-ribbon empty ; no crest.
    Of Chellowe, Va. Illustrated in " Curio," page 15.

89. BONAPARTE. *Jerome Napoleon Bonaparte.*
    A plain label, with an ornamental type border.
    Nephew of Napoleon the Great. Born in England,
    1805 ; died in Baltimore, Md., 1870.

90. BOND. *T. Bond, Surgeon.*
    Armorial. Chippendale. Signed, *W. H.* Native
    of Maryland ; 1712–1784. A distinguished physi-
    cian and surgeon of Philadelphia.

91. BOOTH. *Benjn. Booth.*
    Crest only. Autograph in a wreath under the
    crest. Of New York, until the Revolution broke
    out.

92. BOOTH. *George Booth.*
    Literary. A lighted candle and books in con-
    fusion are placed upon a table. The name is
    carved upon the edge of the table. On one of the
    book-covers appears the Booth crest. An etched
    plate.

93. BOSTON. *Shakspeare Circulating Library, Charles Cal-
    lender, No. 25 School Street, Boston.*
    A very curious old woodcut, with a large oval
    medallion of the famous writer for whom the
    library was named placed in the centre against a
    rough rock background ; the masks of Comedy
    and Tragedy lie at the foot, and the hilts of foils
    can be made out ; a garland of roses falls at the
    right hand, and the rays of the sun come over the
    top. This is a rough engraving, very black and
    indistinct.

94. BOSTON. *Social Law Library. Boston.*
    The name appears on a curtain looped up and held
    by cord and tassel ; above this a small oval encloses
    a view of four waterspouts, each from behind a
    rock ; above this the circular frame encloses a hand
    bearing a lighted torch ; on the frame is the motto,
    Vestra cura alitur, and the date 1804 ; a pile of
    books above for crest, with *S.L.L.* on the cover
    of one.

95. BOUCHER. *Jonathan Boucher.*
Armorial. Chippendale. Motto, *Non vi sed voluntate.* A Loyalist clergyman in Virginia, whose estates were confiscated, after which he returned to England whence he had come in 1754. Published a tract on the causes and consequences of the Revolution, and compiled a glossary of Provincial and Archæological Words, which was purchased of his family in 1831, for the proprietors of Webster's Dictionary.

96. BOUDINOT. *Boudinot.*
Armorial. Ribbon and Wreath. Motto, *Soli Deo gloria et honor.* Elias Boudinot, born in 1740, in Philadelphia, of Huguenot extraction. Sided strongly with the colonies in the Revolution, and was President of Congress in 1782. A signer of the Treaty of Peace. Died, 1821. This plate is not signed, but it is the work of Maverick. Illustrated in "Curio," page 111.

97. BOWDOIN. *Honble. James Bowdoin. Esqr.*
Plain armorial. Motto, *Ut aquila versus coelum.* The same plate as the Bowdoin College, whose benefactor he was.

98. BOWDOIN. *Bowdoin College.*
Plain armorial. The arms of the Hon. James Bowdoin are given with his motto, *Ut aquila versus coelum.* The sun in splendor shines above the crest, and the name of the college is engraved over it. This college was chartered in 1794, and then presented with eleven hundred pounds and one thousand acres of land, by Hon. James Bowdoin, son of the governor of the colony. By his will a further gift was made to the college.

99. BOYLSTON. *Boylston Medical Library.*
Plain armorial. The arms of the Boylston family are given without ornamentation or motto. Signed, *Annin & Smith.* Ward Nicholas Boylston, a patron of medical science, gave to the medical school of Harvard College a valuable collection of anatomical and medical books and engravings, in the year 1800.

100. BOYLSTON. *Property of the Boylston Medical Library Cambridge.*

Armorial. The arms of the Boylston family are given. Signed, *Callender Sc.*

101. BOZMAN. *John Leeds Bozman. Esqr of the Middle Temple.*

Armorial. Ribbon and Wreath. Motto, *Sine virtute vani sunt honores.* Lawyer, poet, and historian; born in Maryland in 1757, died in 1823. University of Penn., 1783. Completed his studies in London. His chief work is the "History of Maryland to the Restoration in 1660." An "Historical and Philosophical Sketch of the Prime Causes of the Revolutionary War" was suppressed; in this Washington was praised and Franklin depreciated. This same copper has been used more recently with the following words added: on either side of the crest, "John Leeds Kerr of Talbot Co. Md. 15th Jan. 1780, 21st Feb. 1844;" at the bottom, under the name of Bozman, "The Maryland Historian, 25th Aug. 1757, 20th April, 1823."

102. BRASHER. *Philip Brasher.*

Armorial. Ribbon and Wreath. Motto, *Beata Domus, Custodita Sic Cuja Deo Domino Est.* The shield, with its motto-ribbon and flowery ornamentation, seems to be held up by the winged female who grasps the portcullis of the crest. Below the shield a patch of ground is strewn with books and writing material. A dwarfed weeping willow bends mournfully at the left. Signed on an unrolled sheet of paper, *Maverick Scp.* Was a prisoner in a sugar-house in New York during the Revolutionary War, which suggested the crest; he had no right to the arms.

103. BRAZER. *John Brazer.*

Plain armorial. Shaded mantling. Motto, *Try.* Of Salem, Mass.

104. BREARLY. *David Brearly.*

Armorial. Ribbon and Wreath. Motto, *Honor virtutis praemium.* A large plate; attributed to

Vallance.   Jurist, of Trenton, N.J.   A brave officer in the Revolution.

105. BRIDGEN.   *Charles Bridgen.*
Plain armorial.   Motto, *Probitate et industria.* This plate is not signed, but it is very probably the work of Maverick.

106. BRIMAGE.   *William Brimage.*
Plain armorial.   Impaling Gilbert.   Arms closely surrounded by a garter on which the name appears. Motto below, *Deus dux certus.*   Of Virginia.

107. BRISBANE.   *William Brisbane.*
Armorial.   Ribbon and Wreath.   Motto, *Dabit otia Deus.*

108. BROOKS.   *Benjamin S. Brooks.*
Armorial.   Ribbon and Wreath.   Motto, *Sustinere.* Signed, *A. D.* (Amos Doolittle).

109. BROWN.   *David Paul Brown.*
Plain armorial.   Motto, *Patria cara, carior libertas.* Signed, *C. P. H.   St.*   Lawyer, of Philadelphia.

110   BROWN.   *The Property of Jacob Brown.*
Pictorial.   The interior of a library is depicted, within an oval frame which is ornamented above with a ribbon and a spray of holly ; the name is given on the fluttering ends of the ribbon.   The central portion of the library is occupied by a couch, covered with striped cloth, on which a youth, dressed in the height of the fashion, reclines ; a book is laid upon the convenient corner of the table, and he is reading from this ; behind him the shelves of books are seen partly covered by a curtain ; through the window are seen the nodding pines ; the carpet is adorned with thirteen stars.   The following lines are given below the frame : —

Weigh well each thought, each sentence freely scan,
In Reason's balance try the works of man;
Be bias'd not by those who praise or blame,
Nor, Servile, Yield opinion to a Name.

Signed, *Engrd. by P. R. Maverick 65 Liberty Street.* As the name *Jacob Brown* is not engraved, but is printed by hand, it is quite likely that this plate was for promiscuous use ; either to be filled up with the name of any who ordered it, or to be pasted in the books sold by some bookseller.

111. BROWN. *John Carter Brown.*
Crest only. Motto, *Gaudeo.*

112. BROWN. *Thomas Brown.*
Armorial. Arms, ... on a chevron, between three leopards' heads cabossed, or as many escallops . . . . . . Crest, an eagle's head erased or. Motto, *En esperance je vie.* Signed by Hurd.

113. BROWNE. *Peter A. Browne.*
Literary. A plain table, with the scull and cross-bones carved in two places upon it, supports several large volumes, on the side of one of which is the name of the owner. On the side of the table the motto is cut, *Fiat Justitia.* A wreath of laurel rests upon the books, and the all-seeing eye looks upon the scene from above. Signed, *Engraved by James Akin.* A prominent lawyer in Philadelphia, and the author of "Browne's Reports."

114. BROWNSON. *Oliver Brownson's Property.*
An engraved label with the name curved over a peacock which is perched on a scroll.

115. BRUEN. *M. Bruen.*
Plain armorial. Motto, *Fides scutum.* Matthias Bruen was a clergyman in New York City; ordained in London, 1819.

116. BRUFF. *The Property of J. G. Bruff, Portsmouth, Va. 183–.*
Pictorial. On this, a weeping elm supports a large shield on which the inscription is given; so large is the shield that only a little of the tree shows around the edge of the shield. A woodcut.

117. BUCHANAN. *W. B. Buchanan.*
Armorial. Motto, *Clarior hinc honos.*

118. BULL. *Martin Bull.*

Armorial. A plain armorial plate with the mantling extending down the side of the shield. Motto, *Virtus basis vitae.* This is the plate of one of the engravers of the old Farmington book-plate, Deacon Bull. See "Ex Libris Journal," Vol. III, page 187.

119. BURKE. *James Henry Burke Esqr.*

Armorial. Ribbon and Wreath. Motto, *Sola salus servire Deo.* Of Virginia.

120. BURNET. *John Burnet. Attorney at Law New York.*

Armorial. Jacobean frame; mantling. Motto, *Virescit vulnere virtus.* This plate is earlier than the succeeding one by Dawkins.

121. BURNET. *John Burnet Esqr New York.*

Armorial. Chippendale. The usual pastoral scene which Dawkins used is found here; the shepherdess, and the cupids making music on the flute, and bringing books for leisure moments. Motto, *Virescit vulnere virtus.* Signed, *H. Dawkins Sculp. 1754.* Illustrated in "Curio," page 13.

122. BYAM. *Francisci Byam, ex Insula Antigua.*

Armorial. Jacobean. Motto, *Claris dextera factis.* Rich mantling continued around the whole shield; the background shell-lined. Printed in brown ink.

123. BYRD. *William Byrd of Westover in Virginia Esqr.*

Armorial. Jacobean. A very interesting specimen of its class. The profuse mantling thrown high in the air, the shell-lined background, and the curtain upheld at the ends (on which the name and address are given) are prominent characteristics as pointed out by Warren. A rich abundance of fruit overflows from two cornucopiæ, and the motto-ribbon is twined in and out through the scrolls at the base. Motto, *Nulla pallescere culpa.* Colonel Byrd was a very distinguished Virginian: was born to an ample fortune, liberally educated, and became the patron of science and literature in his native state. President of the Council of the colony;

author of the "Westover Manuscripts," and of other essays. Born, 1674; died, 1744. Illustrated in "Curio," page 14.

124. CABELL. *Doct.r Geo. Cabell Richmond Virga.*

Allegorical. In the centre of the design a flaming heart rests upon the shank of an anchor. A thin patch of ground, which grows a few trees, and looks like an island, upholds these emblems of hope. The motto is just above, — *Spes mea in Deo.* Above this again the all-seeing eye, wreathed in clouds, appears. The whole is enclosed in a design of Ribbon and Wreath arrangement. Evidently the work of Brooks, who engraved the plate of Dr. I. Dove of the same city.

125. CABELL. *Samuel Jordan Cabell, of Soldier's Joy.*

Pictorial. The name is printed from type upon a large oval medallion; this is supported by the half-draped figure of Liberty holding the pole with the cap upon it, and an officer in the uniform of the Continental Army. The arms of the United States are above the medallion. The pictorial parts of this are cut in wood.

126. CABOT. *William Cabot.*

Armorial. Wild Chippendale. No motto. Of Massachusetts.

127. CADENA. *M. V. C.* (Mariano de la Cadena.)

Plain armorial. An ordinary square shield supported by a very peculiar frame. Motto, *Fidem servat vinculaque sulvit.* A Professor of Spanish in Columbia College.

128. CADENA. *Don Mariano Valazquez de la Cadena.*

Plain armorial. No motto. Of New York City.

129. CADENA. *Mariano Valazquez de la Cadena.*

Small, plain armorial. Of New York City.

130. CAILLAUD. *John Caillaud. Esqr.*

Armorial. Ribbon and Wreath. The frame enclosing the arm is oval in form and quite peculiar in construction; an eagle with a chaplet in his beak appears as a crest.

131. CALLAWAY. *Thomas Callaway.*
  Plain armorial. Motto, *Aliis quod ab aliis.*

132. CALLENDER. *John Callender.*
  Armorial. Pictorial. The shield rests against a rock, mossgrown and over-topped by shrubs. Signed, *Callender Sc.* Of Massachusetts.

133. CALVERT. *Thos. Calvert.*
  Armorial. Chippendale. Motto-ribbon empty.

134. CAMPBELL. *Donald Campbell. Jamaica.*
  Armorial. The shield affixed to the mast of a lymphad. (The crest of this family of Campbells.) Motto, *Fit via vi.*

135. CARMICHAELL. *The Honourable Wm Carmichaell Esqr.*
  Armorial. Early English. The very full mantling nearly surrounds the shield. Motto, *Toujours prest.* Diplomatist. Born in Maryland. Delegate to Congress, 1778–1780. Foreign minister. Illustrated in "Curio," page 16.

136. CARROLL. *Charles Carroll.*
  Armorial. Chippendale. No motto. The last surviving signer of the Declaration. Died, 1832. This was the Charles Carroll who added " of Carrollton " after his signature to the Declaration, that no mistake might ever be made in recognizing him. Illustrated in " Book Lovers' Almanac," 1894. Duprat and Co., New York.

137. CARROLL. *Charles Carroll Barrister at Law.*
  Armorial. Jacobean. No motto. The same arms as the Charles Carroll.

138. CARROLL. *Charles Carroll of ye Inner Templer Esqr, Second Son of Daniell Carroll of Litterlouna Esqr. in the Kings County in the Kingdom of Ireland.*
  Armorial. Early English. Elaborate mantling all about the shield. Motto-ribbon empty. Grandfather of Charles Carroll of Carrollton, the signer. Emigrated to Maryland about 1686.

139. CARROLL. *Ephm. Carroll.*
  Armorial. Ribbon and Wreath. Motto, *In fide et in bello fortes.*

140. CARY. *Alpheus Cary. Jr.*
  Plain armorial. The shield surrounded by an oval frame of sun's rays. Signed, *A. Cary del. H. Morse Sc.* Of Massachusetts.

141. CARY. *Miles Cary.*
  Armorial. Chippendale. Motto, *Sine Deo careo.* Of Virginia.

142. CARY. *Thomas Cary.*
  Armorial. Ribbon and Wreath. Motto, *In medio tutissimus ibis.* Signed, *Callender Scp.* Of Massachusetts.

143. CAY. *Gabriel Cay.*
  Crest only. Name enclosed in Jacobean frame. No motto. Of Virginia.

144. CHALMERS. *Geo. Chalmers.*
  Armorial. Motto, *Spero.* A resident of Maryland ; a stiff Loyalist ; author of " Chalmers' Annals."

145. CHAMBERS. *Benjamin Chambers's Book.*
   Armorial. False heraldry. Plain armorial plate
   with supporters, surrounded by a circular wreath.
   Motto, *Spiro.* Founder of Chambersburg, Penn.

146. CHAMBERS. *John Chambers Esqr.*
   Armorial. Arms not in Burke. Az. a chevron or.
   bet. three cockle shells of the last. Chippendale.
   Motto, *Vincit veritas.* Signed, *E. Gallaudet Sculp.*
   Chief Justice of New York, 1754.

147. CHANDLER. *Gardiner Chandler.*
   Armorial. Chippendale. Motto-ribbon empty.
   Signed, *P. Revere Sculp.* Of Massachusetts.

148. CHANDLER. *John Chandler Junr Esqr.*
   Armorial. Chippendale. A very handsome design
   in the best of Hurd's styles. Has the characteristic
   flow of water from the large shell at the bottom.
   No motto. Signed, *N. Hurd Sculp.* Of Massachusetts.

149. CHANDLER. *Rufus Chandler.*
   Armorial. Attributed to Hurd.

150. CHASE. *Sl. Chase.*
   Armorial. Chippendale. Motto, *Ne cede malis.*
   Signed, *Boyd Sc.* A signer of the Declaration
   from Maryland.

151. CHAUNCEY. *Chauncey.*
   Plain armorial. Motto, *Gloria.*

152. CHAUNCEY. *Charles Chauncey.*
   Plain armorial. Motto-ribbon empty.

153. CHAUNCEY. *Charles Chauncey M.D.*
   Plain armorial. Motto, *Sublimis per ardua tendo.*
   Two fierce lions couch upon the ends of the motto-
   ribbon, and the mantling envelopes the shield.
   The initials *C. C.,* in cipher, are given between the
   two names.

154. CHAUNCEY. *J. St. Clair Chauncey.*
   Plain armorial. Motto, *Gloria.* An officer of the
   United States Navy.

155. CHAWNEY. Armorial. Of Pennsylvania.

156. CHESTER. *John Chester.*
>   Plain armorial. On a ribbon tied above, *By the name of Chester.* No motto. Of Wethersfield, Conn. Colonel in the Continental Army ; commander of the " elite corps" ; was in the battle of Bunker Hill.

157. CHILD. *Francis Child.*
>   Armorial. Chippendale. Motto, *Pro lege et rege.* Signed, *H. Dawkins. Sculpt.* Very fine work.

158. CHILD. *The Property of Isaac Child.*
>   Under the name is the verse beginning —
>
>   > *If thou art borrowed by a friend,*
>   > *Right welcome shall he be,* etc.
>
>   Signed, *Sold by N. Dearborn & Son.* Undoubtedly engraved by Dearborn.

159. CHILD. *Isaac Child, Boston.*
>   Literary. Four shelves of books. Probably by Dearborn.

160. CHILD. *Thomas Child.*
>   Armorial. Chippendale. Motto, *Fari aude.* Not signed, but evidently the work of Nathaniel Hurd. First Postmaster of Portland, Me.

161. CHILD. *William Henry Child.*
>   Armorial in form, but displaying no arms on the shield. Crest, two doves with olive branches in their mouths. The initials *W. H. C.*, in cipher, occupy the shield. Ribbon and Wreath. No motto. Very similar in design to the plate of George Grote, the historian. Illustrated in "Art Amateur," April, 1894.

162. CLARK. *D. Lawrence Clark.*
>   Armorial. Ribbon and Wreath. Motto, *Semper idem.* Undoubtedly the arms are not genuine : the argent field of the shield is charged with a branch of holly, and the crest is the American eagle, with a star above its head.

163. CLARK. *John Clark. M.D.*
>   Plain armorial. Motto, *Semper idem.* The arms are undoubtedly assumed ; az. an oak branch ppr. Crest, an American eagle, with a star (mullet) above.

164. CLARKE. *Alfred Clarke.*
    Crest only. Motto, *Soyez ferme.* Of Coopers-town, N.Y.

165. CLARKE. *George Clarke.*
    Crest only. Motto, *Soyez ferme.* Signed, *J. F. Morin. Sc. N.Y.*

166. CLARKE. *Peter Clarke.*
    Armorial. Chippendale. Motto, *Coronat virtus cultores suos.* Printed in blue ink.

167. CLARKSON. *David Clarkson Gent.*
    Armorial. Jacobean. No motto. Of New York. Illustrated in " Curio," page 66.

168. CLARKSON. *M. Clarkson.*
    Armorial, plain. No motto. Matthew Clarkson was for twenty-one years the President of the Bank of New York.

169. CLEBORNE. *C. I. Cleborne. M.D.*
    Armorial. The shield canted to one side, surmounted by the helmet; it and the mantling is enclosed within a circular ribbon, on which the motto, *Clibor ne sceame,* is given. A second ribbon over the design bears the motto, *Virtute invidiam vincas.* Signed, *Jarrett London.*

170. CLEVELAND. *Stephen Cleveland.*
    Pictorial. A very unusual plate : a full-rigged British man-of-war, with ten guns peering from the loop-holes, is hastening from the observer ; the English ensign flies from the stern. A very spirited piece of work. It is said that his commission as Captain in our Navy just after the Declaration was the first one issued. Born in Connecticut, 1740, died in Massachusetts, 1801.

171. CLINTON. *De Witt Clinton.*
    Armorial. Ribbon and Wreath. Motto, *Patria cara carior libertas.* Signed, *P. R. Maverick. sculpt.* Governor of New York, 1817–1822, and 1824–1827. Illustrated in " Art Amateur," February, 1894.

172. COCK. *William Cock.*

Armorial. Ribbon and Wreath. Motto, *Quod fieri non vis alteri ne fueris.* Signed, *Maverick Sculpt.* The tinctures in the crest — which looks like a leghorn — are indicated by the words, gules and or. engraved outside, and connected with the parts thus tinctured by dotted lines, — a new method. Of New York. Illustrated in "Art Amateur," March, 1894.

173. COFFIN. Coffin arms : name erased. Armorial. Ribbon and Wreath. Motto, *Post tenebras speramus lumen de lumine.* Signed, *J. Akin Sculp.* The name *N. W. Coffin* is written upon the copy at hand. The arms are of the family of Sir Isaac Coffin, who was born in Boston, 1759.

174. COFFIN. *Hector Coffin.*

Armorial. Ribbon and Wreath. Motto, *Exstant recte factus praemia.* Signed, *J. Akin del. F. Kearny Sc.* Of Boston.

175. COFFIN. *John Coffin. 1771.*

Armorial. A frame of Jacobean tendencies. Motto-ribbon empty. Of Massachusetts.

176. COLDEN. *Cadwallader D. Colden.*

Plain armorial. Motto, *Fais bien crains rien.* Mayor of New York City in 1818. Friend and coadjutor of De Witt Clinton.

177. COLUMBIA COLLEGE. *Columbia College Library New York.* Allegorical. The scene is out-of-doors ; a throne placed on rising ground is occupied by the Goddess of Learning ; the Shekinah blazes above and the rising sun peeps over the horizon. Three little nude beginners in learning stand before the Goddess, in whose hand an open book is extended bearing the motto, Λογια Ζὼνζα. From her mouth a scroll issues bearing in Hebrew the motto, אוריאר *Let there be light.* Beneath this scene is the reference *I Pet. II 1. 2 &c.* The name of the library appears upon the circular frame which encloses the whole scene ; the motto, *In lumine tuo videbimus lumen,* follows the inner line of the circle. Above,

an urn is overfilled with the blossoms of knowledge, while the background of the whole is a brick wall. Signed, *Anderson sculp.*

178. CONNECTICUT THEOLOGICAL INSTITUTE. *Theol. Institute of Con. 1833. Presented by*

Pictorial. The representation is of a pulpit with winding stairs on either side, and a very tall solemn-looking sounding-board behind it, partially hid by a curtain. The front panel of the pulpit has the following, ΚΗΡΥΣΣΟΜΕΝ ΧΡΙΣΤΟΝ ᾿ΕΣΤΑ-ΥΡΩΜΕΝΟΝ.

179. CONNECTICUT THEOLOGICAL INSTITUTE. *Society of Inquiry. Theological Institute of Connecticut.* Three book shelves disclosed by a drawn curtain.

180. CONNOLLY. *Charles M. Connolly.*

Armorial. Motto, *En Dieu est tout.* Signed, *J. G. Bolen, 104 B'way.*

181. CONSTABLE. *William Constable.*

Plain armorial. Motto, *Post tot Naufragia portus.* Of the early New York family that owned large estates near Utica, N.Y. This plate is circa 1783 and was engraved in New York. It is interesting as a specimen of twisted heraldry ; the correct arms are " Quarterly, gu. and vaire, over all a bend or." (Flamburgh. Co. York. descended from Robert De Lacy, second son of John De Lacy, Baron of Halton, and Constable of Chester). See Burke. In this plate the arms are " Quarterly vaire and gu. over all a bend sinister or.," which are manifestly incorrect. It was not probably the purpose of the engraver to make this alteration, but not understanding heraldic drawing he drew the arms correctly on the copper, which reversed them in the print.

182. COOLEY. *Abial A. Cooley's Property.*

An elaborate plate of its kind, which is unusual ; it is regular die-sinker's work, and is printed in red ink. The word *Property* is on a ribbon which is arched over a peacock and a dove ; scrolls abound in convenient places. The only copy seen is in a Boston imprint, 1742.

183. COOPER. *Myles Cooper LL.D. Coll. Regis Nov. Ebor. in America. Praefes, et Coll. Reginae de Oxon. Socius &c.*
   Armorial. Chippendale. No motto. Second President of King's College (now Columbia). His Loyalist inclinations resulted in a hasty flight from the college ; he escaped to England, where he was an honored preacher. Illustrated in " Art Amateur," April, 1894.

184. COURTENAY. *Henry Courtenay.*
   Armorial. Chippendale. No motto. Very similar in style to the Philip Dumaresque. Not signed, but undoubtedly by Hurd. Of Massachusetts.

185. COX. *Chris. C. Cox. A.M. M.D.*
   A name-label with the skull and crossed bones above the name. The motto, *Lectorem delectando paritque monendo,* is given below.

186. COX. *Chris. C. Cox. A.M. M.D. LL.D.*
   Armorial. Crest only. Motto, *Fortiter et fideliter.*

187. CRANCH. *Richd. Cranch. Braintree.*
   An engraved label. The name is within an oval frame, formed of oak and laurel leaves. This plate was engraved by William Bond of Falmouth (now Portland), in 1786. Richard Cranch was a brother-in-law of John Adams, and lived in Quincy, and also in the adjoining town of Braintree.

188. CRAVEN. *Craven.*
   Armorial. Motto, *Verus in actione consistit.* This is the plate of Lord William Craven, one of the Lords Proprietors of South Carolina.

189. CROOKSHANK. *Judge Crookshank.*
   Armorial. Chippendale. Motto, *Lege et ratione.*

190. CUNNINGHAM. *James Cunningham, Junior.*
   Armorial. Jacobean. No motto. Printed in blue ink.

191. CUNYNGHAM. *Robert Cunyngham, of Cayou in ye Island of St. Christopher in America, Esqr.*
   An old armorial plate ; no further information at hand.

192. CURWEN. (Anonymous.)

Armorial. Jacobean. No motto. A crude piece of work. Of Salem, Mass.

193. CUSHING. *Jacob Cushing, His Book. 1746.*

A plain printed label with border of ornamental type.

194. CUSHMAN. *Cushman.*

Plain armorial. Motto, *Habeo pro jus fasque.* Signed, *Pulini Inc.* The famous actress, Charlotte Cushman.

195. CUSTIS. *Geo. Washg. Park Custis.*

Armorial. Chippendale. No motto. The last of Washington's family — builder of "Arlington." Son of the following.

196. CUSTIS. *John Park Custis.*

Armorial. Presumably assumed arms ; arg. an eagle displayed ppr. Crest, an eagle's head erased ppr. Chippendale. No motto. Son of Mrs. Washington by her first husband, Daniel Parke Custis. The engraver omitted the *e* from the middle name.

197. CUTTING. *James S. Cutting.*

Armorial. Ribbon and Wreath. Motto, *Postero ne credo.* Signed, *Maverick Sct.* Of New York.

198. CUTTING. *William Cutting.*

Armorial. Ribbon and Wreath. Motto, *Carpe diem : postero ne crede.* Signed, *P. R. Maverick Sct.* Of New York.

199. CUYLER. *John Cuyler.*

Armorial. Ribbon and Wreath. Motto-ribbon empty. Signed, *Maverick Sculpt.* Of New York.

200. DANA. *Edmund Trowbridge Dana.*

The same copper as the following plate, with slight alterations. In the upper left-hand corner the date *A.D. 1569* is given. Presumably the date of the grant of arms. Son of R. H. Dana. Translator and editor of works on International Law.

201. DANA. *Francis Dana.*

Armorial. Chippendale. Motto, *Cavendotutus.* Signed, *N. H. Scp.* A handsome plate in Hurd's best style. Statesman and jurist. Born, Charlestown, Mass., 1743 ; died in Cambridge, 1811.

202. DANA. *Richard Henry Dana.*
> The same old copper again retouched. The date *1569* is in new type, and the name is changed to the present user. Poet and essayist.

203. DANFORTH. *Danforth.*
> Armorial. Chippendale. Motto, *Ubi plura offendar maculis nitent non ego paucis.* Signed, *N. H. Scp.* At the upper left-hand corner, outside the design, the sun shines in full strength. Presumably the plate of Dr. Samuel Danforth of Boston. Born, 1740; died, 1827.

204. DARTMOUTH COLLEGE. *Library of Dartmouth College. Presented by Isaiah Thomas Esq A.D. 1819 in his Donation of 470 Volumes.*
> These words printed from type within a border of ornamental type disposed in an oval.

205. DARTMOUTH COLLEGE. *Social Friends Library.*
> A plain shield with thistles for decoration bears the number of the volume. Motto, *Sol sapientiae nunquam occidet.* The full sun above the shield.

206. DAVENPORT. Armorial. Of Virginia.

207. DAVIDSON. *Henry Davidson.*
> Armorial. Ribbon and Wreath. Motto, *Sapienter si sincere.* A very neat plate. The wreath has not the proper twisted effect, but appears more like a row of eggs than an heraldic wreath.

208. DAVIS. *Davis.*
> Plain armorial. Motto, *Auspice Christo.*

209. DAY. *John Day.*
> Plain armorial. Signed, *J. Smithers. Sculp.* Of Philadelphia.

210. DAY. *M. W. Day.*
> Pictorial. A collection of literary property is grouped in an open space where the rising sun shines strongly; the name is given upon a ribbon which floats above; from it depends a lamp; to the right, a book-case; to the left, a bust of Franklin, a large globe, books, ink-pot and quills;

in front, an unrolled parchment which purports to be a list of books. The following motto : —

> '*Tis education forms the common mind,*
> *Just as the twig is bent, the tree's inclined.*

Signed, *W. Chapin del & Sc.*

211. DEANE. *John Deane.*

Armorial. Ribbon and Wreath. No motto. Name on motto-ribbon.

212. DE BLOIS. *Lew's. De Blois.*

Armorial. Jacobean. No motto. Signed, *Nathaniel Hurd Sculp.* The mantling is well conceived but rudely engraved ; the shell-lined background is here, and the curtain upheld at the corners, on which the name is given. The whole appearance of the plate shows it to be quite early, and among the first attempts of Hurd.

213. DE BLOIS. *N. J. De Blois.*

Armorial. Jacobean, with handsome mantling. Motto, *Je me fie en Dieu.* "These arms are assumed by some members of the family of this name living in Newport, R.I. The first of the name in America was born in Fort George, N.Y., some time before the Revolution ; his descendants in New York and Newport carried on a great hardware business with their parents in England, but when the troubles occurred they became Tories and left the country. Some of the wax seals on their old letters bear the impression of a Moor's head, which may have been correct. Others had either the conceit or ignorance to assume the armorial bearings of the famous and noble family of Châtillon of France, which historical race became extinct in 1762. As, during the 14th century some members of the Châtillons were Comtes de Blois, this title, extinct in 1364, over 500 years ago, is most unwarrantably used as if it were the family name, and the Châtillon arms adopted in a most extraordinary way, reversing the ordinary way of acquiring arms ; so audacious and arrogant is the assumption and so sublime the impudence it entitles the fact to a high place in the Curiosities of Heraldry." (These notes are found accompanying the copy of the plate in the collection of the late Mr. James Eddy Mauran.) This plate is apparently copied from the one by Hurd, and as that is much earlier, it may be that the assumption of the arms was due to him instead of to the later users, who simply copied what appeared to be the legitimate plate and arms of an ancestor.

214. DEDHAM. *Library of the " Young Men's and Young Ladies' Societies for the Study of the Sacred Scriptures." Dedham, (Ms).*
The above inscription is printed from type within an oval frame which is cut on wood ; elongated cornucopiæ extend their blossoms above and around the central panel ; above in a small frame a lute and some music books.

215. DENNY. *William Denny.*
Armorial. Motto, *Et mea messis erit.* Governor of the Province of Pennsylvania.

216. DE PEYSTER. *Frederick De Peyster.*
Armorial. A plain, heart-shaped shield supported by two eagles on palm branches, which are crossed under the shield and extend upwards on either side. No motto. Signed, *P. R. Maverick Sct.* Of New York. Illustrated in "Art Amateur," February, 1894.

217. DERBY. *Martha Derby.*
The name printed within a border of flowers and sprays. A group of musical instruments above.

218. DERING. *Nicoll H. Dering.*
Armorial. No motto. The Thomas Dering plate by Hurd, with the name altered.

219. DERING. *Thomas Dering.*
Armorial. Chippendale. No motto. Signed, *N. Hurd Sculp 1749.* This is the earliest plate by an American engraver which is both signed and dated. But one copy is known at this writing. Illustrated in " Curio," page 14.

220. DERING. *Thomas Dering.*

Crest only, enclosed within a circular ring. The half-date *17* . is given. Resembles the work of Hurd somewhat.

221. DE WITT. *Richard Varick De Witt.*

A small pictorial plate, representing Minerva standing helmeted and with spear and shield in hand. On some copies of this plate the following additional inscription is found engraved, *From his uncle Richard Varick.*

222. DEXTER. *Samuel Dexter's. MDCCLXXXV.*

A printed label, with a border of ornamental type. Eminent lawyer and statesman. Secretary of War 1800, and Secretary of the Treasury, 1801.

223. DILL. *John E. Dill. Boston.*

A name-label in which the name is printed within a border made up of ornamental type, although it does not look so at first glance. The back of the design resembles a brick wall; the frame is made up of bouquets in holders, hearts, and an assortment of odds and ends.

224. DINWIDDIE. *Rob't. Dinwiddie.*

Armorial. Chippendale. Motto, *Ubi libertas ibi patria.* Lieutenant-Governor of Virginia, 1751–1758. See " Ex Libris Journal," Vol. II, pages 89, 125.

225. DOLBEARE. *Benjamin Dolbeare of Boston in New England. Oxford. Printed at the Clarendon Printing House. October, 6. 1739.*

A very large printed label, with three rows of ornamental type border, between which the following is printed, " The Noble Art and Mystery of PRINTING was first Invented by JOHN GUT–TENBERG of *Mentz,* a City of *Germany* in the YEAR 1440 and brought into ENGLAND by JOHN ISLIP of *London* in the year of our LORD 1471." This is very like the plate of Martha Bartlett, illustrated in " The Book-plate Collectors' Miscellany," page 20. See note from Mr. Tuer in same, page 29. There was an Edward Dolbier in the Boston Tea-party, 16th December, 1773.

226. DOVE. *Doct. I. Dove. Richmond. Virga.*

Armorial. Crest only. A dove ppr. holding an olive branch in her bill. Motto, *Deus providebit.* The design is completed by a festoon and crossed branches in Ribbon and Wreath style. Signed, *Brooks Sculp.* The Doct. Cabell plate was evidently the work of this same engraver.

227. DOVE. *Samuel E. Dove. Richmond. Va.*

Pictorial. The dove with the olive branch in her bill flies past mountains with water at their foot. Motto, *Ab initio Deus providebit,* on a circular garter enclosing the picture.

228. DRAYTON. *Drayton, South Carolina.*

Armorial. Ribbon and Wreath. Motto, *Non nobis solum.*

229. DRAYTON. *Jacob Drayton, South Carolina.*

The same copper as the above with the first name added.

230. DRAYTON. *Wm. Drayton, Middle Temple.*

Armorial. Chippendale. Motto, *Non nobis solum.* A smaller plate than the preceding, with the same arms. The name and address are given in a bracket bordered with scrolls and foliations. A jurist of South Carolina and Florida.

231. DRAYTON. *William Henry Drayton.*

Armorial. Statesman. Born at Drayton Hall-on-the-Ashley, near Charleston, S.C., 1742; died, 1779.

232. DUANE. *James Duane. Esqr.*

Armorial. Chippendale. Motto, *Nulli praeda.* Signed, *H. D. fect.* The usual pictorial elements of Dawkins' style are here introduced. The prim shepherdess and attendant swain on one side of the shield, and a lonely young girl singing to herself by a fountain, to the music of her guitar; her home cannot be far away as she wears no .hat and is in décolleté attire. Of New York. Statesman. Member of the Old Congress. Illustrated in "Art Amateur," March, 1894.

233. DUDLEY. *Joseph Dudley 1754.*

Armorial. Early English. The mantling is very full, curling upwards as well as downward and completely envelopes the shield. It is the common type of denticulated mantling, but not so elegant as some examples. Motto, *Nec gladio nec arcu.* The name appears on the usual scroll beneath the shield. Of the family of the Governor of the colony of Massachusetts. This date, *1754*, was added by Hurd, and is much later than the actual date of the plate.

234. DUER. *E Libris Gul. Alex. Duer.*

Plain armorial. Motto, *Esse et videri.* Of New York. Brother-in-law of Beverly Robinson. President of Columbia College from 1829 to 1842. Son of following.

235. DUER. *Willm. Duer. Esq.*

Armorial in form. Crest only. Ribbon and Wreath. Motto, *Esse quam videri.* Attributed to Maverick: the frame strongly resembles the Maturin Livingston. The name is on the shield. Born, 1747. Delegate to Continental Congress.

236. DUMARESQUE. *Philip Dumaresque.*

Armorial. Chippendale. No motto. Signed, *N. Hurd. Sculp.* One of the first officers of old Trinity Church in Boston.

237. DUMMER. *Jer. Dummer Anglus Americanus.*

Armorial. Early English. No motto. In the diary of John Hull, the coiner of the early specie of Massachusetts, the following entry is found: "1659. 1st of 5th. I received into my house Jeremie Dummer and Samuel Paddy, to serve me as apprentices eight years." In the "Heraldic Journal" we learn that Jeremiah Dummer was a goldsmith. Married in 1672 Hannah Atwater. He was the father of Governor William Dummer, and of Jeremiah Dummer the younger, the probable owner of this plate, who was Massachusetts agent in England, 1710–1721.

238. DUNCAN. *James H. Duncan.*
>   Armorial. Ribbon and Wreath. Motto, *Disce pati.* Very crude work.

239. DUNKIN. *Robert Henry Dunkin.*
>   Armorial. Motto, *Disce pati.* Signed, *I. H.* (Hutt.) Of Philadelphia.

240. DUNNING. *Charles E. Dunning.*
>   Armorial. Chippendale. Motto, *Semper paratus.* Foliage, roses and a griffin in the ornamentation.

241. DUNNING. *Charles S. Dunning.*
>   Armorial. Impaling Wijnkoop. Chippendale. (Late.) Motto, *Semper paratus.* More elaborate design than the above.

242. DURAND. *John Durand. Esqr.*
>   Armorial. Chippendale. Very fine. Presumably by the brother of Asher B. Durand, who was a fine engraver. A medallion beneath the shield shows cupids in a corn-field.

243. DUVALL. *E Bibliotheca Gabrielis Duvall. A.D. 1778.*
>   The name printed from type within a woodcut border, in which thirteen stars form a patriotic allusion. Signed, *T. S.* (Sparrow.) Of Huguenot descent. Born in Maryland, 1752. Jurist and Federal officer.

244. DYCKMAN. *Dyckman.*
>   Armorial. Ribbon and Wreath. The crossed branches are under the shield, and its edge is embellished with close festooning. *J. G.* written before the name. Motto, *Zyt bestindig.* Illustrated in "Art Amateur," April, 1894.

245. DYCKMAN. *States Morris Dyckman.*
>   Armorial. Ribbon and Wreath. Motto, *Zyt bestendig.*

246. EAST WINDSOR. *Miscellaneous Literary Association, East Windsor.*
>   Allegorical. Minerva in repose. A Greek mask near by.

247. EDWARDS. *Bryan Edwards Esqr. Greenwich Park, Jamaica.*

> Armorial. Chippendale. Very ornate. Motto, *Nosce te ipsum.* Signed, *Ashby Sculp, Russel Court, London.* Historian, and wealthy merchant in Jamaica.

248. EDWARDS. *Charles Edwards.*

> Plain armorial. Motto, *The North against the World.* Lawyer and author of New York. Born in 1797.

249. EDWARDS. *Isaac Edwards. North Carolina.*

> Armorial.

250. ELAM. *Samuel Elam. Rhode Island.*

> Armorial. Pictorial. A bit of landscape is introduced, and the shield hangs from a ring around the bole of a shattered oak. A very pretty design and well engraved, reminding one somewhat of the book-plates by Bewick.

251. ELIOT. *William H. Eliot.*

> Armorial. Crest only, within an oval garter on which is given the motto, *Non nobis solum.*

252. ELLERY. *Benjamin Ellery.*

> Armorial. Chippendale. No motto. Of New York. The same plate is found bearing the name Harrison Ellery.

253. ELLIOTT. *Barnard Elliott.*

> Plain armorial. Colonel in the Revolution. Signed, *P: R. Maverick.*

254. ELLISTON. *Robert Elliston Gent. Comptrolr. of his Majesties Customs of New York in America.*

> Armorial. Jacobean. A very handsome plate indeed, engraved in an excellent manner. The shield is set against a diapered background, and the ornamental moulding of the side is lined with shell-work; the shield rests upon an upturned shell, and two eagles have alighted upon the upper arms. The motto, *Bono vince malum,* is given upon a ribbon under the frame, and there is no curtain or scroll to receive the inscription, which in engraved plainly in three lines beneath all.

255. ELLISTON.   *Robert Elliston Gent. Comptrolr. of his Majestie's Customs of New York in America.*

This is very similar to the preceding, but is a trifle larger, and in some respects superior. As before, the shield is placed within the enfolding arms of a Jacobean frame, but the diapered pattern is succeeded by an all-over shell pattern, and a grinning canephoros head supports the shield. On a ribbon above the crest the date is given, *M.DCC.XXV.* The motto, *Bono vince malum,* as before, is on its ribbon under the frame. Again the usual curtain is omitted and the inscription is engraved in three lines below all, with a little more attention to grammatical marks, and in bolder type. The eagles have disappeared. The copy before me has the following in handwriting : — *His gift to the library of St. Georges' Ch: in . . . Queens County province of New York. 1730.* Illustrated in "Curio," page 65.

256. EMERSON.   *William Emerson.*

Armorial. Ribbon and Wreath. The work looks very much like Callender's. Motto, *Fidem servabo.* Father of Ralph Waldo Emerson.

257. ERASMUS HALL.   *Erasmus Hall Library.*

Allegorical. Signed, *Maverick Sculpt New York.* The plate is divided into two sections : the upper one is enclosed within a circular frame, and contains the allegorical picture. Diana is seen in the foreground directing the attention of a youth to the glories revealed upon the heights above them. Two temples are seen which bear dedications to Fame and to Virtue. Surrounded by clouds the angel of Fame is even now appearing above her sacred fane. The implements of study are at the foot of the youth, and under this scene are the words, FORTITER ! ASCENDE. The lower part of the design is simply a wreath enclosing the name. The Erasmus Hall Library belonged to an Academy which was founded at Flatbush, L.I., in 1786.

258. ERVING. *William Erving. Esqr.*

Plain armorial. Mottoes, *Quo fata vocant,* and *Flourish in all weathers.* Signed, *Callender Sct.* Undoubtedly of the Boston family of Loyalists.

259. ERVING. (Anonymous.)

Plain armorial. Quartering, " Ar. an eagle displayed sa. within a border invected of the last." The first and third quarters are the Irvine arms.

260. EUSTACE. *Colonel John Skey Eustace, State of New York.*

Armorial. Ribbon and Wreath. Motto, *In hoc signo vinces.* The arms are not correct, as one cross-crosslet is missing, and it is not certain that the crest which hangs in unusual style on a plate, from the festoon, belongs to this family. The crest is balanced by a plate on the other side of the shield, on which a letter *E* is engraved. The whole is contained within an elongated wreath. The name appears above the shield following the curve of the wreath, and at the bottom two additional lines in Latin serve as another motto,

Ignotis errare locis, ignota videre, Flumina gaudebat: studio minuente laborem. A variant of the above, — the same copper altered, — gives this motto in place of *In hoc signo vinces,* — *Sans Dieu rien.* A Revolutionary officer whose bravery was recognized by Congress.

261. EVARTS. *Jeremiah Evarts.*

A simple name-label with the motto under the name and a festoon of cloth above it. Motto, *Nil sine magno vita labore dedit mortalibus.* Father of the Senator.

262. EVERDELL. *William Everdell.*

Armorial in form, though no real arms are shown. Motto, *Semper paratus.* The four quarters of the shield are occupied with implements of the draughtsman's art. Of New York.

263. EVERETT. *Edward Everett.*

Plain armorial. Motto, *Patria veritas fides.* Scholar and orator. Born, 1780 ; died, 1851.

264. EWING. *Ewing.* (John.)

Armorial. Chippendale. A very porky lamb, books, two cooing doves, and a quadrant are introduced into the framework. Motto, *Audacter.* A Philadelphia clergyman.

265. FAIRFAX. *Bryan Fairfax.*

Armorial. Motto, *Fare fac.* Eighth and last baron ; friend of Washington.

266. FARMINGTON. *Library in the First Society in Farmington.*

A large engraved label.

267. FARMINGTON. *This Book belongs to Monthly Library in Farmington.*

Allegorical. Signed, *M. Bull's & T. Lee's Sculp.* A large plate in which the Laws and the names with the attendant flourishes take a good deal of the space. In the centre a shelf of books separates two groups of figures. At the right a very stiff youth, in the court costume of the period, with wig, ruffles, and buckled shoes, is seen under the guidance of a portly female figure who impersonates Wisdom.

AUDACITER

J.H. Ewing

She appears to be warning the youth of the dangers of pursuing the two sirens who beam at him across the shelf; or else they are meant to represent the sources of Knowledge, and the youth is being conducted to them. As Deacon Bull was not a great engraver we may be pardoned if we do not clearly understand his allegory. However, the LAWS of the Library are very plain, and are neatly engraved under the row of books mentioned.

1. Two pence pr day for retaining A Book more than a Month.
2. One penny for folding down a Leaf.
3. 3/ for lending a book to a Nonproprietor.
4. Other Damages apprais'd by a Committee.
5. No person allowed a Book while indebted for a Fine.

Below these stringent rules the following verse is given : —

The Youth, who, led by WISDOM'S guiding Hand,
Seeks VIRTUE'S Temple, and her Laws Reveres :
He, he alone, in HONOUR'S Dome shall Stand,
Crown'd with Rewards, & rais'd above his Peers.

The design is very ambitious, but is rather poor in execution.

268. FARMINGTON. *Village Library.*

Library · Interior. A young lady, very prim, and exceptionally neat and austere in her virtuous demeanor, sits upright in a chair beside a table, on which a few books are laid, and an ink-pot with the quill in it. An open case of books on the wall, a closed writing-desk under it, and a print of Washington complete the furniture of the room. Out of the window can be seen the inspiring sight of a steep hill, upon the summit of which the pillared Temple of Honor stands.

The following verse is given : —

Beauties in vain their pretty eyes may roll :
Charms strike the sense, but merit wins the soul.

Also of Farmington, Conn.

269. FAUQUIER. *Francis Fauquier. Esqr.*
    Armorial. Chippendale. No motto. Lieutenant-Governor of Virginia from 1758 to his death in 1768. Regarded by Jefferson as the ablest executive of Virginia. Illustrated in "Art Amateur," May, 1894.

270. FENDALL. *Philip Richard Fendall.*
    Armorial. Arms very doubtful. Ribbon and Wreath. Motto, *Esse quam videri.*

271. FENWICK. *Fenwick.*
    Armorial. Chippendale. Motto, *Perit ut vivat.* Signed, *J. Smither. Sc.* A plate showing fertility of design in the engraver, but not much skill with the burin.

272. FISH. *Hamilton Fish. Stuyvesant Square New York.*
    Plain armorial. Mantling. Motto, *Deus dabit.* Governor of New York State, 1849–1851.

273. FISHER. *Joshua Fisher.*
    Armorial. Ribbon and Wreath. No motto, name on motto-ribbon. Native of Delaware. A leading merchant of Philadelphia during the Revolution.

274. FITZHUGH. (Anonymous.)
    Plain armorial. Motto, *Pro patria semper.* Of Virginia.

275. FITZHUGH. *Willm. Fitzhugh Junr.*
    Armorial. Chippendale. Motto, *Pro patria semper.* Of Virginia.

276. FOOT. *Ebenezer Foot.*
    Armorial. Ribbon and Wreath. Signed, *Maverick. Sct.* Of New York.

277. FOOTE. *Ebenezer Foote.* Plain armorial. No motto.

278. FOOTE. *Foote.*
    Plain armorial. No motto. The name *John P.* is written in before the family name on the copy at hand.

279. FORBES. *Eli Forbes.*
    Armorial. Chippendale. Motto, *Omni fortunae paratus.* Signed, *T. M. Furnass, St.* This is the only specimen so far discovered of the work of

this engraver, who was a nephew and pupil of Hurd. The owner was Chaplin in the army of the Revolution and a missionary to the Indians. (1800.)

280. FORMAN. *Forman.*
Armorial. Chippendale. Motto, *Deo et amicitiae.* An officer of the Revolutionary army. Had an estate named "Rose Hill," in Maryland.

281. FOSTER.
A plate of this family name is owned in Boston, but no information concerning it can be obtained. It is said to be the work of Furnass.

282. FOSTER. *Isaac Foster.*
Armorial. Jacobean. Motto, *Mille mali salutis habeo, species mille.* Signed, *N. Hurd. Scpt.*

283. FOWLER. *C. Fowler.*
Armorial. Ribbon and Wreath. No motto. Name on motto-ribbon. A small plate. Of Rhode Island.

284. FOWNES. *From the Library of the late Rev. Joseph Fownes, of Shrewsbury, 1790.*
A printed label.

285. FOXCROFT. *John Foxcroft.*
Armorial. Of Boston.

286. FRANCIS. *John Francis.*
Plain armorial. Motto, *Manet amicitia florebit que semper.* Signed, *Callender Sculp.*

287. FRANKLIN. *John Franklin Boston New England.*
Armorial. Jacobean. Motto, *Exemplum adest ipse homo.* Signed, *J. Turner Sculp.* The shield rests upon a very elaborately ornamented frame, the background of which is covered with a diaper pattern. As supporters, Artemis, the goddess of the moon, with spear and arrow in hands appears upon the left hand, and Apollo, likewise with spear, attends upon the right. Both are represented with the lower part of the figure diminishing into a vase, in the manner of the Termini. They stand upon an ornamental bracket which encloses a sketch of Diana sounding the hunter's horn, while an attendant unleashes the hound. The points upon which

the figures of Artemis and Apollo rest are supported by female busts in profile. The whole design is very ornate, and the plate is perhaps the rarest of our early Americans. John Franklin was the brother of Benjamin of greater fame.

288. FRANKLIN INSTITUTE. *Library of the Franklin Institute.*
Portrait plate. A very fine portrait of Benjamin Franklin enclosed in a typical picture-frame of the day.

289. FRAUNCES. *Andrew G. Fraunces.*
Armorial. Mantle of estate. Motto, *Procurator industria.* Signed, in the flourishes under the owner's name, *Maverick Scp.* An unusual style for Maverick.

290. FREEMAN. *Nathaniel Freeman.*

>   Armorial in form, but no arms displayed. The
>   shield hangs upon a dwarfed tree, and has the
>   initials *N. F.* in cipher upon it. A long ribbon
>   trails on the ground and over the shield and tree,
>   bearing the motto, וראת וחררו דאשיו דעת.

291. FRENCH. *Jonathan French.*

>   Armorial. Late Chippendale. Motto-ribbon empty.
>   Of Massachusetts.

292. GALLATIN. *Gallatin.*

>   Plain armorial.   Motto, *Persevere.* This is the
>   plate of Albert Gallatin (1761–1849), the states-
>   man. He is said to have adopted this motto in
>   place of the family motto.

293. GALLAUDET. *Gallaudet.*

>   Plain armorial.   Motto, *Ut quiescas labora.* Not
>   signed, but engraved by Edward Gallaudet.

294. GARDINER. *By the name of Gardiner.*

>   Armorial.   Chippendale.   No motto, the name
>   occupying the motto-ribbon. This is the plate of
>   John-Lion, the seventh proprietor of Gardiner's
>   Island, who was born November 8, 1770, and who
>   died November 22, 1816.   The arms are the same
>   as those of John Gardiner, but the tinctures differ;
>   the bugle-horns are *gules* in this plate, and *sable*
>   in the other.   This plate is also found with the
>   autograph of David, the eighth and last proprietor,
>   under the will of Mary, the widow of Lion.

295. GARDINER. *John Gardiner.*

>   Armorial.   Chippendale.   Motto-ribbon empty.
>   This is the plate of the fifth proprietor of Gardi-
>   ner's Island.   Born, 1714; died, 1764.

296. GARDINER. *John Gardiner of the Inner Temple.*

>   Armorial.   Chippendale.   Motto, *Pro patria mori.*
>   A witty and eloquent lawyer of Boston.

297. GARDINER. *Samuel Gardiner.*

>   Plain armorial.   No motto.   Of the Maine family.

298. GARNETT. *John Garnett.*

>   Armorial.   Chippendale.   Motto-ribbon empty. No
>   crest.

299. GEORGETOWN COLLEGE. *Georgetown College.*
Pictorial. An eagle just rising from the stump of a tree carries a ribbon floating in his beak, on which the legend, *Presented to the P. Society Library.* Motto above, *Lex libertas salusque gentis.*

300. GEORGETOWN COLLEGE. *Collegium Georgiopolitanum, ad ripas Potamaci in Marylandia.*
The American eagle displays the shield of our country on his breast; one talon is upon a globe, the other grasps a cross. The motto, *Utraque unum,* is given upon a ribbon which flutters from the beak of the eagle. Above, in a blaze of glory, an ancient lyre is seen. Branches of oak rise on either side of the design.

301. GHITON. *William R. Ghiton. 1718.*
Armorial.

302. GIBBES. *Edmund A. Gibbes.*
Plain armorial. No motto. Of South Carolina.

303. GIBBES. *James S. Gibbes.*
Plain armorial. Motto, *Amor vincit naturae.* Of Charleston, S.C.

304. GIBBS. *John Walters Gibbs.*
Armorial. A very peculiar frame showing Jacobean, Chippendale, and Ribbon and Wreath features. No motto. Crude work.

305. GIBBS. *John Walters Gibbs. Charleston. So. Carolina.*
Armorial. Ribbon and Wreath. Motto, *Beware my edge,* in reference to the battle-axes of shield and crest. Signed, *Abernethie Sculpt.* The edge of the shield is close-trimmed with festooning, and tall vases rest upon the scrolls at the sides.

306. GIBS. *James Gibs.*
Armorial. Of New York. Signed by Maverick.

307. GILES. *Daniel Giles.*
Armorial. Ribbon and Wreath. Motto, *Toujours le même.*

308. GILES. *James Giles.*
Armorial. Military trophies with slight Ribbon and Wreath ornamentation. Motto, *Libertas et patria*

mea. Signed, *Maverick Sculp.* Behind the shield a plentiful supply of munitions of war are arranged. The flags of the United States and of England, swords, pikes, lances, muskets, bayonets, cannon in the act of discharging, trumpets, drums, wormers, ramrods, cleaners, piles of cannon-balls, and kegs of powder are in the assortment.

309. GILMER. Armorial. Of Virginia.

310. GILPIN. *Henry D. Gilpin.*
Pictorial. The arms are carved upon a large fragment of the adjacent ruins, and which lies at the base of a broken column. The ribbon under the shield bears the motto, *Dictis factisque simplex.* A large tree rises behind the broken column and cuts off the view, but a part of a castle is visible, and between it and the fore view a knight on horseback assisted by one on foot is chasing a wild boar, which is a plain reference to the charge on the shield. Signed, *C. G. Childs.* Attorney-General of the United States. 1840–1841.

311. GILPIN. *Henry D. Gilpin.*
A plate so nearly identical with the preceding as to be taken for it without close examination. This plate is not signed.

312. GILPIN. (Anonymous.)
The plate of John Gilpin, English Consul at Newport. Motto, *Dictis factisque simplex.*

313. GOELET. *John Goelet.*
Armorial. Jacobean. A beautiful example. No motto. Not signed, but probably by Maverick.

314. GOODWIN. *George Goodwin.*
Pictorial. A bracket of graceful design and ornamentation supports two substantial piles of books, between which ensconced in branches of flowers and holding a lyre in his hands, sits a pleasant-faced cupid. Attributed to Doolittle. Publisher of " The Courant," Hartford, Conn.

315. GORHAM. *Joseph Gorham.*
Armorial. Chippendale. Motto, *Par espérance et activité nous surmontons.* Signed, *W. Smith Sculp.*

At the right hand, standing on the name scroll, is an Indian with his feet upon a snake which is stretched at full length. The savage is in civilized clothing, and carries a tomahawk in his folded arms; behind him the ends of bows, arrows, quiver, and tomahawk stand out from behind the shield. On the other

side is a British regular with drawn sword in his folded arms; for a background he has a powder-horn, drum, lances, and the British flag.

316. GOURGAS. *J^N. J^S. J^H. Gourgas.*

Armorial. Apparently of French make. No motto. Signed, *P. L.* In the New York Directory of 1837, the name of John J. J. Gourgas is given;

a merchant. This plate is from the same copper as the Jean Louis Gourgas, which is a French plate seen in several collections.

317. GRACIE.   *Robert Gracie.*

Crest only. Motto, *God grant grace.* Signed, *Lewis Sculp.* In the New York Directory of 1826 as a merchant.

318. GRAEME.   *Elizabeth Graeme.*

Armorial. The arms are in a lozenge with Chippendale ornamentation of exceeding gracefulness. No motto. Of Philadelphia. An accomplished woman in literature.

319. GRAHAM.   *Henry Hale Graham.*

Armorial. Signed, *J. Smither sc.* Eminent lawyer of Chester, Penn.

320. GRAHAM.   *John A. Graham. M.D.*

Armorial. Ribbon and Wreath. Motto, *Ne oublie.*

321. GRANT.   . . . . . *Grant.* (First name erased.)

Plain armorial. Motto, *Stand sure.* Of Scottish descent.

322. GRAY.   *Gray.*

Armorial. Ribbon and Wreath. Motto, *In Deo fides.* Probably by Callender.

323. GREEN.   *Francis Green.*

Armorial. Chippendale. Motto, *Aestate hyeme que idem.* A Boston merchant. Signed, *N. Hurd Sculp.*

324. GREEN.   *Garrett Greens' Private Library. 809 Greenwich Street.*

A printed label with the following motto, *When we are deprived of friends we should look upon good books (they are true friends that will neither flatter nor dissemble :), and we should study to know ourselves. The borrower will please read and return this Book uninjured and without delay.* Circa, 1822.

325. GREEN.   *John Green Jr. of Worcester.*

A grotesque plate. The name is enclosed within a frame which is filled with mementoes of the dissecting room, and with various mottoes.

326. GREENE. *Benjamin Greene.*
    Armorial. Jacobean. Motto-ribbon empty.
    Signed, *N. H. Scp* A very neat and pretty plate.
    A wealthy merchant of Boston; of a branch of the
    Rhode Island family.

327. GREENE. *Benjamin Greene. 1757.*
    The same copper as the above but with the date
    1757 added beneath the name; this was probably
    placed there some time subsequent to the date of
    engraving, although very likely the correct date.
    Signature unchanged. Illustrated in "Art Ama-
    teur," April, 1894.

328. GREENE. *B. D. Greene.*
    Armorial. Ribbon and Wreath. No motto. A
    small plate, very neat in appearance.

329. GREENE. *David Greene.*
    Armorial. Chippendale. Motto, *Nec timeo nec
    sperno.* Signed, *Revere scp.* Of Massachusetts.

330. GREENE. *Thomas Greene Junr.*
    Armorial. Jacobean. Motto, *Study to know thy-
    self.* Signed, *N. Hurd Scp.* Very similar to the
    plate of Benjamin Greene.

331. GREENLEAF. *William Greenleaf.*
    Armorial. Signed, *N. Hurd. Scp.*

332. GREENOUGH. *The Property of David Stoddard Green-
    ough.*
    A printed name label with borders of ornamental
    type. The motto, *Return what thou borrowest,
    with the most sacred punctuality, and withhold it
    not,* is printed between the borders. A woodcut
    pattern of festooning and sprays of flowers encloses
    the whole. Signed, *William Greenough fecit.*

333. GREENWOOD. *Isaac Greenwood.*
    Pictorial. An anchor enclosed within a circular
    frame which bears the name; slight foliations
    within the frame. Resembles an old printer's
    mark somewhat.

334. GRIGGS. *A. Griggs Philadelphia.*

Pictorial.   In a position quite impossible to imagine outside of the picture, are three books thrown upon a huge rock, holding a scroll outspread, which hangs down over a rushing brook.   Indeed, one corner of the scroll dips into the water; a few brushes and stunted or dead trees complete the landscape.   This is a woodcut in the style of Anderson.

335. GUILFORD LIBRARY. *Guilford Library.*

Literary.   Motto, *Improve your hours for they never return.*   A shelf of books very similar to that in the plate of George Goodwin, has a cloth festoon looped above it; the motto is on a circle enclosing the winged hourglass; the scroll-work above this is made into the form of a face.   This plate closely resembles that of the Stepney Society, in Wethersfield, which is by Doolittle, and leads to the conclusion that this is also his work.   In 1737 the towns of Guilford, Saybrook, Killingsworth, and Lyme formed a Library Association. It was dissolved a little before 1800, and Guilford formed one by itself: at about the same time the young people of the town started a library, and these two were united in 1823 and formed the Union Library whose plate is noticed below.

336. GUILFORD. *Union Library.*

Pictorial.   The American eagle, with shield, olive branch, bunch of arrows, and the ribbon with the motto, *E pluribus unum,* is printed from a woodcut; the motto, *Improve your hours for they never return,* is printed from type beneath.

337. GUINAUD. *Henry Guinaud.*

Armorial.   Chippendale.   Motto, *Sans venin.*   A bow and quiver of arrows and a Gainsborough hat with a stick thrust through it are seen in the ornamentation.   The arms are peculiarly unpleasant, being a huge ten-legged scorpion printed very black.   This is repeated in the crest.   Of Baltimore.

338. GURNEY. *Henry Gurney. Esqr. Philadelphia.*
 Armorial. Ribbon and Wreath. Motto, *Sperne successus alit.*

339. HALE. *Robert Hale Esqr of Beverly.*
 Armorial. Chippendale. No motto. Signed, *N. Hurd Scp.* Prominent man in Massachusetts; under Pepperell at Louisburg. From this family of Hales came Nathan Hale.

340. HALL. *James Hall.*
 Armorial. Chippendale. No motto. Not signed, but attributed to Turner. Lawyer and author of Philadelphia.

341. HALL. *Thomas Hall. 1787.*
 Armorial. Ribbon and Wreath. Believed to be the first postmaster under Washington, in Charleston, S.C.

342. HALL. *William Hall.*
 Armorial. Arms, Quarterly 1st and 4th, Sable, three talbot's heads erased argent, collared gules, 2nd and 3rd, Sable, three leopard's heads jessant-de-lys, orgeant. Crest, a talbot's head erased sable.

343. HALLOWELL. *Robert Hallowell.*
 Armorial. Ribbon and Wreath. Motto-ribbon empty. This plate is not signed, but is probably the work of Callender. Comptroller of the Customs in Boston. A Loyalist whose home was mobbed. One of his sisters married Samuel Vaughn, whose plate impales the Hallowell arms.

344. HAMERSLEY. *J. W. Hamersley.*
 Plain armorial. Motto, *Honore et amore.* Signed, *Faithorne.* A New York lawyer.

345. HAMILTON. *William Hamilton.*
 Armorial. Ribbon and Wreath. No motto. Of Pennsylvania. A Loyalist. Nephew of Governor James Hamilton. His country seat was "The Woodlands," now the Woodland Cemetery of Philadelphia.

344. HANCHETT.   *John Hanchett.*
> Armorial.   Ribbon and Wreath.   No motto.
> Taken from a book containing the autograph of
> the owner, with the date, Aug. 28, 1768, and the
> residence given as Hartford.

347. HARRIS.   *Alexander Harris, Architect, Boston.*
> An engraved label.

348. HARISON.   *Richard Harison.   Esqr.*
> Armorial.   Chippendale.   Motto, *Nec te quaesiveris
> extra.*   A large plate, very pretty in appearance,
> but strange in the tincture of the arms.   Of New
> York.

349. HARRISON.   *Rich'd. Harrison.*
> Crest only.   Motto, *Nec te quaesiveris extra.*   A
> lambrequin looped up with cord and fasteners
> above.   Signed, *Rollinson Sculpt.*   Presumably
> belonging to the same owner as the last.

350. HARTFORD.   *Hartford Library Company.*
> An engraved name-label ; the name within an oval
> frame, with a festoon of roses about it, and sprays
> of palm crossed beneath.   Now the Hartford
> Public Library.

351. HARVARD.   *Sigill: Coll: Harvard: Cantab: Nov: Angl:
> 1650.*
> Armorial.   Signed, *N. Hurd Sculp.*   Motto, *Christo
> et ecclesia.*   The design is in the form of a seal, and
> is enclosed within branches of holly.   Above all a
> ribbon bears the words, *Detur digniori,* showing the
> use and purpose of the plate to have been for
> insertion in books presented as prizes to the stu-
> dents.   This is the earliest of the Harvard plates.

352. HARVARD.   *Sigill: Coll: Harvard: Cantab: Nov: Angl:
> 1650.*
> Armorial.   The arms of the college enclosed within
> a double circle which bears the inscription.   The
> motto, *Christo et ecclesia,* is just inside the border.
> The framework is embellished with a profusion of
> fruit and flowers ; in the place of the crest, a pile
> of three books with the sun in splendor above them ;

NEC TE QUÆSIVERIS EXTRA

Richard Harison Esqr.

on each side of the books two slender vases standing upon an upward curl of the ornamentation hold bouquets; below this whole design a gorgeous curtain is spread out to contain the name of the giver of the book; this is backed by a frame whose edge only is seen; this is elaborately scrolled, and is finished at the bottom with the canephoros head and shell pattern; two globes at the uppermost part, on either side, complete the decoration. Signed, *N. Hurd Boston.* Several plates are known very similar to this, but having different names upon the curtain. One of them has simply the words *Ex Dono,* with the curtain left blank for the writing of the giver's name. Others have the name of donors of quantities of books engraved upon the curtain; among these are, *Hancock* and *Thorndike.*

353. HARVARD. *Sigill: Coll: Harvard: Cantab: Nov: Angl: 1650.*

A very close copy of the above in all particulars; indeed, a fac-simile of it. Signed, *A. Bowen.* On some of them appear the name of *Shapleigh,* and on others, *Ex Dono Samuelis A. Eliot.*

354. HARVARD. *Sigill: Coll: Harvard: Cantab: Nov: Angl: 1650.*

This is again a copy in the main of the plate by Hurd, but is later than the last. The ornamentation is similar to that used by Hurd, but is changed in some particulars; the canephoros head is replaced by a bunch of grapes, the sun is missing above the pile of books, and all the work has lost in beauty of execution. Signed, *Andrew Filner.* This plate is used to record the gifts of many persons, among them being : —

Samuel Shapleigh. (Class of 1789.)
Joshua Green. M.D. (Class of 1818.)
Samuel Abbott Green. M.D. (Class of 1851.)
Jonathan Brown Bright. (1884.)

355. HARVARD. *Academiae Harvardianae Sigillum. 1638.*

The arms of the college as usual, with the addition of the word *Veritas* upon the open books. This plate in its general design was suggested by the plate of Hurd, but is quite different in details. The curtain, simpler in make, is still here, and the shield is in the usual position, but the fruit and flowers are replaced by an august assemblage of the gods and goddesses who are the special patrons of learning. Signed, *H. Billings del. C. G. Smith Sc.*

356. HARVARD COLLEGE. *Hasty Pudding Library.*

Pictorial. Two Doric pillars uphold a large curtain which is looped at the top, and left plain in the centre for the writing in of donors' names. Above this a circular frame encloses a picture of an iron pot, supposedly full of pudding, towards which two hands, one with a bowl in its clasp, and one holding a spoon, approach. The motto, *Seges votis respondet,* is given upon the frame. Directly under this is the date, *1808.* Below the curtain a figure of the Sphynx is seen surrounded by books in curved shelves. The bases of the pillars bear the words, *Concordia discors.* Signed, *Callender Sc.* A Harvard College Society plate.

357. HARVARD COLLEGE. *Porcellian Library.*

A large and handsome curtain looped up with cord in large bow-knots is left as usual for the donors' names ; above it two small pillars with the Greek letters on their bases, 'Oμ 'Eλ ; the pillars are joined by a chain which passes behind an oval medallion on which the clasped hands are shown ; above this the circular frame bearing the name encloses the hog ; the frame is ornamented with sprays of palm and roses, and a pile of three books, as so often in plates of Harvard College, form the crest. This plate is not signed, but it strongly resembles the work of Callender.

358. HARVARD COLLEGE. *Porcellian Club. 1803.*

Allegorical. Two stone pillars support a circular frame within which the hog is pictured. On the frame the name of the club is given ; below hangs a poor curtain for the name of the donor of books ;

above are the arms surrounded by the grape-vine, and having books, a loving cup, lance, and foil grouped about. The motto across the face of the shield on a bend, *Fide et Amicitia.* Greek letters on the base of the pillars, ʹΟμ ʹΕλ.

359. HARVARD COLLEGE. *Porcellian Library.*
In this plate the curtain is suspended between two very tall amphoræ which rest upon books bearing the Greek letters ʹΟμ ʹΕλ upon their backs ; behind the curtain two hogs disport themselves ; the circular frame is above them and encloses the representation of a punch bowl, under which is the motto, *Dum vivimus vivamus.* Above all, the shield of arms with the motto on a bend, *Fide et Amicitia,* is graced by grape-vine branches, and the crossed lance and sword. Signed, *F. Mitchell. Del.*

360. HAWKS. *Francis L. Hawks.*
Armorial. Motto, *Never check.* Clergyman and author. Left a large collection of books to the New York Historical Society, where they are kept in a room appropriated to their sole occupancy.

361. HAY. *Mr. George Hay.*
Armorial. Chippendale. Motto, *Serva jugum.* Jurist of Virginia. Prosecutor of Aaron Burr.

362. HAY. *Peter Hay. M.D.*
Armorial. Chippendale. Motto, *Serva jugum.*

363. HAY. *William Robert Hay. M.A.*
Plain armorial. No motto. Was a student at the Inner Temple, London, in 1781.

364. HAYNE. *Isaac Hayne.*
Armorial. Revolutionary patriot. Born, 1745 ; hanged by the British in Charleston, S.C., 1742.

365. HAYNE. *Robert Hayne.*
Armorial. Ribbon and Wreath. No motto.

366. HAYS. *Barrack Hays.*
Landscape. The shield rests against a shattered tree. In the distance, hills and water. Signed, *I. Hutt Sculp.*

LHutt sculp

Barrak Hays

367. HAYWARD. *Benjamin Hayward.*
Of Charleston, S.C.

368. HAYWARD. *George Hayward.*
Armorial. Ribbon and Wreath. No motto.
Flags, cannon, a trumpet, and a lance form the
background to the shield ; the mantling runs down
and joins the flowering branches which are crossed
beneath the shield. Below the name which is on
the motto-ribbon, hangs a small curtain, probably
for the number of the volume.

369. HAYWARD. *Sarah Hayward.*
Armorial. The same copper as the above with the
first name altered.

370. HAYWARD.   *Thomas Hayward.*
     Armorial.   Chippendale.   No motto.   A signer of
     the Declaration from South Carolina.

371. HEATH.   *John Heath.   Boston.*
     An engraved label in which the sun rises above the
     name, which is enclosed in festoons and sprays.

372. HEMING.   *Samuel Heming. de sancta Anna Parochia in
     Jamaica.   Armigr.*
     Armorial.   Chippendale.   Motto, *Aut nunquam
     tentes aut perfice.*   Very fine work.

373. HENDERSON.   *James Henderson, Williamsburg.*
     Pictorial.   Military.   A woodcut very similar to
     the Timothy Newell.

374. HERBERT.   *Herbert.*
     Armorial.   Chippendale.   Motto, *Un loy, un roy,
     un foy.*   Not signed, but probably the work of
     Maverick.

375. HERMAN.   *Sum Ex Libris Frederici Hermani, Sapientia
     praestat divitiis.*
     Printed label.   Of Pennsylvania.

376. HICKS.   *Elias Hicks.*
     Plain armorial.   Behind the shield a sword is seen
     and on its belt the motto is given, *Tout en bonne
     heure.*   Signed, *P. Maverick.   S.*   Distinguished
     Quaker preacher.

377. HICKS.   *Elias Hicks.*
     Armorial.   Ribbon and Wreath.   Motto, *Judicemur
     agendo.*   Signed, *Rollinson Sct.*

378. HICKS.   *Whitehead Hicks.   Esqr.*
     Chippendale.   Motto, *Pro lege et rege.*   Signed,
     H. Dawkins.   Sculpt.   At the left a cupid is play-
     ing a flute; to which accompaniment his com-
     panion sings from a sheet of music held in his
     hand.   At the right, a female in a costume of
     extreme simplicity sits under a jutting rose branch,
     while awaiting a cupid who is seen struggling
     towards her with a large volume.   Of the same
     Quaker family.   Mayor of New York City, 1766–
     1776.

379. HILL. *Marcus Samuel Hill.*
    Armorial. Ribbon and Wreath. Motto, *Non sibi sed patriae.*

380. HILL. *Sam'l. Hill.*
    Literary. Within an oval formed by branches of palm and holly, two books with quill and ink-pot upon them. Probably the plate of the engraver.

381. HOAR. *Richard Hoar.*
    Armorial. Jacobean. No motto. This plate is not signed, but it bears a strong resemblance to the work of Hurd.

382. HOFFMAN. *Philip L. Hoffman. Esqr.*
    Armorial. Ribbon and Wreath. Motto, *Carpe diem.* Signed, *Maverick Sculpt. New York.* A bit of landscape introduced below the shield, as was often Maverick's way ; a stretch of water, trees, books, and writing materials complete the adjuncts. The name is signed on an open scroll ; this lower part of the plate is very similar to the plate of Prosper Wetmore by the same engraver. Of New York.

383. HOLLADAY. Armorial. Of Virginia.

384. HOLLINGSWORTH. *Levi Hollingsworth.* Armorial. Chippendale. No motto.

385. HOLYOKE. *Edward Augustus Holyoke.*
    Armorial. Chippendale. Motto, *Duce natura sequor.* Not signed, but without doubt the work of Hurd. Eminent physician and surgeon of Massachusetts. Lived to a great age and performed an operation at the age of 92.

386. HOLYOKE. (Anonymous.)
    Armorial. Ribbon and Wreath. Motto, *Sacra quercus.* This plate is presumably of the Holyoke family, as the motto is the family motto, the arms are meant to be the Holyoke arms, and the crest is correctly an oak-tree. The design and execution of this plate are poor.

387. HOOPER. *Swett Hooper.*
    Pictorial. Over a vase full of flowers, two cupids bearing a scroll on which is the motto, *The wicked borrow & return not.*

388. HOOPER. *William Hooper.*
    Armorial. Chippendale. Motto, *Haec etiam par-entibus.* Signed, *N. H. Scp.* Plate of the signer of the Declaration from North Carolina.

389. HOPKINS. (Anonymous.) Plate of Reuben Hopkins.
    Armorial. Ribbon and Wreath. Motto, *Piety is peace.* The frame which supports the shield rests upon two books; other books, a globe, and a telescope are among the decorations.

390. HOPKINSON. *Francis Hopkinson.*
    Armorial. Chippendale. Motto, *Semper paratus.* Signed, *H. Dawkins Sculp.* The frame is very like that of the Bushrod Washington plate in some respects. This type is not uncommon; the peculiar cant of the shield, the hissing griffin perched threateningly upon the corner of the frame, and the very form and arrangement of the flowers and spray are duplicated in several instances. Son of Thomas Hopkinson, the Councillor of Pennsylvania. A signer of the Declaration from New Jersey.

391. HOPKINSON. *Joseph Hopkinson.*
    Armorial. The same copper as the last, with the name changed. The first name, Francis, is not well removed and shows in the printing of the plate. Son of Francis. A distinguished lawyer. Author of " Hail Columbia."

392. HORANIAN SOCIETY. *Horanian Society Library.*
    Allegorical. The large shield displays a picture of the Madonna; the supporters are Diana and the Muse of History; the crest is a pile of three books with an owl perched upon them. A large pediment supports the shield and the figures, and on its face the name is given within an elliptical frame; festoons and a curtain of cloth hang about it, and the motto, *Mutual Improvement,* is given upon a ribbon which is draped across the top of the frame. Signed, *P. R. Maverick Sct. No. 3 Crown Street. N. Y.*

393. HORRY. *Dan Horry. Esqr.*
    Armorial. Chippendale. Motto, *Toujours fidele.*
    Of South Carolina.

394. HORSMANDEN. *Daniel Horsmanden. Esqr.*
    Armorial. Jacobean. Motto, *De interior templo socius.* Author of "Negro Plot of New York, 1741." Published in 1810. Born, 1691 ; died, Flatbush, 1778. Illustrated in "Curio," page 65.

395. HUBARD. Armorial. Of Virginia.

396. HUMPHREY. *Henry B. Humphrey.*
    Pictorial. A very graceful framework encloses several spaces which are occupied by decorative features. Above the name, Minerva, helmeted and robed, with shield and spear, is seated attended by the owl. Beneath her the motto appears on a curved portion of the frame, *Inter folia fructus.* Beneath this again is the name within an oval formed by two writhing snakes ; at either side of this are female griffins, sejant. At the very lowest point of the design a grotesque canephoros head is seen. Of Boston.

397. HUNTER. *Archibald Hunter.*
    Armorial. Signed by Dawkins.

398. HUNTER. *John Hunter.*
    Plain armorial. No motto. A small plate.

399. HUNTER. *His Excellency, Robert Hunter. Esqr.*
    Armorial. Jacobean. Motto, *At re non impetu.* In writing, *the General and Chief General of Jamaica.* Author of the famous letter on "Enthusiasm," which was attributed to Shaftesbury and to Swift. Became Governor of Jamaica in 1728.

400. HUNTER. *William J. Hunter.*
    Armorial. Ribbon and Wreath. Motto, *Sola bona quae honesta.* Signed, *Engrd. by P. R. Maverick 65 Liberty St. N.Y.*

401. HURD. *Name of Hurd.*
    Armorial. The arms seem to be wholly imaginary, or at least borrowed from some other family.

Arms, Az. a lion ramp. or. on a chief ar. a stork ppr. between two mullets sa. Crest, A bird sa. on a garb fess-ways ppr. No motto. The name occupies the ribbon. This plate is crude in appearance, and not unlike the work of Nathaniel Hurd; it may have been an early attempt of his for himself or some member of his family. The copy before me has written upon it, "Isaac Hurd's presented to Barzillai Frost."

402. HYSLOP. *By the name of Hyslop.*
Armorial. Ribbon and Wreath. No motto, the name occupying the motto-ribbon.

403. HYSLOP. *Robt. Hyslop.*
Armorial. Ribbon and Wreath. Motto, *Vincit omnia veritas.* A rude piece of engraving. The garland draped behind the shield is very stiff, and the oak branches at the sides are ungraceful.

404. INGERSOLL. *Jared Ingersoll Esqr. of New Haven Connecticut.*
Armorial. Chippendale. Motto, *Fama sed virtus non moriatur.* Lawyer; born, 1749; died, 1822. Studied in the Middle Temple, London. Member of the Old Congress, 1780–1781. In 1812 was the Federal candidate for Vice-President of the United States. Author of a rare pamphlet on the Stamp Act, New Haven, 4to, 1766.

405. INGLIS. *Inglis.*
Plain armorial. Motto, *In tenebris lucidor.* Of New York.

406. INGLIS. *Alexr. Inglis.*
Armorial. Chippendale. Motto, *Lucidor in tenebris.* The heraldry is mixed and the motto twisted. Of South Carolina.

407. INGLIS. *George Inglis. Petersburg.*
A woodcut border with the name in type within it. The border is elaborate, with cornucopiæ of flowers at either side, and ornamental pieces in the corners. In the copy at hand the type is set in wrongly, so that the frame is bottom up.

408. INGLIS. *John Inglis.*
> Armorial. Chippendale. Motto, *Recte faciendo securus.* Of Pennsylvania.

409. INGRAHAM. (Anonymous.)
> Armorial. Chippendale. Motto, *Magnanimus esto.* Name bracket empty.

410. INGRAHAM. *Edward D. Ingraham.*
> Armorial. Chippendale. Motto, *Magnanimus esto.* It was said of him that if he wanted a book, he would prefer to buy it; if he could not buy, he would borrow (not to return), and if necessary would even steal it. A man of great learning and eccentricity. Lawyer of Philadelphia. Illustrated in "Art Amateur," April, 1894.

411. INGRAHAM. *Edwd. D. Ingraham.*
> Crest only.

412. INGRAHAM. *Edward D. Ingraham.*
> Plain armorial. No motto.

413. INGRAHAM. *Edward D. Ingraham.*
> Crest only, enclosed in a garter on which the motto is given, — *Magnanimus esto.*

414. INNES. *Colonel Innes.*
> Plain armorial. Motto, *Je recois pour donner.* Of North Carolina.

415. IREDELL. *James Iredell.*
> Armorial. Chippendale. No motto; name on motto-ribbon. Jurist of North Carolina. Illustrated in "Art Amateur," March, 1894.

416. ISELIN. *Helen Iselin.*
> Plain armorial. Crude work; the mantling very scraggly. No motto.

417. IZARD. *R. S. Izard.*
> Armorial. Pictorial. The arms are carved on what bears strong resemblance to a gravestone; a draped female figure stands leaning upon the stone holding a book open, on which the motto, *Hoc age,* is given.

418. JACKSON. *James Jackson.*
> Armorial. Ribbon and Wreath. Motto, *Bona quae honesta.*

419. JACKSON. *Jonathan Jackson.*
>
> Armorial. Ribbon and Wreath. Motto, *Bona quae honesta.* Signed, *N. H. Scp.* A Massachusetts statesman. Member of Old Congress. Illustrated in "Art Amateur," April, 1894.

420. JACKSON. *W. Jackson.*
>
> Ribbon and Wreath. A shield is suspended from a wall-pin under the crest, on which assumed arms are shown; in chief a group of thirteen stars surrounded by the word *Independence;* in base is a plough, indicative of the spirit of the owner. Motto, *Meliora non opto.* Perhaps the plate of Major William Jackson, a prominent patriot of the Revolution; held many offices.

421. JAMAICA. *The Bishop of Jamaica.*
>
> Armorial. Motto, *Simplius sicut columbae.* Signed, *Griffiths & Weigalls 3 St James St Londn.*

422. JARVIS. *Jarvis.*
>
> Armorial. Pictorial. A very handsome and peculiar plate, in which the shield resembles a wind-filled sail; angry waves roll at the foot, and a part of a mast and sail are seen. The ornamentation at the sides takes the form of trees and sprays of holly, while roses appear at the sides. Motto, *Adversis major par secundis.*

423. JARVIS. *Samuel Farmar Jarvis. D.D.*
>
> Armorial. Literary. Mottoes : *Hora é sempre,* and see *Sola salus servire Deo.* The shield rests against a pile of books, and above the cross and crown are seen in a blaze of glory. Son of Bishop Abraham Jarvis.

424. JAUNCEY. *Jauncey.*
>
> Armorial. Ribbon and Wreath. Motto, *Quo vocat virtus.* The name *William* is written in on the copy at hand. He was a merchant in New York. His father was an eminent ship-captain.

425. JAY. *John Jay.*
>
> Plain armorial. Motto, *Deo duce perseverandum.* Statesman.

426. JEFFRIES. *Dr. John Jeffries.*

Plain armorial. No motto. It is said that he was the surgeon who recognized the body of Warren at the battle of Bunker Hill. This plate is not signed, but bears strong resemblance to the work of Callender.

Samuel Farmar Jarvis. D.D.

427. JEFFRIES. *J. J.*

Crest only. Plate of John Jeffries.

428. JEFFRY. *James Jeffry.*

Armorial. Early Chippendale. **Motto-ribbon** empty. Same arms as the succeeding.

429. JENKINS. *Robert Jenkins.*

Armorial. Jacobean. Motto, *Non reverter invitus.* Signed, *N. Hurd.* Some copies are dated *1751* in mss. A very handsome plate in which the arms are placed against a diapered background, enclosed by ornamental scroll-work, set off at the bottom by a spirited scene in which a ship under full sail hastens from view. At the upper part of the frame two grotesque female faces peer at each other from across the space in which the crest is given. In the steeple of Christ Church, Boston, in which the lanterns of Paul Revere were hung, a chime of eight bells, made by Abel Rudhall of Gloucester, England, was placed in 1744 ; each bell bears an inscription ; on the sixth we read that the subscriptions for these bells was completed by Robert Jenkins and John Gould, Church Wardens, Anno 1744.

430. JOHNSON.　(Anonymous.)

Armorial. Chippendale. Motto, *Deo regique debeo.* The shield rests upon an elaborately carved pedestal, on which the supporters, American Indians, stand. This is very probably the plate of Sir William Johnson, nephew of Admiral Sir Peter Warren, and colonial agent of George II. for the control of Indian affairs in the colony of New York (1756). Still, the plate seems hardly old enough to have been his, and may have been his son's. Only one copy is known to the writer.

431. JOHNSON.　*John I. Johnson.*

Pictorial. A cherub coming down on the clouds carries a curtain before him, spread out, and on this the name is given. A brick wall frames the oval which holds the picture. Signed, *Maverick. St.*

432. JOHNSON.　*Thomas Johnson.*

Armorial. Chippendale ; rather wild. No motto. The design is supported upon four short columns which rest upon a large shell. Query : Is this an early effort of Hurd's (as it resembles his work), or is it the work and plate of Johnson, the engraver and herald painter?

433. JOHNSON.　*W. L. Johnson.*

Armorial. Chippendale. Motto, *Per aspera ad astra.* Of South Carolina.

QUO
VOCAT VIRTU

William Jauncey

434. JOHNSON. *Wm. S. Johnson of Connecticut Esqr.*
Armorial. Chippendale. Motto, *Per aspera ad astra*. Born in Connecticut. Distinguished jurist and scholar. Delegate to Congress, 1765 ; agent of Connecticut in England, 1766–1771.

435. JOHNSON. *Wm. S. Johnson LL.D.*
The same plate as the above with the inscription altered. President of Columbia College, 1787–1801.

436. JOHNSTON. *Johnston.*
Armorial. Book-pile. Motto, *Nunquam non paratus*. This is in the conventional book-pile style, and is the only example we have of this peculiar arrangement of books. The volumes are piled in three tiers about an open scroll which is suspended in the centre and which bears the arms. On the copy before me the letter *G* is written before the name. Of Maryland.

437. JOHNSTON. *John Johnston.*
Armorial. Ribbon and Wreath. Motto, *Nunquam non paratus*. Signed, *Maverick Sculpt*. Not so striking as the Thomas Johnston.

438. JOHNSTON. *Robert Johnston.*
Armorial. Of Turkey Island.

439. JOHNSTON. *Thomas Johnston.*
Armorial. Ribbon and Wreath. Motto, *Nunquam non paratus*. Signed, *Maverick Sculp N.Y.* A beautiful plate.

440. JONES. *Gabriel Jones. Attorney at Law in Virginia.*
Armorial. Early Chippendale. Motto, *Pax hospitia ruris.*

441. JONES. *Gardner Jones.*
Armorial. Ribbon and Wreath. Motto-ribbon empty. Of Boston.

442. JONES. *Samuel Jones Esqr.*
Armorial. Chippendale. Motto, *Trust in God.* Signed, *Dawkins Sc.* This plate has none of the extraneous ornamentation so common to Dawkins. Member of Constitutional Convention. Illustrated in " Art Amateur," March, 1894.

2

443. JONES. *William G. Jones.*
Armorial. Ribbon and Wreath. Motto, *Pax et copia.* Born Aug. 5, 1787. Of New York. The same copper as the Gardner Jones with the name altered, and the motto placed on the ribbon.

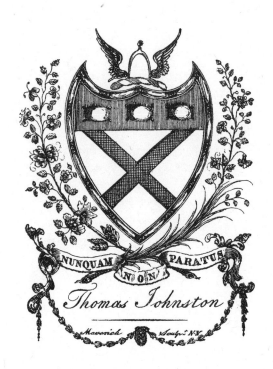

NUNQUAM NON PARATUS

Thomas Johnston

Maverick   *Sculp: N.Y.*

444. JUDAH. *Benjamin S. Judah.*
Armorial. Ribbon and Wreath. Motto, *Fortitudo et justitia.* Signed, *Maverick Sculpt.*

445. JUDAH. *Benjamin S. Judah.*
Armorial. Ribbon and Wreath. Motto, *Fortitudo et justitia.*

446. KEESE. *John Keese.*
    A small engraved label, with Chippendale frame,
    and books at either side. Signed, *Maverk. Sct.*
    Earlier than the following; a very unusual signa-
    ture for Maverick.

447. KEESE. *John Keese.*
    Armorial. Ribbon and Wreath. Motto, *Bello
    virtus.* Signed, *Maverick Sculpt.* Of New York.

448. KEFFER. *John C. Keffer.*
    Pictorial. A figure representing Commerce is
    seated on a rock with implements of Agriculture
    around her; in the distance can be seen an
    expanse of water with boats upon it.

449. KEITH. *Ex Libris Gul. Keith.*
    Armorial in form, though no arms are shown.
    Early English; heavy mantling. On the shield
    the inscription is given. The only copy known
    (Loganian Library) is dated 1727 in ms. Gov-
    ernor of Pennsylvania, 1717–1726. He was a
    "desperate intriguer." See "Franklin's Auto-
    biography."

450. KEMBLE. *Peter Kemble.*
    Armorial. Chippendale. Motto-ribbon empty.
    Signed, *J. Lewis.* Rather crude work. An illus-
    tration apparently from the original copper may be
    found in "The Pilgrims of Boston," etc., by
    Thomas Bridgman.

451. KEMPE. *John Tabor Kempe. Esqr.*
    Armorial. Early Chippendale. Motto, *Labour to
    rest.* Last Royal Attorney-General of New York.
    A Loyalist whose estates were confiscated.

452. KERR. *John Leeds Kerr.* (See John Leeds Bozman.)

453. KEY. *F. S. Key, Georgetown, Columbia.*
    Label with type border. Lawyer and poet, born
    in Maryland, 1779; writer of "The Star Spangled
    Banner."

454. KING. *Miles King.*
    Armorial. Of Norfolk, Va.

455. KING. *Morris King.*
    Armorial. Chippendale. Motto, *Loyall au mort.*

456. KING. *Rufus King.*
    Armorial. Ribbon and Wreath. Motto, *Recte et suaviter.* Signed, *Maverick Sculpt.*

457. KING. *Sally King, Owner.*
    Pictorial. A peculiar plate, drawn in ink, by hand. Two columns support an entablature, in the centre of which a large representation of a mariner's compass is given. The motto, *Cherish Virtue,* is on the circular frame enclosing it. The work on all parts of the design is very fine, and shows a master hand. Not many of these plates are known, but a few are certainly known to have been in use. They were, presumably, the work of some member of the family who was efficient with the pen, and had time and inclination to use his talent thus. Although dating probably about 1800, the ink is fresh, and the plate clear and excellently drawn.

458. KINGSTON. *Kingston.*
    Plain armorial. No motto. Of Pennsylvania.

459. KINGSTON, CANADA. *Santa Johanis Evangelistae Sigilum Collegi Latomorum. Kingston, Canada, 1794.*
    Vesica-shaped shield, on which a robed figure holds an open book, which shows masonic emblems on its pages.

460. KINLOCH. *Francis Kinloch. Esqr.*
    Plain armorial. Motto, *Altius tendo.* A student at Gray's Inn in 1774.

461. KIP. *Isaac L. Kip.*
    Armorial. Ribbon and Wreath. Motto, *Victoris aut mors.* Signed, *Maverick Sculpt.* The signature is on a scroll upheld by a winged cherub, who rests against a stump. Among the accessories are a book labelled LAW, an ink-pot, etc.

462. KIP. *Leonard Kip, New York.*
    Pictorial. Two quills are crossed above a scroll on which the name is given. Signed, *B. Brown. Sc.* President of the North River Bank.

463. KIP. *Leonard Kip.*

Plain armorial. Motto, *Vestigia nulla retrorsum.* Same as preceding.

464. KIRKPATRICK. *James Kirkpatrick.*

A woodcut label; books and other literary property are distributed about; the name is on an opened scroll.

465. KISSAM. *Benjamin Kissam.*

Armorial. Chippendale. Motto, *Honestum Praetulit util.* Signed, *H. Dawkins. Inv. et Sculp.* This is in the happiest vein of this engraver. At the left a young lady in the low-necked, hooped dress of the period, carrying a shepherd's crook, and at the right the shepherd himself, but having his crook, is seated. By his side a very docile, even weakly appearing lamb, listens while he plays the flageolet. A prominent lawyer in New York in the middle of the last century.

466. KNIGHT. *Jonathan Knight's Book No.*

Armorial. Jacobean. A small plate of rude workmanship. On the motto-ribbon are the words, *By the name of Knight.* A Revolutionary army surgeon; died in Norwalk, Conn., 1829.

467. KNIGHTS. *Knights of the Square Table.*

Armorial. Architectural. A stone canopy is erected in Pointed Gothic style, across the face of which, and hiding from view the long windows, a curtain is stretched, along the top of which the motto, *Cassis Tutis Sima Virtus,* is shown. The shield of arms is placed above the window-tops, and is surrounded by mantling rather straight and original in design. At the very foot the date *1809* appears.

468. KNOX. *William George Knox. Trinidad.*

Plain armorial. Motto, *Moreo et proficio.*

469. L. *Ex Libris L.*

Armorial. The shield is enclosed within a large letter L, a French crown surmounts it, and on a ribbon at the foot is seen *Joe L—.* Signed, *P. Riera.* Of South Carolina.

470. LADD. *Ladd.*
    Armorial. Chippendale ; rough. No motto, the
    name occupying the motto-ribbon. Signed, *S.
    Felwell. Sculpt.* Of New Hampshire.

471. LAMB. *John Lamb.*
    Armorial (?). A gallant soldier of the Revolution.

472. LARDNER. *Lynford Lardner.*
    Armorial. Pictorial. Landscape. The shield rests
    against the bole of an oak, and around it are sparse
    bushes and grass. Motto, *Mediocria firma.* Of
    Philadelphia. Probably the grandson of the Pro-
    vincial Councillor.

473. LAURENS. *Edward R. Laurens.*
    Armorial. Belongs to no particular style. The
    shield is highly ornamented with scrolls and
    flowers. Motto, *What is, is best.* Signed, *Stout
    del et Sculpsit.* Of South Carolina.

474. LAWRENCE. *J. Tharp Lawrence.*
    Plain armorial. Motto, *In cruce salus.* An ermine
    mantle behind the shield.

475. LEAVENWORTH. *Capt. Gideon Leavenworth.*
    Armorial. Jacobean. No motto, the name on the
    motto-ribbon. Very crude work, resembling the
    Elijah Backus plate.

476. LEE. Armorial. Of Virginia. (Richard Henry Lee ?)

477. LEE. *Edward Lee. Esqr.*
    Plain armorial. No motto, the name occupying
    the motto-ribbon. Of Virginia.

478. LEE. *Cpt. John Lee.*
    A crude name-label, with a border suggestive of
    nothing. Signed, *S. Mcintire.*

479. LEE. *Philip Ludwell Lee, Esqr of the Inner Temple*
    LONDON.
    Armorial. Chippendale. Motto, *Non incautus
    futuri.* Of Virginia.

480. LEIPER. Armorial. Of Virginia.

481. LENTHALL.   *John Lenthall.*

Armorial.   Ribbon and Wreath.   Motto-ribbon empty.   Signed, *Thackara.*   A large plate, the only signed specimen of this engraver's work. Very probably the plate of John Lenthall, an Englishman employed by Latrobe on the public buildings at Washington, and a very valuable architect.

482. LENOX.   *David Lenox.   Philadelphia.*

Armorial.   Ribbon and Wreath.   Motto, *Auctor pretiosa facit.*

483. LENOX.   *James Lenox.*

Plain armorial.   Motto, *Auctor pretiosa facit.* The founder of the Lenox Library, New York City.

484. LEWIS.   *Joseph S. Lewis.*

Literary.   No motto.   Four large books in an impossible position ; the topmost one has the name engraved upon the side ; an ink-pot and two quills, with a sprig of holly, complete the ornamentation.   A prominent merchant of Philadelphia seventy-five years ago.

485. LEWIS.   *Mordecai Lewis.   No.*

A very handsomely engraved name-label.   A frame of Chippendale gracefulness surrounds the name. A canephoros head of pleasant expression appears in the lower edge.   A Philadelphia merchant. Born, 1784 ; died, 1851.

486. LEWIS.   *Morgan Lewis Esqr.*

Armorial.   Ribbon and Wreath.   Motto, *Courage sans peur.*   This plate is not signed, but it is undoubtedly the work of Maverick.   Soldier and jurist.   Was on the staff of General Gates in the Revolution, and was in action again in the War of 1812.

487. LIGHTFOOT.   *Philip Lightfoot.*

Armorial.   Of Virginia.   Tomb at Sandy Point, dated 1784.

488. LIGHTFOOT.   *Wm. Lightfoot Esqr.   Tedington.   1750.*

Armorial.   Chippendale.   No motto.

489. LINN. *Rev. Matthias Linn.*
Armorial.

490. LISLE. *Henry Maurice Lisle, Attorney at Law.*
Armorial. Ribbon and Wreath. Motto, *Legibus viro.* Of Hingham, Mass. Circa 1800

491. LIVERMORE. *Edmund St. Loe Livermore.*
An engraved name-label, with the motto on an ornamental ribbon above, *Miseris succurrere disco.* Lawyer of Boston.

492. LIVINGSTON. *Brockholst Livingston Esqr.*
Armorial. Chippendale. Motto, *Spero meliora.* Son of Governor William Livingston. Accomplished scholar and lawyer. Of New York. Illustrated in "Curio," page 63.

493. LIVINGSTON. *Edward Livingston.*
Landscape. The shield upheld against a shattered oak by a ribbon; the ship in distress for crest; *Spero meliora* on a dainty ribbon among the twigs. At the foot of the tree, close to which a marsh is seen, a pointer barks at a squirrel sitting unconcernedly on a bough eating acorns. Signed, *Maverick Sculpt.* A beautiful plate. Jurist and statesman. Son of Robert R. Illustrated in "Curio," page 64.

494. LIVINGSTON. *John R. Livingston.*
An engraved label, the name being within an oval frame.

495. LIVINGSTON. *Maturin Livingston.*
Armorial. Ribbon and Wreath. Motto, *Spero meliora.* Signed, *Maverick Sculpt.* Of New York.

496. LIVINGSTON. *Mortimer Livingston.*
Plain armorial. Motto, *Spero meliora.*

497. LIVINGSTON. *Peter R. Livingston.*
Armorial. Jacobean. Motto, *Prestat opes sapientia.* Signed, *N. Hurd. Scp.* The whole within an oblong frame. Illustrated in "Curio," page 62.

498. LIVINGSTON. *Robert L. Livingston.*
Armorial. Chippendale. Motto, *Spero meliora.* Crest, a demi-barbarian with a bludgeon raised in

his right hand, and a coiling serpent in the other. Illustrated in " Curio," page 64.

499. LIVINGSTON. *Rob't. R. Livingston Esqr. of Cleremont.* Armorial. Ribbon and Wreath. Motto, *Spero meliora.* Not signed, but probably the work of Maverick. Illustrated in " Curio," page 63.

Edward Livingston

500. LIVINGSTON. *Rob't. R. Livingston. Esqr. Of Clermont.* Armorial. Pictorial. The shield rests against a broken column; at its base a large globe, caduceus, scrolls, and vellum-bound books. A garland of roses falls across the shield, and a view of the distant plain is afforded through the bushes at the

side. A large palm above droops over all. Motto, *Spero meliora.* Crest, the ship. A very beautiful plate. Eminent lawyer. Illustrated in "Curio," page 63.

501. LIVINGSTON. *Walter Livingston.*

Armorial. Chippendale. Motto, *Spero meliora.* Not signed, but undoubtedly the work of Maverick. Books and a lighted lamp among the ornamentations.

502. LIVINGSTON. *William Livingston of the Middle Temple.*

Armorial. Chippendale. Motto, *Aut mors aut vita decora.* Born in Albany, 1723; graduated from Yale at the head of his class, 1741. Intending to go to London, he obtained permission to enter the Middle Temple, but seems to have never done so. The book-plate must have been engraved about this time (1742). Statesman. Illustrated in "Curio," page 62.

503. LIVINGSTON. *Willm. Smith Livingston.*

Armorial. Ribbon and Wreath. Motto, *Spero meliora.* Signed, *Maverick Sculpt.* A peculiarly shaped frame. Illustrated in "Curio," page 63.

504. LIVIUS. *Livius.*

Plain armorial. Motto, *Colendo crescent.* Of New Hampshire. Peter Livius; same as following.

505. LIVIUS. *Livius Chief Justice of Quebec.*

Plain armorial. Motto, *Non flectere a vero.* The same copper as the above with the name changed, the motto altered, and an in-escutcheon added. A Loyalist. Chief Justice, 1777–1786.

506. LIVIUS. *George Livius.*

Armorial. Chippendale. No motto. Illustrated in "Art Amateur," May, 1894.

507. LLOYD. *Jno. N. Lloyd.*

Armorial. Early English. No motto. Very tempestuous mantling completely encircles the shield. An old family of Long Island; the manor of Queen's Village was in their possession as early as 1679. Of this family came Dr. James Lloyd, of

Boston, a Loyalist, friend of Sir William Howe, and whose estates on Long Island were seized by the Royal Army, who allowed three thousand acres of woodland to be cut off. When redress was offered upon his swearing allegiance to England, Dr. Lloyd refused. Name in fac-simile of autograph.

ABRAHAM   LODGE

508. LLOYD.   *John Nelson Lloyd.*
     Pictorial.   Urn, festoons, and sprays of palm.
509. LLOYD.   *Richd. Bennett Lloyd. Esqr.*
     Armorial.   Pictorial. No crest, and no motto. The shield is oval, and is held upright by a female clad in the Greek manner; an anchor at her feet.
510. LODGE.   *Abraham Lodge.*
     Armorial.   Jacobean. No motto.

511. LOGAN. *Charles Logan.*

> Armorial. Chippendale. No motto. Of Philadelphia ; lived also in Powhatan County, Va. He freed all his slaves in Virginia upon his marriage.

512. LOGAN. *James Logan.*

> Armorial. Chippendale. No motto, the name occupying the motto-ribbon. Books and a globe at the base as ornamentation, and as indicative of the owner's tastes. Of Philadelphia. Came to this country at the suggestion of William Penn. A scholar and statesman ; left his library to the public, which was the foundation of the Loganian Library. His translation of Cicero's " De Senectute " was the especial pride of Benjamin Franklin's press. He printed it with a preface by himself. Illustrated in " Curio," page 13.

513. LOGAN. *William Logan.*

> Armorial. Of Philadelphia. Librarian of the Library.

514. LOGANIAN LIBRARY. *Loganian Library.*

> Armorial. Arms not the ones on the plate of James Logan, the donor of the Library. No motto, the name occupying the motto-ribbon. Chippendale. Started by James Logan in 1743, who gave books to the value of £1000 and a building. Illustrated in " Curio," page 12.

515. LONGBOTTOM. *Abram P. Longbottom.*

> Plain armorial. Two shields of arms side by side under a large American eagle. Mottoes, *Labor omnia vincit,* and *Pro rege et lege.*

516. LORD. *William Lord's East Haddam.*

> An early engraved copper-plate ; the name and address only within an oval frame of twisted vines.

517. LORING. *Loring.*

> Armorial. Chippendale. No motto. Not signed, but bears some of the characteristics of Hurd's work. Undoubtedly his.

R

518. LOTBINIERE. *M. le Marquis de Lotbiniere.*

Armorial. French heraldic. A lion crouches below the escutcheon, while eagles scream at either side. Motto, *Fors et virtus.* A large landowner in New York City at the beginning of the century.

519. LOW. *Cornelius Low. Esqr.*

Armorial. Chippendale. Motto, *Ex necessitate.* Not signed, but undoubtedly by Dawkins. The frame is the same in ornamentation and style as the Whitehead Hick plate.

520. LOWELL. *John Lowell.*

Armorial. Chippendale. Motto, *Occasionem cognoscere.* Signed, *N. Hurd. Scp.* Jurist and statesman of Massachusetts. Member of Old Congress.

521. LOWELL. *John Lowell Jr.*

Armorial. Chippendale. Motto, *Occasionem cognoscere.* A second motto is given, *Deo dirigente cresendum est.* Signed, *Annin & Smith Sc.* Founder of the Lowell Institute, Boston. Illustrated in "Art Amateur," May, 1894.

522. LOWELL. *John Lowell. Jr.*

Armorial. Chippendale. Mottoes as the preceding. Signed, *A. & S.* This seems to be a lithograph made from the above.

523. LOWELL. *John Amory Lowell.*

Armorial. Chippendale. Motto, *Occasionem cognoscere.* Very similar to the design of the John Lowell by Hurd ; evidently copied from it.

524. LUDLOW. *Cary Ludlow.*

Armorial. Chippendale. Motto. *Fide sed cui vide.* Signed, *W. Smith Sculp.* Somewhat in the style of Dawkins.

525. LUDLOW. *Charles Ludlow. A.M.*

Armorial. Chippendale. Motto, *Fide sed cui vide.* Signed, *W. Smith.* The arms are the same as on the John Cooke Ludlow. At the left a scantily robed female is playing the flute, while a cupid holds the book of music. The surroundings are indicative of a desert.

526. LUDLOW. *Gabriel Verplank Ludlow.*
Armorial. Crest only. Motto, *Naturae convenienter vivere.*

527. LUDLOW. *Gab : Wm : Ludlow.*
Armorial. Chippendale. Motto, *Spero meliora.*
Signed, *H. D. Sc.* (Dawkins.) A very fine plate.

528. LUDLOW. *George Ludlow.*
Armorial. Ribbon and Wreath. Motto, *Decus virtuti soli.* The festoon of cloth draped above the shield is trimmed with a string of laurel. Signed, *Rollinson Sct.*

529. LUDLOW. *John Cooke Ludlow.*
Armorial. Chippendale. Motto, *Spero meliora.*
Signed, *H. D. Sc.* (Dawkins.)

530. LUDWELL. *Philip Ludwell of Greenspring in Virginia Esqr.*
Armorial. Late Jacobean. Motto, *I pensieri stretti ed il viso sciolto.* Of Virginia.

531. LUKENS. *John Lukens.*
Armorial.

532. McALISH. Armorial.

533. McCOMB. *John McComb.*
Plain armorial. No motto. The plate is enclosed within a frame made of a festoon of oak leaves above, and straight lines below.

534. McCOUN. *Wm. T. McCoun.*
Plain armorial. Motto, *Semper paratus.* Signed, *Rollinson. S.* Of New York.

535. McDOWALL. *William McDowall. Esqr. One of His Majtes. Council in ye Island of St. Christopher in America.*
An old armorial plate of which no further information has been noted.

536. McFARLAN. *Frederick Mc. Farlan.*
Armorial. Ribbon and Wreath. Motto, *This I'll defend.* Of Pennsylvania.

537. MCILVAINE. *Bloomfield McIlvaine.*
Pictorial. An angel seated among the clouds holding a tablet upright upon her knee, is writing upon it with a quill. A very pretty design. Signed, *I. F. Barralet, inv. F. H. Seymour Sc.* Lieutenant United States Navy.

538. MCKELDEN. *Andrew McKelden.*
Pictorial. The arms of the United States finely engraved within a circular frame. Motto, *E pluribus unum.* The name of the owner written within the circle. Signed, *Leonard Sculpt.*

539. MCKENZIE. *Kenneth McKenzie.*
Armorial. A Virginia physician.

540. MCKENZIE. *William McKenzie. Surgeon.*
Armorial. Chippendale. Mottoes, *Luceo non uro.* The date *1766* is written on the copy before me.

541. MCLEAN. *Hugh McLean.*
Armorial. Ribbon and Wreath. Motto, *Altera merces,* and *Virtus durissima terit.* Signed, *Maverick Sct.* Oak leaves and branches used in the decoration.

542. MCMURTRIE. *Henry McMurtrie.*
Pictorial. Landscape. The frame is oval in form ; the rising sun discloses a small island on which are five trees in a straight row ; the bank at the left hand also has a similar row of five trees, and in the immediate foreground a few piles of stone and more trees are seen. The name is on a ribbon under the picture. Signed, *Smither Sculpt.* A physician of Philadelphia.

543. MCMURTRIE. *Henry McMurtrie.*
Literary. Books are piled upon a table ; the serpent of Æsculapius carries the motto-ribbon on which are the words, *Respice finum.* Cupid weeps beside a mortuary urn whose tip is aflame. An open book seems to have two words on the pages. The first one is *Rush.* The whole design is enclosed in a circle about which numerous clouds hover. Signed, *Fairman del. Kearny Sc.* The Philadelphia physician.

544. MCTAVISH. *John McTavish.*
     Plain armorial. Motto, *Non oblitus.* Of Maryland.

545. MACKAY. *James Mackay. Belfast.*
     Armorial. Chippendale. Motto, *Delectando pariterque monendo.* A resident of Virginia about the year 1760.

546. MACKEY. *Albert G. Mackey. M.D.*
     Plain armorial. Motto, *My might makes right.*
     Physician and author of Charleston, S.C.

547. MAGILL. *John Magill.*
     Armorial. Chippendale. Motto, *Perit ut vivat.*
     Signed, *J. Smither Sct.* Of Maryland.

548. MANIGAULT. *Peter Manigault of the Inner Temple, Barister at Law South Carolina.*
     Armorial. Chippendale. Motto, *Prospicere quam ulcisci.* Signed, *Yates Fecit Royal Exchange.*
     There is no official grant of these arms; they were engraved in 1754; the crest, an American Indian, had not then been decided upon.

549. MANN. *John Preston Mann.*
     Literary. A peculiar out-of-door scene, in which the foreground is occupied with a very tall case of shelves filled with books; the corner post of the case is made of a pile of books carefully arranged; in the distance is seen the temple of Honor, upon the summit of a hill, the ascent to which is rocky and steep; the American eagle rests upon a globe which is placed upon the tall pile of books; the whole design is enclosed within an oval border, which is decorated with scrolls, etc. The last name only is engraved upon the plate, the first ones being written in.

550. MANN. *The property of Timothy Mann. Walpole. Oct. — 1810.*
     The name is printed from type within a woodcut border; festoons and sprays of palm compose the frame, in the centre of which, above, is a small circle with the arms of the United States within it; two ink-pots with quills in them are on either side of the arms.

551. MANNING. Armorial. Of Virginia.

552. MARCH. *Charles March.*
Plain armorial. Motto, *Fortis et veritas.* Charleston, S.C. Circa 1819.

553. MARCHANT. *Henry Marchant.*
Armorial. Chippendale. Motto, *Patria cara carior libertas.* Signed, *N. H. Sc.* Very similar to the John Marston plate, below mentioned. Attorney-General of Rhode Island, 1770–17—. Member of Old Congress, 1777–1780 and 1783–1784.

554. MARSH. *Frederick Marsh.*
Literary. Identical with the George Goodwin plate mentioned above.

555. MARSHALL. *John Marshall A.M.*
Armorial. Chippendale. Motto, *Ex candore decus.* Chief Justice United States, 1801.

556. MARSTON. *John Marston.*
Armorial. Chippendale. Motto-ribbon empty. Signed, *N. Hurd, Sculp.* Illustrated in "Art Amateur," May, 1894.

557. MARTIN. *The Honble. Josiah Martin of Antigua Esqr.*
Armorial. Jacobean. Motto, *Pugna pro patria libertas.*

558. MARTIN. *Luther Martin A.M.*
Armorial. Chippendale. Motto, *Initium sapientiae est timor Dei.* Inside the name-frame an open book at either end ; one labelled *Black's Comms.* Very similar to the Bloomfield plate, and undoubtedly by Trenchard. Lawyer ; Member of Old Congress ; defended Samuel Chase.

559. MARTIN. *Thomas Martin.*
Armorial. Chippendale. Motto, *Initium sapientia est timor domini.* The same arms as the above, but the crest different.

560. MASON. *Jonathan Mason Junr.*
Simply the name engraved within a flourish. One of the witnesses of the Boston Massacre. The book from which the copy before me was taken

had the autograph of the owner in it and the date,
1774. Eminent lawyer and statesman.

561. MASSACHUSETTS. *Library of the General Court. Sigillum
Reipublicae Massachusettensis.*
The shield of the State, surrounded by the motto
of the State, *Ense petit placidam sub libertate
quietem,* is placed within the circular frame which
bears the name. Above, a pile of three books,
similar to those on the Harvard plate by Hurd, and
a globe upon them stand in lieu of a crest; a blaze
of glory flashes out from these symbols of learning.

562. MASSACHUSETTS. *This Book is the Property of the Historical Society, Established in Boston. 1790.*
A printed label with ornamental type border.

563. MASSACHUSETTS. *Property of the Massachusetts Medical
Society, incorporated November 1781.*
A large curtain, similar to that in the Harvard College plate by Hurd, is upheld by festoons; this is
left blank for the recording of donors' names.
Above this an oval medallion presents a picture of
the efficacy of Nature's cures; a wounded stag
with the arrow still in his side has come to Æsculapius for healing. He, in rough garb, with the
serpent entwined around his rod, has directed the
distressed animal to an herb, which he is lying
down to eat. A motto, *Natura duces,* is seen
over the picture. Signed, *Callender Sc.*

564. MASSACHUSETTS. *The First State Normal School.*
The arms of the State of Massachusetts surrounded
by an oval garter, on which the name is given. In
the clouds above the motto appears, *Live to truth.*

565. MASTERTON. *Peter Masterton.*
Armorial. Ribbon and Wreath. Motto, *Cogi posse
negat.* Signed, *Maverick Sculpt.* Thistles used in
the decoration.

566. MATTHEW. *William Matthew Esqr. Lt. Genl. of His
Majtes. Leeward Carribee Islands: and Lt. Govnr.
of St. Christopher in America.*
An old armorial plate; no further information
obtainable.

567. MATTHEWS. *Wm. Matthews of Philada. N°.*
> A copper-plate engraving; no design, except a border of scrolls and flourishes enclosing the inscription.

568. MAYO. *John Mayo.*
> Armorial. Chippendale. Motto, *Virtus sola nobilitate.* Mantling about the helmet.

569. MAXCY. *Virgil Maxcy.*
> Plain armorial. Motto, *Nullus in verba.* Of Maryland.

570. MAXWELL. (Anonymous.)
> Armorial. Maxwell arms and motto. The arms are enclosed in an oval frame studded with pearls, and a profusion of flowers is used in the ornamentation, which comes as near to the Ribbon and Wreath style as to any. Motto, *Riviresco.* Signed, *Maverick, Sculpt.*

571. MERCER. *Hugh Mercer.*
> Armorial. Of Virginia. A gallant General of the Revolution; was killed at the battle of Princeton, at which the daring plan of crossing the river was undertaken and carried out upon his suggestion.

572. MERCER. (Anonymous.)
> Armorial. Rich mantling encompassing the whole shield. Motto, *Per varios casus.* John Mercer of Marlboro, near Fredericksburg; a witness to the will of Mary Washington.

573. MEREDITH. *Jonathan Meredith Junr.*
> Armorial. Ribbon and Wreath. Motto, *Integra mens augustissima possessio.* This plate is not signed, but is apparently the work of Maverick.

574. MIDDLETON. *John Izard Middleton.*
> Armorial. Born at Middleton-Place-on-the-Ashley, near Charleston, S.C., 1785; died, 1849. Author; intimate in the circles of Mesdames De Staël and Récamier.

575. MIDDLETON. *Peter Middleton. M.D.*
> Armorial. Chippendale. Signed, *J. Lewis Sc.* Mantling profuse and reaching well down the

shield. Motto, *Fortis & fidus.* Of New York.
Born in Scotland. Made the first dissection on
record in America.

576. MILLER. *Ferdinand H. Miller.*
Literary. Very similar to the Thomas Robbins plate.

577. MILLER. { *Bruder Jaebez. 178–.*
{ *Petrus Heremit. 1791.*
These plates, simple printed labels, were the prop-
erty of J. Peter Miller, the Prior of the Convent at
Ephrata, Penn.

578. MILNER. *James Milner.*
Armorial. Chippendale. Motto-ribbon empty.
Of Virginia.

579. MINOT. *Minot.*
Armorial. Early English. Rough mantling all
about the shield. Motto, *Ad astra per aspera.*
George Richard Minot, historian, Boston.

580. MINOT. *Minot.*
Armorial. Early English. Mantling all about the
shield. Motto, *Ad astra per aspera.* A better
plate than the above. The copy before me has an
S written before the name. Of Massachusetts.

581. MINTURN. *William Minturn.*
Plain armorial. An elaborate frame, with mantling
reaching far down the sides. Motto, *Esse potius
quam haberi.*

582. MITCHELL. *A. Mitchell Ejus Liber.*
Armorial. Chippendale. An early settler of Chester County, Penn.

583. MITCHELL. *Jacobum Whitely Mitchell.*
Literary. The central panel of this design bears
the name and the following lines : —

> *Hujus si capias dominum*
> *Cognoscere libri, si infra,*
> *Inspicida nomen habebis ibi.*

At the left shelves of books are seen, and at the
right what seems to be a heavy press. Above, on
a bracket, are grouped several implements of music,
art, etc. This is a rude woodcut.

584. Moat.　*Horatio Shepheard Moat.*

> Armorial.　Ribbon and Wreath.　Motto, *Nil desperandum.*　Signed, *Rollinson.*

585. Moore.　*Lambert Moore. Esqr.*

> Armorial.　Chippendale.　Motto, *Virtus interrita pergit.*　This plate is not signed, but is unmistakably the work of Dawkins.　The half-draped female on the left side is the same as that on the Whitehead Hicks plate, and the music-making shepherd on the right is reversed from the Benjamin Kissam plate.

586. Moore.　*Nathl. F. Moore.*

> Armorial.　Ribbon and Wreath.　No motto.　Signed, *P. Maverick.*　Of New York.　President of Columbia College, 1842–1849.

587. Moore.　*Saml. W. Moore.*

> Plain armorial.　Motto, *Non est vivere sed valere vita.*　Of New York.

588. Moreau.　*John B. Moreau.*

> Literary.　The name on an open book, floating in the clouds.

589. Morgan.　*John Morgan.　M.D.　Philadelphia.*

> Armorial.　Chippendale.　Motto, *Fama praestante praestantior virtus.*　This plate is not signed, but is very much in the style of Dawkins' work.　A cupid sits on a flourish of the decoration and pats a large bust on its crown, presumably representing sculpture.　At the other side two cupids discuss astronomical problems with a globe for reference.　One of these little fellows is an African evidently.　Eminent physician educated abroad.　One of the founders of the American Philosophical Society, 1769.

590. Morong.　*Thomas Morong.*

> Literary.　A pile of books, some open, some closed, lies at the foot of a cross, above which the crown is seen in glory.　A ribbon runs over the face of one book, bearing the motto, *Sola salus servire Deo.*　A line of Hebrew is given across the open book.

591. MORRIS. *Gouverneur Morris.*
   Armorial. Chippendale. Motto, *Tandem vincitur.*
   One fold of the ribbon empty, as if possibly made
   for a larger motto ; a stock pattern. This is the
   same copper as the Lewis Morris mentioned below,
   with the first name changed. Statesman and orator.
   Illustrated in " Art Amateur," February, 1894.

592. MORRIS. *J. M.*
   Crest only. (Morris of Philadelphia.)

593. MORRIS. *James Morris.*
   Armorial. Chippendale. No motto. A very
   handsome plate, rich in appearance, and full of decorative features. Open books, globe, and scrolls at
   the base indicate a literary taste. The sides of the
   frame are embellished with the caduceus and a
   cornucopia of fruit. Of New York.

594. MORRIS. *Lewis Morris Esqr.*
   Armorial. Chippendale. Motto, *Tandem vincitur.*
   Father of Gouverneur Morris.

595. MORRIS. *Roger Morris.*
   Armorial. Early Chippendale. No motto. The
   mantling is present, very straight and stiff; the
   shell-work is prominent, and the whole design is
   rather formal than graceful. Illustrated in " Curio,"
   page 112.

596. MORRIS. *William Morris.*
   An engraved label, the name being within an oval
   frame of laurel leaves. Signed, *Shallus Sculpt.*

597. MORRISON. *John Morrison. Portland. U. S. America.*
   Armorial. Chippendale. Motto, *Dum spiro spero.*
   A very neat design. The sprays which are crossed
   beneath the shield are connected above by a row
   of thirteen stars.

598. MURRAY. *James Murray.*
   Armorial. Chippendale. Motto, *Mens sibi conscia recti.* Of Virginia.

599. MURRAY. *John Murray.*
   Armorial. Ribbon and Wreath. No motto.

600. MURRAY.   *The Revd. John Murray.*

Armorial in form, but no true arms shown. The motto, *Malo mori quam foedari*, is on a circular band which encloses a space, divided into quarters, colored heraldically and charged with absurd charges ; in the first quarter, which is tinctured az., a shield with a helmet above is supported by a row of fence posts with cinquefoils between them ; the second, which is tinctured ar., is divided per saltire, and is charged with a powder-horn, a crescent and stars, an ox-bow, and a crown; the third, which is tinctured gu., has Gabriel and Apollyon in combat, with a crown above them ; the fourth, which is tinctured az., has the dove with the olive branch on a peculiar cross which holds thirteen spots (for lack of a better term) ; disposed about· are three flaming hearts. This whole design is enclosed in a large shield ; the crest is a man on a prancing steed, carrying a tomahawk ; the supporters are a nude Indian with a wreath about his loins, his feet chained, and the end of the chain and a shield in his hands ; and a crowned lion with three stars on its body. Motto, under all, *Juncta virtute fides*. This plate is not signed. What a pity ! Very probably the plate of the Father of American Universalism, who it is said was greeted with a shower of stones when he first tried to preach in Boston.

601. MURRAY.   *Joseph Murray.*

Armorial. Chippendale. Motto, *Virtute fideque*. Not signed, but evidently by Maverick.

602. MURRAY.   *Murray Earl of Dunmore.*

Armorial. Supporters, mantling, and crown. Motto, *Furth — Fortune*. John Murray, fourth Earl. Made Governor of New York, 1770 ; and of Virginia, 1771.

603. MUSGRAVE.   *Richard Musgrave.*

Plain armorial. Motto, *Sans changer*. On the copy before me is written, *of New Haven Connecticut.*

THE REV,^D IOHN MURRAY.

604. NELSON. *The arms of the Rt. Hon. George Nelson Esq. Ld. Mayor.*
    Armorial. Late Jacobean. No motto. Of Virginia.

605. NEWBERRY. *Roger Newberry's Property.*
    An engraved label with a festoon above, and the following motto below :—

    > *To Virtue & Science attend,*
    > *And Truth & Justice befriend.*

606. NEWBURYPORT. *Newburyport Athenæum.*
    Pictorial. A large American eagle about to rise from a pile of rocks bears a ribbon in his beak with the name upon it.

607. NEWELL.   *Timothy Newell.*

Military.   The name is given within a frame, behind which are seen a various assortment of military implements, — flags, swords, guns, drums, trumpets, etc.   Signed, *I. Thomas print.*   This is a woodcut, and was printed by Isaiah Thomas, the early printer of Worcester, Mass.

608. NEWPORT, R.I.   *Redwood Library. Newport. R.I.*

Pictorial.   A large picture of the library building. Signed, *Drawn by James Stevens Civil Engr. Engd. by W. D. Terry Newport.*   The library used other smaller plates, a simple label, and also another view of the building with the rules governing the use of volumes printed with it.

609. NEWTON.   *Lucretia E. Newton.*

Armorial.   Ribbon and Wreath.   Motto, *Cognosce occasionem.*   This is the plate of John C. Williams, by Hurd, with the name and signature erased, and the present name printed from type under the shield.   An unwarrantable proceeding.

610. NEW YORK.   *Apprentices' Library.*

A pictorial plate of great beauty.   In the immediate foreground an aged man, clad in classic garb, accosts two youths who have evidently but just risen, at his approach, from a moss-covered rock on which they had been studying, if the scattered books are an indication : with uplifted hand, the old man directs them to the temple of knowledge, which can be seen in the distance crowning the summit of a lofty hill : at the foot of the declivity the spires and houses of a village can be discerned : between it and the place of meeting a broad expanse of water stretches : a beehive at hand indicates activity, and the broken column behind the preceptor is a link connecting classic history with present time.   Above the picture the muscular arm holds the hammer, and oak branches are about it.   Signed, *A. Anderson. Sc.*

611. NEW YORK.   *The Property of the New York College of Pharmacy.*

An oblong name-label, with flourishes.   Above, a

crucible is placed, with the rays of the sun spreading out behind it. Signed, *Rollinson Sc. New York.*

612. NEW YORK. *The Property of the College of Physicians and Surgeons of the University of the State of New York.* An oblong printed label with type border. This college was established in 1807, and is now a part of Columbia College.

613. NEW YORK. *New York Society Library.* This plate is armorial in form, but presents no real arms. The central frame, of Chippendale design, contains four quarterings, which represent the arts of Astronomy, Navigation, Geography, Mathematics, and Literature; Religion also is represented. Mercury and Minerva support the frame, standing upon the ribbon which bears the name; above the frame sits Apollo with his broad back to the full-shining sun; clouds which resemble toy balloons rise about him. Beneath the frame appear the outskirts of a city, with spires and towers visible; directly under this is the word *Athenia* in Greek (presumably to suggest that New York City was the modern Athens); a closed chest with a lighted candle upon it has these words on it, *sed in candelabro*, and an open book bears across its face the motto, *Nosce teipsum.* Signed, *E. Gallaudet. Sc.* Illustrated in " Ex Libris Journal," Vol. III, page 141.

614. NEW YORK. *New York Society Library.* Pictorial. The interior of the library is shown; Minerva, helmeted, and with spear resting against her arm, leans upon a pillar; before her, in obeisance, an American Indian, half draped, with tomahawk under his foot, receives from the hand of the gracious goddess a book. The well-filled shelves of the library are disclosed behind them, as the drawn curtain, upheld by cords, lets the sunlight stream in. This view is contained within an oval frame which rests upon a pedestal bearing on its face the name of the library; the whole is filled out to the edges of the plate by a background

representing a brick wall. Signed, *Engd. by P. R. Maverick 65 Liberty Street.* A large painting of this design hangs in the library at present.

615. NEW YORK. *New York Society Library.*

Allegorical. Minerva, just alighted from the clouds, with garments somewhat displaced by her flight through the air, and with clouds still about her, finds an Indian waiting to receive the volume she holds out to him ; as he lays hold of it he seems to be offering his tomahawk in exchange. The shelves of the library are seen behind them, and in the gable the motto, *Emollit mores,* is painted. The oval frame enclosing this scene is upheld by ribbon and festoons, branches of oak are crossed beneath, and the plate is signed, *Maverick. Sct. Crown Street.*

616. NEW YORK. *New York Typographical Society.*

Allegorical. A picture of Franklin's press with the American flag and a liberty pole crossed before it ; above, a large eagle with a medallion of Franklin depending from his beak. Not signed, but attributed to Anderson.

617. NORRIS. *George W. Norris.*

Armorial. Chippendale. The same copper as the Isaac Norris, with the name changed. Signed, *W. G. M.*

618. NORRIS. *Isaac Norris.*

Armorial. Chippendale. No motto. Signed, *Jas. Turner Sc.* Of Philadelphia. Prominent statesman. He directed the placing of the prophetic inscription upon the old Liberty Bell. His library went to the Dickinson College. Illustrated in "Art Amateur," February, 1894.

619. NORTH CAROLINA. *This book is the gift of . . . . . . to the University of North Carolina. Anno Dom.*

These words appear within a frame of Chippendale ornamentation. Several books disposed about give a literary flavor to what is otherwise a rather meaningless design.

620. OGDEN. *Lewis Morris Ogden.*

    Armorial. Ribbon and Wreath. Motto, *Et si ostendo non jacta.* Signed, *P. Maverick Sc 1801.*

621. OGDEN. (Anonymous.) The Ogden arms.

    Chippendale. Motto, *Et si ostendo non jacto.* Of New Jersey.

622. OLCOTT. *George Olcott.*

    Literary. Very nearly the same as the George Goodwin and the Frederick Marsh.

623. OLMSTED. *Charles H. Olmsted.*

    Pictorial. The beehive surrounded by flowers. Motto, *Non sibi sed aliis.* The whole design enclosed in foliated scrolls.

624. OLMSTED. *H. B. Olmsted.*

    Pictorial. A beehive beneath low bushes.

625. OLIVER. *Andrew Oliver.*

    Armorial. Chippendale. Attributed to Hurd. Motto, *Pax quaeritur bello.* Of Massachusetts. Colonial statesman. Distributer of stamps under Hutchinson.

626. ORPHAN ASYLUM. *Orphan Asylum.*

    Pictorial. A beautiful little picture of the Christ blessing the little ones. The line, *Forasmuch as ye did it unto one of the least of these ye did it unto me,* is given under the vignette. Signed, *L. Simond del. Seney, Sc.*

627. OSBORNE. *Peter Osborne.*

    Armorial. Chippendale. No motto. Of Philadelphia. Master of ship " Pennsylvania Packet," sailing between Philadelphia and England. Lost in a gale in September, 1775.

628. OSBORNE. *Samuel Osborne.*

    Armorial. Early Chippendale. Motto-ribbon empty. Signed, *N. Hurd. Scp.* Of Boston. Brother of Captain Jeremiah Osborne, who died July 25th, 1768, on his passage from Isle of May to Newport. The only copy of this plate known to me is in the Mauran-Deats collection, and was taken by Mr. Mauran from a folio ledger of 1764.

s

629. OTIS. *Harrison Gray Otis.*
Crest only. No motto. A graceful festoon on either side of the crest. Of Massachusetts. Statesman and orator.

630. OTIS. *James Otis. Feby 1773.*
Plain name-label, belonging to the orator and patriot of Massachusetts.

631. OTIS. *James Otis, junr's BOOK.*
A large name-label with the name in big type, with the request, *Please return this with care.* An ornamental type border.

632. PACE. *Henry Pace.*
The only information obtainable concerning this plate is the solitary fact that it is the work of Hurd. It is given in Warren's " First List of English Engravers."

633. PAGE. *Francis Page of the Inner Temple Esqr. 1703.*
Early English. Full mantling envelopes the shield. Motto-ribbon empty. Of Virginia.

634. PAGE. *The Property of Samuel Page.*
A frame of Chippendale decoration enclosing simply the name. Resembles the work of Hurd.

635. PAINE.
A pictorial plate of the celebrated political and deistical writer, Thomas Paine, is said to be known. Copied from a tail-piece in the " Gentleman's Magazine."

636. PANTON. *Frans. Panton.*
Armorial. Chippendale. Motto, *Meliora spero.* Of New York. A hair-dresser. Had no right to the arms. Not signed, but undoubtedly by Maverick.

637. PANTON. *Francis Panton Junr.*
Landscape. A very peculiar design. The shield is borne by two ducks, who have each an end of a ribbon in their bills, the shield being upheld by it over a stream ; mountains in the background, each

having one tree on its peak ; ducks are swimming in the marsh, and four men in a boat seem in no hurry to get anywhere. Motto, *Spes meliora.* Signed, *Maverick Scp.* Of New York.

Francis Panton Jun.

638. PARKE. *John Parke. Esqr. A.M.*
  Armorial. Chippendale. Motto, *Terra aut mari.* Signed, *I. S. Sculp.* This was engraved by Skinner, the famous engraver of Bath.

639. PARKER. *B. Parker.*
  Armorial. Jacobean. Motto, *Aude fieri justum.*

640. PARKER. *James Parker. Esqr.*
  Armorial. Ribbon and Wreath. Motto, *Cave.* A very handsome plate.

641. PARKER. *Jas. Parker.*

> Pictorial. Landscape. In the immediate foreground a group of laborers are discussing the first railroad train, which is passing at a safe distance; the old-fashioned engine and car are moving to the left of the picture; behind, mountains, and lakes with shipping, and a distant village are seen. A very elaborate border encloses the scene.

Samuel Parker's. Nº 45.

802

642. PARKER. *Samuel Parker's. No.*

> Pictorial. *Clio*, the Muse of history, sits upon a bank of earth on which her name is given, under the spreading branches of a tree; a youth on bended knee receives from her fair hand a volume; other books and a lyre would indicate that the Muse had further gifts to distribute, or was enjoying a stay at this place. In the dim distance rises

the spire of the school, over which wheels an arrow of wild ducks. Of Roxbury, Mass.

643. PARKMAN. *John Parkman, BOSTON.*
Pictorial. A large scroll is laid over a low bush, which it almost hides from view, and on this the name is printed. This is a woodcut border, with the name printed from type within it. Signed (cut in the wood), *Russell and Cutler printers.*

644. PARSONS. *Gorham Parsons.*
A very pretty name-label; engraved on copper. The name, with appropriate flourishes, is enclosed within an oval wreath, festooned above, and with a cherub's face among the flowers.

645. PARSONS. *William Parsons.*
Name-label; engraved. Name in an oval frame and festooned above with flowers.

646. PASLEY. *William Pasley.*
Armorial. Ribbon and Wreath. Motto, *Be sure.* The thistle and rose used in the ornamentation. Not signed, but undoubtedly by Maverick. Of New York.

647. PAULDING. *J. K. Paulding.*
Armorial in form, although no real arms are shown. Ribbon and Wreath. Motto, *Fidelity.* The design of this plate is from the "Captor's Medal." An ancestor of the owner of this plate was the principal captor of Major André. A fine estate of the Pauldings' lies on the Hudson River, with a castellated mansion of white marble, in which the notable library was housed. Author and politician.

648. PAULDING. *W. Paulding.*
Armorial. Signed by Maverick.

649. PEIRSON. *A. L. Peirson.*
Armorial. Ribbon and Wreath. Motto, *Consilio manuque.* Signed, *Annin & Smith Sc.* Of Massachusetts.

650. PEASE.   *Lewis Pease.*

> *The PROPERTY of the REV*
>
> **L** *ong may you live to spread a Saviour's name :*
> **E** *ach day be hallow'd by a serious frame.*
> **W** *isdom assigns the task — His call obey :*
> **I** *n fear and meekness, point the narrow way :*
> **S** *trong are your foes, but Christ is strong as they.*
>
> **P** *ursue with pious zeal th' road that Jesus trod,*
> **E** *nforce his truths — Exalt a Saviour's blood :*
> **A** *ngelic spirits wait to guide you home,*
> **S** *ustain the cross — shew Men their certain doom,*
> **E** *nsnar'd by Sin a fatal end must come.*
>
> *J . . . . h   B . . . n.*

The above verse is printed from type and enclosed in a border of ornamental type.

651. PEASE.   *Oliver Pease, Owner.*

Pictorial.   Motto, *Read and return.*   Of Suffield, Conn.   A physician.   Date probably about 1800. Very similar to the Sally King, which see for a description.

652. PEASE.   *Oliver Pease, Owner.*

Pictorial.   Motto, *Read and return.*   A variety of the above, in which but one-half of the compass is shown, and a tessellated floor is laid under the pillars.

653. PELL.   *William F. Pell.*

Crest only.   Motto, *Deus amici et nos.*

654. PENN.   *Edmd. Penn.*

Pictorial.   A number of books rest upon a shelf ; with them, an hour-glass, a sickle, and two sheaves of wheat ; a wreath of oak leaves and palm is erected above them, and the name is given upon a scroll which falls over the edge of the shelf.   Signed, *T. Baddick.*

655. PENN.   *Thomas Penn of Stoke Pogeis in the County of Bucks First Proprietor of Pensilvania.*

Early English.   Arms and motto as in the succeeding plate, that of his father.   Illustrated in " Curio," page 14.

656. PENN. *William Penn Esqr Proprietor of Pennsylvania.*
1703.
Armorial. Early English. Full mantling envelop-
ing the whole shield. Motto, *Dum clavum teneam.*
Illustrated in "Curio," page 13.

657. PENN. (Anonymous.) Penn arms.
Supposed to be the plate of Thomas Penn, the son
of William. The volume in which the only copy
of this plate has been seen has the autograph of
J. Logan, and the statement that the book was
given to him by Thomas Penn. The William Penn
plate is also in the book.

658. PENNINGTON. *Pennington.*
Plain armorial. Motto, *Vincit amor patriae.* Of
Pennsylvania.

659. PENNINGTON.   *Edward Pennington.*
     Name-label; engraved.   Festoon above, and sprays
     of palm and grape-vine below.

660. PENNINGTON.   *Edward Pennington.   Philadelphia.*
     Pictorial.   A reservoir, from which the water is
     escaping, is overshadowed by palms of some kind.
     The significance of this design is mysterious.
     Signed, *J. J. Plocher.   Sc.*

661. PENNINGTON.   *T. H. Pennington.*
     The name is printed from type within a circular
     frame which is engraved.   The peculiarity of the
     plate is that after the abbreviation *No.* for the
     number of the volume, the word *Plates* is given.
     Whether this was to be erased in volumes which
     were not illustrated, or the number of illustrations
     was to be given in those which had them, is hard
     to say.

662. PENNSYLVANIA.   *The Historical Society of Pennsylvania.*
     Armorial.   The arms of William Penn impaling
     those of the state.   Motto, *Dum clavum teneam.*

663. PENNSYLVANIA.   *The Historical Society of Pennsylvania.*
     A very handsome steel engraving of the coat-of-
     arms of the state of Pennsylvania.   Motto, *Vir-
     tue, Liberty and Independence.*   Another variety of
     this plate is intended as a gift-plate.

664. PEPPERELL.   (Anonymous.)   Sir William Pepperell.
     Armorial.   Chippendale.   Motto, *Virtute patria
     tuemini.*   A beautiful plate.   On a ribbon at the
     very top, *Peperi.*   William P. Sparhawk, grandson
     of the first Sir William Pepperell, assumed his name
     and was created a baronet, Oct. 29, 1774.   This
     was undoubtedly his plate.   The vast estates of the
     family were confiscated in 1778, as they were
     Loyalists.   The crown allowed five hundred pounds
     to Sir William.

665. PERKINS.   *Thomas Handasyd Perkins.*
     Armorial.   Ribbon and Wreath.   No motto.   A
     prominent merchant of Boston.   Born, 1765.

666. PETIGRU. *James Louis Petigru.*
Plain armorial. Motto, *Verité sans peur.* Prominent lawyer of Charleston, S.C. Born, 1789 ; died,
1863.

667. PHILADELPHIA. *Apprentices Library Co. of Philada.*
A group of implements indicative of the work done
by the patrons of the Library. On a panel of a
desk are the words, *Instituted 1820;* below this,
Science, Art, Virtue. An open book upon the
desk displays these words, *Take fast hold of instruction let her not go for she is thy life. Proverbs. Ch. 1.
ver. 17.*

668. PHILADELPHIA. *Apprentices Library Company of Phila.
Instituted 1820. Opened for girls 1842.*
This plate is a little later than the former, and the
scene is shifted from the class-room to the forest :
here by the running brook, overshadowed by the
pines and oaks of the forest, a scroll is found upon
a rock bearing the same quotation from Proverbs
that appears upon the preceding plate. This is a
woodcut very much in the style of Anderson.

669. PHILADELPHIA. *The Carpenters Company of Philadelphia,
1724.* Armorial in form. On the shield a square
is used as a chevron, and is placed between three
pairs of dividers. No tinctures. The full sun
shines powerfully from above.

670. PHILADELPHIA. *The Library Company of Philadelphia.*
The name printed from type within a border made
up of ornamental type. Motto, *Communiter bona
profundere Deorum est.* Signed, (*Printed by
Zachariah Paulson jun. No 106 Chestnut-street.
May. 1801*).

671. PHILIPSE. *Frederik Philipse. Esqr.*
Armorial. Jacobean. No motto. The shield is
backed by a brick wall, the foliations are shell-lined,
and the upturned shell is in place under the shield.
Of New York. Illustrated in "Curio," page 111.

672. PHILLIPS. *Dinwiddie B. Phillips.*
Plain armorial. Motto, *Ducit amor patriae.* Of
Virginia.

673. PHILLIPS. *Samuel Phillips His Book 1707.*

Name-label, with ornamental type border. Grand-father of the founder of the Academy at Andover and of the American Academy of Arts and Sciences at Boston. Born at Salem, 1690.

674. PHILLIPS ACADEMY. *In usum Academiae Phillipsiae Exoniensis.*

Armorial. (Phillips arms.) Chippendale. This plate is not signed, but is very similar to the Holyoke plate by Hurd, and is undoubtedly his work. Motto, *Pia mente studeatur.* Phillips Academy of Andover, Mass.

675. PHILLIPS. This plate was used in some of the books of Phillips Academy, at Exeter, N.H., and has a representation of the arms of the Phillips family, with a festoon of flowers above it, and below it is appended the following statement and exhortation : —

The Trustees of Phillips Academy to whom is committed the distribution of the pious bounty of the late LT. GOV. PHILLIPS wishing to co-operate in the same benevolent and useful design, affectionately recommend this inestimable book to the serious and careful perusal of every person into whose hands it may fall.

Reader, whoever thou art, the work before you is the pro-duction of one of the ablest and best of men, whose praise is in all the churches. Though dead, he is instructing thou-sands by his numerous and excellent practical (?) writings which have survived him. Among these, *The Saints' Rest* has been most highly esteemed. He wrote it in the near view of death, when in feeble health, and for his own immediate use; and he testifies that he derived "more benefit from it, than from all the other studies of his life." Few books have ever received higher commendations, been translated into more languages, passed through more numerous editions, been more read, or more useful in the Christian church than this. No person of a serious mind can read it without profit.

"*To allure our desires*, it unveils the sanctuary above, and discovers the glories and joys of the blessed in the Divine presence, by a light so strong and lively, that all the glittering vanities of this world vanish in the comparison, and a sincere believer will despise them, as one of mature age does the toys and baubles of children. *To excite our fears* he re-moves the screen, and represents the tormenting passions of the damned in those dreadful colors, that, if duly considered, would check and control the unbridled licentious appetites of the most sensual." [1]

Reader, the book is in your hands, read, meditate, and then judge for yourself. May the Lord bless the instruction for your spiritual benefit. So will the good design of the pious doner be answered, and the Agents of his bounty have their desired reward.

676. PHŒNIX SOCIETY. *Phœnix Society.*
Pictorial. A large shield, heart shaped, encloses a picture of a large plantation, evidently with a considerable settlement on the rising ground ; a stream meanders through the estate, and various kinds of crops are under cultivation ; a little summer-house is seen at the end of a long path. A large curtain is draped over the shield, and a stag and a lion guard it at the foot. Under all, a tablet shows a second smaller shield quartered heraldically, and bearing a hunter's horn, a right arm, a quill and roll of paper, and a twig from an oak tree on the four quarters ; this is draped with a festoon of holly leaves, and a line in Greek impossible of translation is given above it. The meaning and use of this plate is mysterious. It came from Charleston, S.C.

677. PICKERING. *Henry Pickering.*
Armorial. Crest only. Poet.

678. PICKERING. *John Pickering Junr.*
Plain armorial. No motto.

679. PICKERING. *T. A. Pickering.*
Armorial. Ribbon and Wreath. No motto. Possibly by Callender.

680. PIERCE. *William L. Pierce.*
Armorial. Ribbon and Wreath. Motto, *In futura spector.* Signed, *Maverick Sculpt.* Of New York.

681. PIERPONT. *Charles Pierpont.*
Armorial. Ribbon and Wreath. Motto, *Manet amicitia florebit que semper.* Signed, *S. Hill.*

[1] Dr. Bates.

682. PIERPONT. *John Pierpont.*
    Simply a name-label engraved on copper. Minister
    and poet of Litchfield, Conn. Born, 1785.

683. PINFOLD. *Charles Pinfold. LL.D.*
    Armorial. Chippendale. Motto-ribbon empty.
    Two different plates are known, but they are very
    similar.

684. PINFOLD. *Charles Pinfold LL.D. Governor of Barba-
    does.*
    Same as above, with title added.

685. PINTARD. *John Pintard, LL.D.*
    Armorial. Pictorial. Signed, *Anderson.* The shield
    rests at the foot of a palm tree ; an anchor lies
    behind it ; the motto, *Never despair,* is given on a
    ribbon and the motto, *Fais bien crains rien,* is on
    the oval shield. The following line in Greek is also
    given, Κατὰ οχοχὸν διωχω, while a fourth motto,
    Depressa resurgo, is seen on a ribbon floating
    over the top of the tree. This is a fine woodcut.
    Founder of the New York Historical Society.

686. PINTARD. *John Pintard.*
    Armorial. Ribbon and Wreath. Motto, *Fais, bien
    crains, rien.* Signed, *Maverick Sct.*

687. POOR. *Benjamin Poor.*
    Plain armorial. Motto, *Pauper non in spe.* Father
    of Major Ben : Perley Poore.

688. POPHAM. *William Popham.*
    Armorial. Ribbon and Wreath. No motto.
    Signed, *Maverick Scp.* Of New York.

689. POULSON. *John Poulson's.*
    A name-label printed wholly from type, the border
    being very elaborate. Signed, *Printed by Zachariah
    Poulson Junior.* Of Philadelphia.

690. POWEL. *Samuel Powel.*
    Armorial. Chippendale. Motto, *Proprium decus
    et petrum.* This is a better plate in execution than
    those made by Dawkins, and as it is almost identical
    with the John Morgan, M.D., plate, which is prob-
    ably by Dawkins, it may have been his model.   He

seems to have copied freely from the designs of other engravers. This plate may have been the work of W. Smith, who engraved the William Spry. The Ryland Randolph, which is undoubtedly English in execution, is similar to all these and better than them all. Of Philadelphia. Twice mayor of the city.

691. POWELL. *Hare Samuel Powell.*
Armorial.

692. POWELL. *John H. Powell.*
The same copper as the Samuel Powell plate, with the name altered. Founder of Pennsylvania Agricultural Society.

693. POWELL. *Philip Powell.*
Armorial.

694. POWER. *James Power of King William County. Price.*
Armorial. Chippendale. Motto, *Impavide*. Of Virginia.

695. POWNALL. *Thomas Pownall.*
Armorial. Book-pile. Motto, *Videte et cavete ab avaritia. Luke. 12. xv.* This is a typical "Book-pile" plate. The books are arranged in tiers, with the shield in the centre; globes stand upon the topmost books at either side; a scroll falls from under the shield and bears the name; the second motto is placed under all, *The Wicked borroweth & payeth not again.* Born in England in 1722; came to America in 1753; Lieutenant-Governor of New Jersey in 1755; Governor of Massachusetts in 1757, and of South Carolina in 1760; returned to England, entered Parliament, and died at Bath in 1805.

696. PRESCOTT. *William Prescott.*
Crest only. Motto, *Nil conscire sibi.* Father of the historian. Lawyer and jurist.

697. PRESCOTT. *William H. Prescott.*
Plain armorial. Motto, *Non conscire sibi.* Signed, *A&S.* The eminent historian.

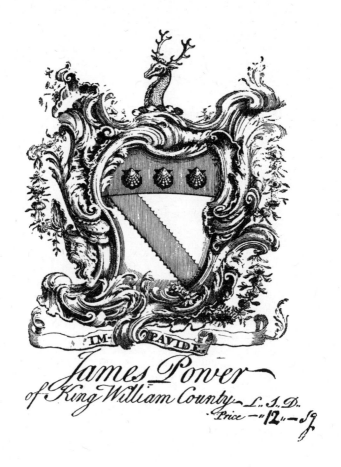

IM· ·PAVIDE

James Power
of King William County L. S. D.
Price — " 12 " — S 9

698. PRESTON. *William Campbell Preston.*
    President of South Carolina College from 1845 to
    1851.

699. PRICE. *Benjamin Price. Esqr.*
    Armorial. Jacobean. No motto.

700. PRICE. *Ezekiel Price.*
    Armorial. Chippendale. No motto. This plate
    is not signed, but is undoubtedly by Hurd. It has
    the flow of water from the shell beneath the shield,
    the peculiar dash after the name, and resembles the
    Dering plate. Of Boston.

701. PRIDE. *Halcott B. Pride.*
    Armorial. Ribbon and Wreath. Motto, *Libertas.*
    Signed, *Maverick Sculp.* Of New York.

702. PRIESTLEY. *Joseph Priestley.*
    Plain armorial. Mantling. Motto, *Ars longa, vita
    brevis.* Of Pennsylvania. Philosopher, chemist,
    and theologian.

703. PRINCE. *By the name of Prince.*
    Plain armorial. Signed, *Wightman. Sc.*

704. PRINCE. *Thomas Prince Liber, Anno Domini: 1704.*
    A printed name-label surrounded by ornamental
    type. See illustration in "Curio," page 12.
    Thomas Prince was pastor of the Old South Society
    (Boston) from 1718 to 1758. His library is one
    of the best known of colonial times; he began to
    collect books as early as 1703, as is shown by the
    following plate: "This book belongs to the New
    England Library, begun to be collected by Thomas
    Prince upon his entering Harvard College July 6th,
    1703," etc. The volumes were deposited in the
    steeple-chamber of the Old South Church, and
    suffered somewhat during the British occupation.
    The remaining volumes are now in the Boston
    Public Library. Illustrated in the "Ex Libris
    Journal," Vol. III, page 152.

705. PRIOLEAU. *Thomas G. Prioleau.*
    Armorial. Ribbon and Wreath. Motto, *Pax in
    bello.* Physician. Of Charleston, S.C.

706. PROCTOR. *Col Thomas Proctor, Artillery.*
Armorial. Motto, *Honor virtutis praemium.*
Colonel of Pennsylvania Artillery during the
Revolution.

707. PROVOOST. *John Provoost.*
Armorial. Jacobean. Motto, *Pro libertate.*

708. PROVOOST. *Saml. Provoost. Esqr. Coll: Pet: Cant.*
Armorial. Chippendale. Motto, *Pro libertate.*
Not signed, but undoubtedly by Maverick. This
plate is earlier than the succeeding.

709. PROVOOST. *Saml. Provoost.*
Armorial. Ribbon and Wreath. Motto, *Pro
libertate.* Signed, *Maverick Sculpt.* First Bishop
of New York; elected, 1786. Consecrated in
England. Illustrated in "Ex Libris Journal," Vol.
III, page 157.

710. PRUYN. *Samuel Pruyn. Albany.*
Pictorial. The scene is towards the close of day,
by the side of the water; Orpheus sits upon a
little knoll playing his lyre as he gazes up into the
sky; the passing ship does not distract him, and
the rising clouds and growing dusk are not
observed. A very pretty plate. Signed, *D. W.
Wilson Sc.*

711. PUTNAM. *The Property of Aaron Putnam, Medford.
178–.*
A printed label with the motto between the borders.
Motto, *The Wicked borrow, but do not return again ;
See thou art not of that Number.*

712. QUINCY. *Josiah Quincy.*
Plain armorial. Motto, *Discretio Moderatrix
Virtutum.* A very fuzzy plate. The mantling
comes well down the sides of the shield, and is
blown above the helmet in very feathery form. An
etching, with the name in fac-simile of owner's autograph: in two sizes with no great dissimilarity,
though the motto is not given on the larger one.
The Massachusetts patriot.

713. RANDOLPH. *John Randolph Esqr of the Middle Temple London.*

Armorial. Late Jacobean. No motto. The name and address occupy a double ribbon at the foot. Signed, *BATH. I. Skinner.* The copy before me is dated in writing, *1742.* Of Virginia. This is the same copper that the Peyton Randolph was engraved on. The lower ribbon is added, and the name imperfectly altered. The old name shows through. Illustrated in " Curio," page 64.

714. RANDOLPH. *John Randolph of Roanoke.*

Plain armorial. Motto, *Fari quae sentiat.* Very pretty mantling. A second motto above the crest, *Nil admirari.* The Virginia orator.

715. RANDOLPH. *John Randolph Junr.*

Armorial. Chippendale. Motto, *Faro quae sentiat.* A very handsome plate. The shield is oval in form and is raised upon an elaborate frame, trimmed upon its upper edge with a garland of roses, and with the shell-edging at the base ; at the left a cupid is just coming into view, holding up the festoon of flowers as he comes. The motto is on a ribbon at the base, and the name on a small curtain whose ends are thrust through the scrolls of the frame. Of Virginia.

716. RANDOLPH. *Peyton Randolph. Esqr.*

Armorial. Late Jacobean. No motto. Signed, *BATH. I. Skinner.* First President of Congress.

717. RANDOLPH. *Ryland Randolph.*

Armorial. Chippendale. Motto, *Fari quae sentiat.* This plate is like the Powell and Morgan plates, but is superior to them in all ways ; undoubtedly of English make. Of Virginia.

718. RAPHAEL. *B. J. Raphael. M.D.*

Pictorial. A hand holding a surgeon's knife ; clouds about. Signed, *Rohun and Co^s. Louisville. Ky.*

719. RAPHAEL. *B. J. Raphael. M.D.*

Pictorial. A skull and crossed bones. Of Kentucky.

720. RAY. *Robert Ray.*
    Plain armorial. Motto, *J'espere en Dieu.* Of
    New York.

721. READ. *Cha. Read of New Jersey, Esqr.*
    Armorial. Ribbon and Wreath. Motto, *Nec spe
    nec metu.* A peculiar plate : the shield is sur-
    mounted by highly rolled mantling from which
    lances depend at either side and suspend the motto-
    ribbon. Father of the Colonel Read who figured
    in the " Joseph Reed Controversy."

722. READ. *Wm. Read.*
    Plain armorial. The shield is fastened to a tree, the
    branches of which are made to resemble mantling,
    though there is no helmet. Motto, *Indefessus vigi-
    lando.* Of Maryland.

723. REED. *Catherine P. Reed. Saybrook, Conn.*
    A printed name-label with ornamental type border.
    On green paper.

724. REED. *Elijah F. Reed's.*
    Literary. An exact reduced copy of the plate of
    Thomas Robbins, even the motto being identical.

725. REVERLY. *Henry Reverly.*
    Armorial. Chippendale. Signed, *F. Kirk Sc.*

726. REYNOLDS. *Hannah Reynolds.*
    A name-label. The oval frame holding the name
    is festooned with flowers and wheat stalks ; an urn
    rests upon the frame.

727. RICHARDS. *The property of Mrs. Sally Richards. 1794.*
    A plain name-label in an ornamental type border.

728. RICKETS. *William Rickets Esqr.*
    Plain armorial. Very copious mantling rises high
    above the shield, and falls low on either side. Of
    New York.

729. RIDDLE'S LIBRARY. *J. Riddle's Circulating Library.
    Shakespear Head, No. 74 South 8th opposite to
    Sansom Strt. Philadelphia.*
    Pictorial. A good head of Shakespeare is in the
    centre of the design ; this copy is numbered 665,
    showing a fair-sized number of books.

730. RIVOIRE. *Paul Rivoire.*
> Armorial. No motto. The family name was spelled thus in France, but was altered very soon upon coming to this country. It is strange that this spelling should come up again in a book-plate unless engraved by the owner himself.

731. ROBBINS. *Philemon Robbins, His Book, A.D. 1755.*
> Printed label. Of Wethersfield, Conn.

732. ROBBINS. *Thomas Robbins.*
> Literary. The name is given upon an oval medallion, above which rise the well-filled book-shelves of the owner. A curtain is draped over them, and sprays of palm are crossed beneath the oval. Under all is the motto on a ribbon, *Nocturna versate manu, versate diurna.* (Hor.) A Connecticut divine, who left his library to the Connecticut Historical Society. A variation of this plate places the name within an oblong frame with indented corners. Otherwise the same.

733. ROBERTS. *G. C. M. Roberts. M.D. Baltimore.*
> Literary. A confusion of books upon a heavy board shelf. A lighted candle at one end; the name on the front edge of the shelf. Motto, *Alere flammam.*

734. ROBERTS. *George C. M. Roberts. M.D. Baltimore.*
> Similar to the above, but no mott

735. ROBERTSON. *Eben Robertson.*
> Plain armorial. Motto, *Virtutis gloria merces.*

736. ROBERTSON. *Eben Robertson. Kingston, Jamaica.*
> Armorial. Chippendale. Motto, *Virtutis gloria merces.* The man in chains below the shield.

737. ROBINSON. *Beverly Robinson.*
> Plain armorial. Motto, *Propere et provide.* Of New York. Wealthy Loyalist concerned in the treason of Arnold.

738. ROGERS. *Fairman Rogers.*
> Plain armorial. Motto, *Dictis factisque simplex.* Illustrated in "Art Amateur," May, 1894.

739. ROOME. *Jacob Roome.*
    Armorial. Chippendale. Motto, *Virtute et fide.*
    Signed, *H. Dawkins. Sculpsit.*

740. ROOME. *John L. C. Roome.*
    Armorial. Chippendale. Signed, *H. Dawkins
    Sculpsit.* At one side, a cupid flies a bird with a
    string tied to it, and on the other side his com-
    panion attempts the capture of another bird. A
    Loyalist lawyer of New York City. Circa 1774.

741. ROSSEAU. *Rosseau.*
    Armorial. A large plate, with the shield upon an
    ermine mantle. Signed, *Karst.* A book-collector
    of New York City. His collection of book-plates
    passed into the hands of a member of the Ex
    Libris Society last year.

742. ROUTH. *David Routh. His Book. Norfolk, 1762.*
    A label with the name within a double border of
    fancy type.

743. ROYALL. *Isaac Royall Esqr of Antigua.*
    Armorial. Jacobean. Motto, *Pectore puro.* Of
    Massachusetts. Loyalist. Benefactor of Harvard
    College. This plate is very similar to the Belcher
    in shape and size. Illustrated in "Curio," page 15.

744. RUFF. *Joanna M. Ruff. Washington City.*
    Printed from type within a border of ten American
    eagles.

745. RUSH. (Anonymous.) Rush arms.
    Armorial. Chippendale. Motto, *Miseris succurrere
    disce.* Name-frame empty ; name evidently erased.
    Probably the plate of the signer of the Declaration
    from Pennsylvania, Benjamin Rush. He is said
    to have destroyed all the copies of his plate which
    he could find.

746. RUSSELL. *Josh. Russell.*
    A simple name-label. The name, with the initials
    above it in a cipher monogram, is enclosed within
    a rectangular frame. This is a woodcut, and is the
    work of Anderson.

747. RUSSELL. *Thomas Russell.*
>Allegorical. Signed, *Callender Sp.* This plate is a copy of the plate of Joseph Barrell.

748. RUTGERS. *Hendrick Rutgers.*
>Armorial. Chippendale. Motto, *Tantes da dir.* Of New York City. Patriot and philanthropist.

749. RUTHERFORD. *John Rutherford.*
>Armorial. Motto, *Nec sorte nec fato.* Born in New York about 1760. One of the proprietors of East Jersey.

750. RUTLEDGE. (Anonymous.) Rutledge arms.
>Supporters, a collared lion and an American Indian. They stand upon the ribbon, which bears the motto, *Progredi non regredi.* Signed, *S. C. Barnes & Co., Coventry St.* Of South Carolina.

751. ST. CLAIR. *Sir John St. Clair Bart.*
>Armorial. Chippendale. Motto, *Quo cunque ferar.* Signed, *Ja. Turner, Philada., Sculpt.* Munitions of war are seen behind the name-bracket. Of Philadelphia. A British officer, associated with Braddock.

752. ST. GEORGE'S CHURCH. *Library of the Sunday Schools attached to St George's Church, established A. D. 1819. Presented by . . . . No. . . . . .*
>Above the words is a pretty little picture of a child on her knees reading from a book on a table before her. This plate is not signed, and seems to be better work than was done on the plate of the Teachers' Union of this same church.

753. ST. GEORGE'S CHURCH. *The property of the Teachers' Union of St. George's Church. Presented by . . . . No. . . . .*
>An engraved label. No ornamentation beyond flourishes. Signed, *Rollinson.*

754. SALTER. *Richard Salter, Esq. Barbadoes.*
>Armorial. Jacobean. Motto-ribbon empty. The name is given on the looped curtain.

755. SALTONSTALL. *Walter Saltonstall.*
    Armorial. Arms, Argent, a bend gules, between two eagles displayed sable. Crest, out of a ducal coronet a demi-pelican vulning herself.

756. SALTONSTALL. *William Saltonstall.*
    Armorial.

757. SAMUELS. (Anonymous.) Plate of James Samuels.
    Armorial. Chippendale. Motto, *L'un Pour l'autre.* Signed, *H. Dawkins, Philada., Fecit.* The hissing griffin, as in the Bushrod Washington plate, is given here.

758. SARGEANT. *Jacob Sargeant.*
    Armorial in form, though no real arms are shown. Chippendale. Motto, *Cito pede praeterit aetas.* Not signed, but engraved on brass by the owner. Of Connecticut. Some dated copies of this plate are about, but the date is not contemporary or correct. Also, the plate was not signed originally.

759. SARGENT. *Daniel Sargent Junr.*
    Armorial. Ribbon and Wreath. Motto, *Nec quaerere honorem nec spernere.* Signed, *Callen der Sc.* Of Massachusetts.

760. SARGENT. *Epes Sargent.*
    Armorial. Chippendale. Motto - scroll empty. Signed, *P. Revere Sculp.*

761. SARGENT. *Winthrop Sargent.*
    Plain armorial. Motto, *Fortior quo rectior.* Of Massachusetts. Statesman and Revolutionary soldier.

762. SCHUYLER. *Philip Schuyler Esqr.*
    Armorial. Early Chippendale. No motto. Major-General in the Revolution, and was, after the war, a Senator. Illustrated in "Curio," page 110.

763. SCHUYLER. *Samuel Schuyler.*
    Armorial. Chippendale. Motto, *Semper fidelis.* Of New York. Born, March 10, 1746 ; died, 1790.

764. SCOTT. *Benjamin Scott.*
    Armorial. Chippendale. No motto.

765. SCOTT. *Gustavus Scott.*
　　　　Armorial. Ribbon and Wreath. Motto, *Gaudia magna nuncio.* A lawyer of Virginia. Died in Washington, 1801.

766. SCOTT. *John V.*
　　　　Armorial. Ribbon and Wreath. Motto, *In God we trust.* This plate is just like the De Witt Clinton by Maverick. The last name is torn out in the only copy seen, but the arms are those of Scott.

767. SCOTT. *Winfield Scott.*
　　　　Plain armorial. Motto, *Amore patriae.* Of Virginia. Famous General.

768. SCOTTON. *John Scotton.*
　　　　Armorial. Jacobean. No motto. Of Boston, Mass.

769. SEARS. *Sears.*
　　　　Armorial. Ribbon and Wreath. Motto-ribbon empty.

770. SEARS. *David Sears.*
　　　　Armorial. A knight in armor and an Indian for supporters. Motto, *Honore et fides.* Circa 1830.

771. SECOMBE. *John Secombe his book 1729.*
　　　　Name-label, with ornamental type border. Clergyman and poet. Of Massachusetts.

772. SEDGWICK. *Theodore Sedgwick Junr.*
　　　　Crest only. The crest is given above an oval garter, within which is the motto, *Confido in Domino.* Publicist and lawyer of Albany, N. Y.

773. SELFRIDGE. *Thomas O. Selfridge Boston 1799.*
　　　　Two fluted pillars are joined at the capitals by festoons of roses; the name is in the open space between them. A woodcut. Selfridge was the Federalist lawyer of Boston who shot Charles Austin.

774. SEMPLE. Armorial. Of Virginia.

775. SETON. *William Seton.*
　　　　Armorial. Ribbon and Wreath. Motto, *Hazard zit forward.* Signed, *Maverick Sculpt.* Of New York.

776. SEWELL. Armorial.

777. SHEPPARD. *John H. Sheppard.*
Armorial. Ribbon and Wreath. Motto, *Nil desperandum.* Of Massachusetts. Lawyer and author.

778. SHERMAN. *Rev. Henry B. Sherman. M.A.*
Armorial. Jacobean. Motto, *Conquer death by virtue.* A very peculiar use is made of the Jacobean features.

779. SHIPPEN. *Edward Shippen Esquire.*
Armorial. Jacobean. No motto. Jurist. Descendant of Edward Shippen, the first Mayor of Philadelphia. Educated in London. Illustrated in " Curio," page 110.

780. SHIPPEN. *Robertus Shippen. S. T. P. Coll. Aen. Nas. Principatis.*
A reproduction of the above. Illustrated in " Art Amateur," May, 1894.

781. SHUBRICK. *Thomas Shubrick, South Carolina.*
Plain armorial. Colonel in the Revolution. Illustrated in " Curio," page 113.

782. SILVESTER. *Peter Silvester Esqr.*
Armorial. Ribbon and Wreath. Motto, *Nec degener.* Signed, *Child Sculpt.* No tinctures. Of New York.

783. SIMPSON. *Jonathan Simpson.*
Armorial. Chippendale. Motto, *Lege et intellige.* This plate is not signed, but is undoubtedly the work of Hurd.

784. SISE. *The Property of Edward Sise.*
Pictorial. An extremely rude home-made etching. A beautiful bird is resting upon a stunted tree ; an ornamented oval encloses the scene.

785. SITGREAVES. *John Sitgreaves of New Bern.*
Armorial in form, but no arms shown. Ribbon and Wreath. Motto, *Libertas et natale solum.* The name occupies the oval space where ordinarily the arms are displayed. Books and writing-material

are introduced below the frame. Signed, *Maverick Scp New York*. Member Old Congress. Revolutionary patriot.

786. SKELTON. *Reuben Skelton Hanover County Virginia.*
 Armorial. Chippendale. Motto-ribbon empty.

787. SKIPWITH. *Fulwar Skipwith.*
 Armorial. Ribbon and Wreath. Motto, *Sans Dieu je ne puis.* Of Virginia. Of the family of Skipwith of Preswould, County Leicester. Baronet.

788. SMITH. *Smith.*
 Armorial. Jacobean.

789. SMITH. *Haziel Smith, Carpenter, New York. Deaf and Dumb.*
 A printed label, within a circular border. This mention of a physical infirmity on a book-plate is unique.

790. SMITH. *Hezekiah Smith.*
 Armorial. Late Jacobean. Motto, *Beauty and Grace.* An open book for crest, with the following Greek on it, Ἐρεονᾶτε τὰς γραφας; the sun in splendor above it. Of Massachusetts.

791. SMITH. (Anonymous.)
 Portrait plate. Showing a young man holding a book, clad in the manner of the studious youth of the early part of the century. Beneath, the motto, *Qui contentus felix.* A very pretty bit of engraving. This was the plate of G. A. Smith, a book-lover, whose library was sold in New York City some thirty years ago.

792. SMITH. *James Scott Smith.*
 Armorial. Ribbon and Wreath. Motto, *Ne crede colori.* Signed, *Maverick Sculp.* Of New York.

793. SMITH. *John A. Smith.*
 A beautiful pictorial plate. On the smooth face of an immense rock the name is carved; the trees grow close to it on the far side, and in the long distance other trees are seen; clouds float lazily, and the effect is sultry. A doctor of medicine in Virginia. Born, 1782; died, 1865. President of William and Mary College, 1814–1826.

794. SMITH. *John Adams Smith.*
Plain armorial. Motto, *Finis coronat opus.* Signed, *Rollinson Sct.*

795. SMITH. *John J. Smith.*
Armorial. Chippendale. No motto; the name occupying the motto-ribbon. This plate is exactly like the James Logan. Great-grandson of James Logan. Librarian of Philadelphia and Loganian libraries.

796. SMITH. *Jonathan Smith. M DCC LX.*
A printed name-label from type with ornamental border.

797. SMITH. *Robert Smith.*
Armorial. Major-General Smith of Virginia.

798. SMITH. *Samuel Smith.*
Name-label; name engraved within an oval, trimmed with a wreath.

799. SMITH. *Samuel Smith, Esquire.*
Armorial. Pictorial. A cherub is seated, busily reading, at the right side, while on the left his companion blows lustily upon a horn, in the direction of the sky, whence a third cherub approaches, displaying a long ribbon upon which is the motto, *Omnes fremant licet dicam quod sentio.* The whole design rests upon a bracket garlanded with roses.

800. SMITH. *Thomas Smith.*
Armorial. Of Gloucester, Va.

801. SMITH. *Thomas Smith Junr. Esqr.*
Armorial. Ribbon and Wreath. Motto, *Nec aspera terrent.* Signed, *Maverick Sculpt.* The customary landscape beneath the shield, and the signature on the open scroll. This plate is a copy of the James Scott Smith plate, and is much better work. Of New York.

802. SMITH. *Thomas J. Smith.*
Armorial. Of New York. Signed by Maverick. Lawyer and scholar.

803. SMITH. *William Smith.*
　　　　Armorial. Chippendale. Motto, *Chacun a son gout.* Not signed, but undoubtedly by Hurd. Of Massachusetts.

804. SMITH. *William Smith.*
　　　　Armorial. Ribbon and Wreath. Motto, *Tutus si fortis.* Signed, *Maverick Sculpt.* Of New York.

805. SMITH. *William Smith A.M.*
　　　　Armorial. Jacobean. Motto, *Nil utile quod non honestum.* Of New York. Rather wild in appearance.

806. SMITH. *William Smith LL.D. Charleston S. Carolina.*
 Armorial. Ribbon and Wreath. Motto, *Fidem servabo genusque.* Statesman and lawyer. Born, 1784 ; died, 1840.

807. SMITH. *William Loughton Smith.*
 Diplomatist. Statesman of Charleston, S.C. Born, 1758 ; died, 1812.

808. SMITH. *William P. Smith A.M.*
 Armorial. Jacobean. Motto, *Deus nobis haec otia fecit.* Signed, *Thomas Johnston Sculp.* The most ambitious Jacobean plate of our early period. Probably the plate of William Peartree Smith of New York. Illustrated in "Art Amateur," May, 1894.

809. SMYTH. *Andrew Smyth.*
 Armorial.

810. SOCIETY FOR PROPAGATING THE GOSPEL. *Sigillum Societatis De Promovendo Evangelio In Partibus Transmarinus.*
 Allegorical. An oval frame bears the Latin inscription and a broad ribbon underneath bears the following, *The Gift of the Society for propagating the Gospel in Foreign parts, 1704.* The scene is off the coast ; a three-masted ship, with all sails set, is within a few feet of the shore ; the missionary, whose height is equal to one half the foremast, stands before that mast with Bible in hand and is already preaching to the natives who, with outstretched hands, come running down the declivity. The imminent danger of the ship is possibly the real cause of the interest on the part of the natives. The full sun bestows his blessing, and a serpentine ribbon in mid-air bears the motto, *Transiens adiuvanos.* Two varieties. Illustrated in "Curio," page 11.

811. SOUTH CAROLINA. *Protestant Episcopal Society for the Advancement of Christianity in South Carolina.*
 A printed label.

812. SPAIGHT. *Spaight.*
 Plain armorial. Motto, *Vi et virtute.* Of North Carolina.

813. SPOONER. *Joshua Spooner.*
     Armorial. Jacobean. Motto, *Follow reason.*
     Signed, *N. Hurd, Scp.* Of Massachusetts. A
     very fine plate.

814. SPOONER. *Wm. Spooner.*
     Pictorial. A play on the name. Two doves are
     billing and cooing, and two hearts are overlapped
     above them. Of Newport. Circa 1825.

815. SPOTSWOOD. (Anonymous.)
     Armorial. Early Chippendale. Motto, *Patior ut
     potiar.* Of Virginia.

816. SPRIGG. *Richard Sprigg junr.*
     Name-label within an ornamental border of foliated
     scrolls, in the top of which a group of thirteen stars
     is fixed. Signed, *T. Sparrow.* Above his name
     are the letters *F. G.,* whose meaning is lost. A
     woodcut.

817. SPRY. *William Spry.*
     Armorial. Chippendale. No motto. Signed, *W.
     Smith's.* Of New York. The design of this plate
     is similar to some by Dawkins, but the execution is
     superior. Probably Dawkins copied from Smith,
     who was without doubt an English engraver.

818. STANFORD. *Thos. N. Stanford.*
     Armorial. Ribbon and Wreath. Motto, *Verum
     dicit.* Signed, *Rollinson.*

819. STEARNS. *Stearns.*
     Plain armorial. Motto, *Firm.* Of Massachusetts.

820. STEARNS. *Benjamin Stearns.*
     Name-label. Above the name a cabalistic arrange-
     ment of the letters W. V. and M. with four hands
     in pairs pointing at them. Motto, *Nihil me tangere,*
     altered to *Noli me tangere.* Dated 1833.

821. STEPHENS. *William Stephens.*
     Armorial. Jacobean. Mantling. Motto, *In corrupta
     fides nudaque veritas.* This resembles the plate of
     William Cowper, Clerk of Parliament. Not signed,
     but possibly by Maverick, although not in his usual
     style.

822. STEVENS.   *Henry Stevens, Barnet. Vt.* (*Walton's Press, Montpelier. Vt.*).

> The arms of the State with its motto, *Freedom and Unity.* Under this, in a frame, is the following poem : —

> > *In Paradise, the tree,*
> > *Of knowledge was the pride :*
> > *By God's supreme decree,*
> > *The man who eat — then died.*

> > *But Heaven in mercy since*
> > *Does him who tastes forgive :*
> > *To know, is no offence :*
> > *Now, he who eats — shall live.*

> The famous bibliographer.

823. STEVENS.   *The Property of Henry Stevens, Barnet, 180–.*
> A simple name-label, printed, with ornamental type.

824. STEWART.   *Anthony Stewart Annapolis Maryland.*
> Armorial. Chippendale. Motto, *Nobilis ira.* A very handsome design, the name-bracket being large and handsomely ornamented ; rows of roses down the sides, and the graceful foliation, make a very handsome plate.

825. STEWART.   *James Stewart. New York.*
> Armorial. Chippendale. Motto, *Nil Desperandum.*

826. STEWART.   *Hon. John Stewart Esqr. Quebec.*
> Plain armorial. Mantling. Motto, *Nobilis ira.* Signed, *S. Jones Sc Quebec.*

827. STILLE.   *Alfred Stille. M.D.*
> Plain armorial. Motto, *Innocenter, patienter, constanter.* A large plate. Of Philadelphia.

828. STITH.   *William Stith.*
> Armorial. Jacobean. Motto, *Rather virtue than learning,* in Greek. The historian of Virginia. Date of plate, circa 1745. Illustrated in "Curio," page 15.

829. STOCKBRIDGE.   *Charles Stockbridge.*
> Name-label. Very much in the style of pen flourishes.

830. STOCKTON. *Richard Stockton, A.M.*
    Armorial. Chippendale. Motto, *Omnia Deo pendent.* Books are shown at either side of the shield. Signer of the Declaration and father of Commodore Stockton of New Jersey.

831. STONE. *Wm. L. Stone.*
    Pictorial. An eagle struggling with a serpent rises into the clouds with it, and bears an open scroll in one talon on which we read, *Demagogues may frown and Factions rage — Traitors may sigh and Tyrants weep, but Freemen will rejoice for . . . .* A ribbon above the eagle bears the motto, *Justice, Truth.* Signed, *R. Rawdon. Alby.* Author and editor.

832. STOTT. *Ebenezer Stott.*
    Armorial. Of Virginia.

833. STOWE. *Stowe.*
    Plain armorial. Motto, *Inter feros per crucem ad coronam.* Calvin Ellis Stowe, clergyman, and husband of Harriet Beecher Stowe.

834. STRINGER. *Samuel Stringer.*
    Armorial. Chippendale. No motto. Signed, *H. D. fecit.* Prominent physician in Eastern New York State. Born in Maryland, 1734.

835. STROBEL. *Martin Strobel. Charleston. S.C.*
    Literary. Identical with the George Goodwin and the Frederick Marsh plates.

836. STURGES. *John Sturges.*
    Armorial. Signed by Maverick. No further information is obtainable.

837. STUYVESANT. *Peter Gerard Stuyvesant.*
    Plain armorial. Motto, *Jovae praestat fidere quam homine.*

838. SULLIVAN. *John Sullivan.*
    Armorial. Ribbon and Wreath. Motto, *Modestia victorix.* Signed, *J. Callender Scp.* Of New Hampshire. Major-General in the Revolutionary army.

839. SUMNER. *Thos. W. Sumner.*
     Name engraved upon a sable tablet; festoon of
     cloth above.

840. SUMNER. *W. H. Sumner.*
     Plain armorial. Motto, *In medio tutissimus ibis.*
     The plate of Gen. William Hyslop Sumner. Born,
     Dorchester, Mass., 1780; died, 1861.

841. SUPREME COUNCIL 33°. *Supreme Council 33° of the
     Ancient Accepted Scottish Rite of Freemasonry for
     the Northern Masonic Jurisdiction U. S. A.*
     Masonic emblems. A triangle with *33* within it;
     above a regal crown is shone upon by the full rays
     of the sun; a double-headed eagle grasps a sword.
     Motto, *Deus meumque jus.*

842. SWAN. *James Swan.*
     Armorial. Pictorial. Supporters, a Scotchman in
     tartan and an Indian holding a tobacco-plant.
     Motto, *Dum spiro spero.* Signed, *Callender Sc.* A
     beehive at the right, and at the left a view of the
     ocean, with distant sail in sight. Merchant, politi-
     cian, scholar, and author before the age of 22.
     Born in Scotland; came to Boston when very
     young; a member of the "Tea Party"; wounded
     at Bunker Hill; went to France and made a fort-
     une; through trouble with a German correspon-
     dent he was imprisoned in St. Pelagie, Paris, for
     fifteen years; died, Paris, 1831.

843. SWETT. *J. B. Swett.*
     A symbolical plate, representing the profession of
     medicine. In the upper part a corpse has been
     laid open for examination, and three cupids are in
     attendance; a fourth reads a book of reference
     with woful face, and a saw and vessel would indi-
     cate that extreme measures were to be tried.
     Below the name the serpent of Æsculapius twined
     about the rod is placed between retorts, and herbs
     growing in flower-pots. The execution of the
     plate is poor. John Barnard Swett of Newbury-
     port, Mass.

844. SWORD. *William Sword.*
    Armorial. Chippendale. Motto-ribbon empty.
    Signed, *H. D. Fecit.*

845. TAYLOE. *Benjn. Ogle Tayloe.*
    Library interior. The shield occupies more room
    than anything else in the library, and is in the
    immediate foreground, standing upright against a
    pillar; a festoon falls over it; behind shelves of
    books are seen; books are on the floor, and a
    globe is in the corner. Of Maryland.

846. TAYLOE. *John Tayloe of Mount Airy Virginia.*
    This plate is the same as the preceding, and is
    probably the older print, the other being from the
    same copper with the name altered.

847. TAYLOR. *George Taylor.*
    Armorial. Of Charleston, S.C.

848. TAYLOR. (Anonymous.)
    Armorial. Ribbon and Wreath. Motto-ribbon

empty. This plate has a guaranteed autograph of George Taylor, the signer of the Declaration from Pennsylvania; also dated by him in the year of Independence, 1776.

849. TAYLOR. *William Taylor.*
Armorial. Ribbon and Wreath. Motto, *Jura sunt mea vindi cabo.* Signed, *Maverick Sct.* Of New York.

850. TAZEWELL. *John Tazewell Virginia.*
Armorial. Chippendale. Motto, *Ne quid nimis.*

851. TEN BROECK. *John C. Ten Broeck.*
Armorial. Ribbon and Wreath. Motto, *Perge coepisti.* Not signed, but very probably by Maverick. Of New York. A soldier of ability in the Revolution; was with Washington at Valley Forge, and was in many important battles. The original copper is now owned by Mr. Beverly Chew, President of the Grolier Club, New York City.

852. THOMAS. *Geo: Thomas. Ex liber, 1798.*
Pictorial. The frame is somewhat of the older Jacobean style, having a large pediment, upon which rests a circular frame, enclosing a little sketch of a beehive with the swarm about it, a mortar as large as the beehive standing beside it, with the pestle in it, and an awkward branch of a rose-bush, with two huge blossoms upon it, bending over the mortar. Oak branches ascend on either side of the frame, and what looks as much like a plum pudding as anything blazes away in place of a crest. The name and date are written upon the face of the pediment. A physician of Lancaster, Pa.

853. THOMAS. *Isaiah Thomas.*
Armorial. Jacobean. Motto, *Nec elatus nec dejectus.* Of Worcester, Mass. Publisher of " Massachusetts Spy." Attributed to Johnson. Illustrated in " Art Amateur," March, 1894.

854. THOMPSON. Armorial. Of Virginia.

855. THOMPSON. *James Thompson.*
    Plain armorial. No motto. Signed, *P. Maverick, Durand & Co.*

856. THOMPSON. *Robert Thompson.*
    Armorial. The arms are those of Count Rumford. (Benjamin Thompson.) No further information obtainable.

John Tayloe, of Mount Airy Virginia.

857. THOMPSON. *Willm. Thompson Esqr.*
    Armorial. Chippendale. Motto, *Ante victoriam ne cane triumphum.* A handsome plate. A cornucopiæ of flowers at the left.

858. THORNDIKE. *Oliver Thorndike.*
    Armorial. Jacobean. Motto, *Rosae inter spinas nascunter.* Of Boston.

859. THORNTON. *William Thornton.*
    Armorial. Jacobean. Motto, *Deo spes meo.* Of
    Virginia. A woodcut. Circa 1745.

860. THRUSTON. Armorial. Of Virginia.

861. TILLOTSON. *Thomas Tillotson.*
    Armorial. Ribbon and Wreath. Motto, *Virtus est
    natale meum.* Signed, *Maverick Sculpt New York.*

862. TOMLINSON. *John Tomlinson.*
    Armorial. Chippendale ; rather wild. Motto, *Cor
    unum ira mea.* Signed, *H. D. fecit.* Similar to
    the Bushrod Washington plate.

863. TRACY. *Nathaniel Tracy.*
    Armorial. Chippendale. Motto-ribbon empty.
    Signed, *N. H. Scp.* Of Massachusetts.

864. TRENCHARD. *Lieut. E. Trenchard. U. S. Navy.*
    Pictorial. The name is given upon an oval
    medallion, back of which are grouped the United
    States flag, pennants, bombs, cannon balls, and an
    anchor, while in the distance the ship of the
    Lieutenant is seen. This plate was probably made
    soon after the War of 1812. Trenchard was born
    in New Jersey in 1784.

865. TRIPP. *Lot Tripp, New York.*
    A simple name-label enclosed in an oval frame, and
    cut on wood by Dr. Anderson.

866. TUBERVILLE. *George Lee Tuberville, Virginia.*
    Armorial. The shield is on the breast of a large
    eagle displayed. Motto, *Omnia relinquit servare
    rempublicam.*

867. TUCKER. *St. George Tucker.*
    Armorial. Poet, jurist, and Revolutionary soldier
    of Virginia. Was called the "American Black-
    stone."

868. TUFTS. *S. Tufts. Newburyport.*
    A very roughly engraved label. The name is
    enclosed within a circular frame.

869. TUTTLE. *The property of Hugh Tuttle, 1822.*
     The name is arranged in the form of a diamond
     with the first letter in the centre and the others
     about it in natural order.

870. TYLER. *Andrew Tyler.*
     Armorial. Jacobean. No motto. Signed, *N. H.
     Sculp.* The shield is placed upon a bracket having
     a handsome diapered pattern; the scrolls are
     graceful, the canephoros head on which the shield
     rests has curled hair, and the upper arms of the
     scroll-work support urns filled with flowers. A
     goldsmith of Boston.

871. TYLER. *Joseph Tyler.*
     Armorial. Motto, *Fari quae sentiat.* By Thomas
     Johnson.

872. TYNG. *Dudley Atkins Tyng.*
     Armorial. Ribbon and Wreath. Motto, *Esse quam
     videri.* Signed, *Callender Sp.* Of Massachusetts.
     Descendant of Governor Dudley.

873. UNIACKE. *Richd. John Uniacke. Esqr. 1801.*
     Plain armorial. Motto, *Faithful and brave.* Gov-
     ernor-General of Canada.

874. UNITED STATES ARMY. *Head Quarters of the Army.*
     The American eagle displays the shield of our
     country upon his breast; the motto, *E Pluribus
     unum,* and the thirteen stars are given above.

875. UNITED STATES CONGRESS. *Library of Congress, United
     States of America.*
     Engraved. Oblong border of oak leaves.

876. UNITED STATES NAVY. *Navy Department.*
     The American eagle rests upon an anchor. A cir-
     cular frame about this holds the words, *Hydro-
     graphic Office, U. S. Navy.* A ribbon below has
     on it, *Bureau of Navigation.*

877. UNITED STATES NAVY. *Navy Department. Bureau of
     Navigation.*
     A large plate. Upon the shield is a representation
     of the mariner's compass; the American eagle

flies over the waves above ; the motto, *Vigilemus ut vigilatis*, is given upon a ribbon below. Branches of oak are used as decoration.

878. VAN BERCKEL. *P. I. Van Berckel.*
Armorial. Supporters, naked barbarians with bludgeons five feet long, and wreaths on their heads ; they stand on the motto-ribbon. Motto, *In silentio et spe.* Signed, *Maverick Scp.* Of New York.

879. VAN BUREN. *M. V. Buren.*
An engraved label ; the name is in script and a thin festoon is draped above it. Very probably the plate of Martin Van Buren, eighth President of the United States.

880. VAN CORTLANDT. *Van Cortlandt.*
Armorial. Military trophies behind the shield. Motto, *Virtus sibi munus.* Of the Manor.

881. VAN NESS. *J. P. Van Ness.*
Plain armorial. Motto, *Pro Deo et nobilissima patria Batavorum.* Mantling comes down well upon either side.

882. VAN RENSSELAER. *Jer. Vn. Rensselaer. Esqr.*
Armorial. Jacobean. Lieutenant-Governor of New York, 1801–1803.

883. VAN RENSSELAER. *K. K. Van Rensselaer. Esqr.*
Armorial. Ribbon and Wreath. Motto, *Vertus est vera vetustas.* Signed, *Maverick, Scp.*, on an open scroll. Of New York.

884. VAN RENSSELAER. *P. V. Rensselaer.*
Armorial. By Billings.

885. VAN RENSSELAER. *Stephen Van Rensselaer.*
Armorial. Mantling. The name on a broad ribbon surrounding the whole. Not signed, but probably by Maverick. The " Patron."

886. VAN WYCK. *Van Wyck.*
Armorial. Jacobean. Supporters. Of New York.

887. VARICK.   *Richard Varick Esq.*
> Armorial.   Chippendale.   Motto-ribbon empty.
> Signed, *A. Billings Sculpt.*   Patriotic features are
> introduced into the ornamentation.   The plate of
> Colonel Richard Varick, a brave officer in the Revo-
> lution : was Mayor of New York in 1801, and with
> Samuel Jones revised the law of the State in 1786.

888. VASSALL.   *John Vassall.   Esqr.*
> Armorial.   Chippendale.   No motto.   This plate
> is not signed, but is undoubtedly the work of Hurd.
> Of Cambridge, Mass. ; inheritor of a large fortune,
> which he augmented largely ; a Loyalist, and a
> refugee ; lived for some time in England, and died

there. His mansion-house at Cambridge became the headquarters of General Washington, and later the home of the poet Longfellow. He would not use the family motto, "Saepe pro rege, semper pro republica," on his coat-of-arms, it is said.

889. VAUGHAN. *Benjamin Vaughan.*

Plain armorial. Motto, *Prudenter et simpliciter.* Of Maine. Educated in London ; gave his library to Bowdoin College.

890. VAUGHAN. *Samuel Vaughan.*

Armorial. Jacobean. Motto, *In prudentia & simplicitate.* Mantling around the helmet. A wealthy planter of Jamaica. Illustrated in "Curio," page 11.

891. VAUGHAN. *Samuel Vaughan Esqr.*

Armorial. Chippendale. Motto, *Christi servitus vera libertas.* The Vaughan arms impaling Hallewell.

892. VAUGHAN. *Samuel Vaughan Junr.*

Plain armorial. Motto, *Prudenter et simpliciter.* Of Maine.

893. VAUGHAN. *William Vaughan.*

Plain armorial. Motto, *Prudenter et simpliciter.* Very similar to the Samuel Vaughan Junr.

894. VAUX. *Edward Vaux.*

Plain armorial. No motto. Of Philadelphia.

895. VAVASOUR. *Josias Short Vavasour.*

Armorial. Chippendale. Signed, *H. Dawkins. Sc.* At the left, a harlequin in a black mask peers around the frame and touches his feathered hat ; at the right a fashionably clad young lady, noticing the intrusion, holds up her hand-glass, in which the black mask of the new-comer is reflected. Motto, *Strive for glory.*

896. VINTON. *John A. Vinton.*

The name is printed within a woodcut border, oval in form, and decorated with a wreath of flowers and a spray of palm. The following quotation is given : *Maximae divitiae sunt prae doctrina et scientia contemnendae : sed virtus omnibus praestat.* Antiquarian.

897. VIRGINIA COUNCIL CHAMBER. *Virginia Council Chamber.*
Armorial. First quarter, the arms of England and
Scotland; second quarter, the arms of France;
third quarter, the arms of Ireland; fourth quarter,
the same as the first. Motto, *En dat Virginia
quartam.* Supporters, two men in complete
armor, their beavers open, three ostrich feathers on
the helmets, their breasts charged with a cross, and
in the exterior hand a lance. Crest, a virgin
queen, couped at the shoulders, hair dishevelled,
and crowned with an Eastern crown. Illustrated
in " Curio," page 14.

898. VIRGINIA COUNCIL CHAMBER. (Anonymous.)
Armorial. Below the arms, which are the same as
those in the preceding plate, is a scene within the
Council Chamber, evidently, as the members are
around the table, and are being addressed by one
of their number. The framework which supports

this is Chippendale in construction, the armed
supporters stand upon the upper part, and the very
lowest panel is occupied by the 249th line of the
first book of Homer's "Illiad," Τοῦ καὶ ἀπὸ γλώσσης
μέλιτος γλυκίων ῥέεν αὐδή. Signed, *Dent— Sculpt.
Bull Alley, Lombard Street. London.* The design
of the plate is attributed to Samuel Wale, R.A.
See "The Book-plate Annual and Armorial Year
Book," 1894. London, A. & C. Black, Soho
Square.

899. VOSE. *Benjamin Vose.*
Armorial.

900. VOSE. *Solomon Vose.*
Armorial. Ribbon and Wreath. Motto, *Quo fata
vocant.* Signed, *Callender Sc.*

901. WALDO. *D. Waldo's.*
Armorial. Jacobean. Motto, *Nil sine Deo.* Of
Connecticut. Soldier in the Revolution.

902. WALKER. *Samuel Walker's.*
Pictorial. Above the plain tablet which bears the
name, and the mottoes, *Ubi plura nitent paucis
non offendar maculis,* and *Vitanda est improba
Siren defidia,* a group of musical accessories is
placed ; below, two sprays of oak branches. A
rude woodcut.

903. WALL. *Wall.*
Plain armorial. Motto, *Par pari refero.* Signed,
J. D. Stout. N.Y.

904. WALLACE. *The Honble. Joshua Maddox Wallace of
Burlington in New Jersey esqr.*
Armorial. Chippendale. Motto, *Pro patria.*

905. WALLER. *Benja. Waller. Virginia.*
Armorial. Chippendale. No motto. A lawyer in
Virginia.

906. WALMSLEY. *I. Walmsley. 1792.*
Armorial. Very crude work. The mantling
encloses the shield. Motto-ribbon empty.

907. WARREN. *G. Washington Warren.*

Armorial. Belongs to no class. Ornamented with scroll-work. The same plate is found with the name of Lucius Henry Warren upon it.

908. WARREN. *John C. Warren.*

Armorial. Pictorial. The shield rests against a boulder, and is shaded by a poplar tree; the serpent and rod of Æsculapius lie on the ground, and the name is given on a ribbon. Eminent surgeon and medical writer of Boston.

909. WARREN. *J. Mason Warren.*

Plain armorial. No motto, the name occupying the motto-ribbon. Same arms as the John C. Warren.

910. WARREN. *The Property of Samuel Warren. jun. Providence.*

The name is printed from type within an engraved border, and the date, *1799,* appears in MS.

911. WARREN. *W. Warren. Theatre.*

Pictorial. The name is given within a frame of shield shape, above which a pair of antlers, trimmed with oak branches and festoons of oak leaves, is seen; resting between them are a book and looking-glass. At the foot of the frame a loving cup.

912. WASHINGTON. *Bushrod Washington.*

Armorial. Chippendale. Motto, *Exitus acta probat.* Nephew of the President, to whom Mount Vernon descended. This plate is almost identical with the Whitebread plate by Dawkins. The dragon changes places with the long spray of flowers, otherwise they are the same. It is not known whether Dawkins did this plate or not, but presumably he copied the other from this, which is likely to have been an imported plate. It is not at all an uncommon type among the English plates.

913. WASHINGTON. *George Washington.*

Armorial. Chippendale. Motto, *Exitus acta probat.* First President of the United States.

914. WATERHOUSE. *John Waterhouse. Halifax.*
      Crest only. Motto, *Veritas vincit omnia.*

915. WATIES. *Thomas Waties.*
      Armorial. Of South Carolina. An eminent judge
      for a period of some forty years. Born, 1760;
      died, 1828.

916. WATKINS. *John W. Watkins. A.M.*
      Armorial. Ribbon and Wreath. Motto, *Fortis et
      fidelis.* Signed, *Rollinson Sct.*

917. WATTS. *John Watts.*
      Plain armorial. Motto, *Forti non deficit telum.* A
      Loyalist of New York, whose estates were confis-
      cated. Statue in Trinity Churchyard, New York
      City.

918. WEBSTER. *Danl. Webster.*
      Plain armorial. Motto, *Vera pro gratis.* Name in
      fac-simile of signature. Statesman, lawyer, and
      orator.

919. WELCH. *D. T. Welch.*
>   Literary. Similar to the M. W. Day plate. Motto, *Literatura mentem expandit.*

920. WELD. *Isaac Weld.*
>   Armorial. Chippendale. Motto, *Verum atque decens.* Traveller and author.

921. WELFORD. *Beverley R. Welford. M.D.*
>   Motto, *The wicked man borroweth and returneth not again.* Engraved name-label. Of Richmond, Va.

922. WENTWORTH. *Wentworth.*
>   Armorial. Chippendale. Motto, *En Dieu est tout.* Signed, *N. Hurd, Scp.* Of New Hampshire.

923. WETHERSFIELD. *Social Library, Stepney Society, Wethersfield.*
>   Literary. A shelf of books is raised upon a frame of Chippendale scroll-work, and has a ribbon draped upon the front of it, bearing the motto, *Waste not a moment.* Above the books on the shelf a winged hour-glass is seen under the folds of a draped curtain. Signed, *Doolittle Sculpt.* This plate is also found with the signature erased, and the following line added in fine letters under the design : *Annual Meeting, 1st Monday in Dec. at 6. P.M. when every book is to be returned.*

924. WETMORE. *Charles H. Wetmore.*
>   Armorial. Ribbon and Wreath. Motto, *Virtus libertas et patria.* Signed, *Doolittle Sculp.* The open field face of the shield is used for the number of the volume. Of Connecticut.

925. WETMORE. *Prosper Wetmore.*
>   Armorial. Ribbon and Wreath. Motto, *Virtus libertas et patria.* The bit of landscape again comes in, as so often in the work of this engraver. Signed on an open scroll, *Maverick Sculpt.* Of New York.

926. WETMORE. *William Wetmore.*
>   Armorial. Ribbon and Wreath. Motto, *Tentanda via est.* Signed, *Revere sc.* Some proofs of this plate are found without the signature, having been printed before it was signed. Of Massachusetts.

927. WHATLEY. *Joseph Whatley.*
Armorial. Ribbon and Wreath. Motto, *Pelle timorem.*

928. WHEELER. *David B. Wheeler.*
A Masonic plate. The full sun, eight-pointed star, and crescent moon are above the name, while below it are the square and dividers, crossed ; the whole enclosed within a frame of ornamental type.

929. WHEELWRIGHT. *Nathl. Wheelwright.*
Armorial. Chippendale. No motto. Of Massachusetts.

930. WHITE. *Daniel A. White.*
An engraved name-label, with the name enclosed in palm branches, and the mottoes on ribbons above and below. *Multum legendum. Esse quam videri.*

931. WHITEBREAD. *W . . . Whitebread.* (First name torn off.)
Armorial. Chippendale. Motto, *Pro lege et rege.* Signed, *Dawkins, Fecit.* Of New York.

932. WHITRIDGE. *The Property of J. B. Whitridge.*
Pictorial. On a bit of ground surrounded by water, Hope stands leaning upon her anchor, and raising her hand towards the motto, *In God we hope,* which floats on a ribbon above her. Under the name a second motto, *Cui est amiens, felix.* Signed, *J. R. Penniman Delt. W. B. Annin. Sc.* Physician at Charleston, S.C., at the beginning of the century.

933. WILKES. *Charles Wilkes.*
Plain armorial. Motto, *Arcui meo non confido.* Signed, *Rollinson sc.* Of New York.

934. WILLIAMS. *Williams.*
Armorial. Late Jacobean. No motto. Of Massachusetts.

935. WILLIAMS. *Azarias Williams.*
Armorial. Ribbon and Wreath. Motto, *Amicitia cum libertate.* Signed, *Rollinson Sculpt.*

936. WILLIAMS. *Gulielmi Williams ex Insula Antigua.*
Armorial. Pictorial. A beautiful granite canopy is erected on the shore of the island ; a view of the sea is afforded, and the palmetto-trees yield a grateful shade ; at the foot of the stone-work are grouped a globe, scrolls, telescope, compasses, books, sextant, and drawing instruments — significant of the tastes of the owner ; the arms are carved upon the face of the stone, and the crest is protected by a hood of graceful design ; flowers in long garlands are trailed over the monument. Signed, *S. Ingram fecit a Paris.* A very beautiful plate.

937. WILLIAMS. *Johannes Williams His Book. 1679.*
The oldest dated book-plate we have ; probably the plate of the first minister of Deerfield, Mass., whose house was raided by the Indians. A printed label.

938. WILLIAMS. *John Williams, Esqr.*
Armorial. Late Jacobean. Motto, *Floriferis ut apes in saltibus omnia libant omnia nos.* Born, Wethersfield, Conn., Sept. 11, 1762 ; Yale, 1802 ; died, 1840. This plate bears some resemblance to the plates of Elijah Backus and Daniel Waldo, both in design, size, and execution.

939. WILLIAMS. *John Williams.*
Armorial. Ribbon and Wreath. Motto, *Floriferis ut apes in saltibus omnia libant omnia nos.* Same as the preceding.

940. WILLIAMS. *John Williams.*
Armorial. Chippendale. Motto, *Y cadam ae cypwyn.* Of Boston. Circa 1767.

941. WILLIAMS. *John C. Williams.*
Armorial. Ribbon and Wreath. Motto, *Cognoscere occasionem.* Signed, *N. H. Scp.* Of Massachusetts. Quite similar to the Jonathan Jackson plate by the same engraver.

942. WILLIAMS. (Anonymous.)
Armorial. Pictorial. The shield is thrown under a tree with a confusion of other things, — a harp, lyre, horn, music-book, violin bow, sword, arrow,

bow, and Indian head-dress. An expanse of water
at the right is illumined by the rising sun. Signed,
Harris. sc. Of Massachusetts.

943. WILLIS. *Willis.*
Armorial. Chippendale. No motto. No crest.

944. WILLIS. *Samuel Willis.*
Armorial. Chippendale. Motto-ribbon empty.
Signed, *Thos. Johnston. Sc.* This design seems
to be a copy of one of Hurd's.

945. WILSON. *David Wilson.*
Armorial. Chippendale. Exactly like the succeeding, and probably the same copper with the
name changed.

946. WILSON. *James Wilson.*
Armorial. Chippendale. No motto. Very handsome plate in the style of Hurd's best design; a
border is added, which is unusual with him, and it
is twined with garlands of roses, and has shells in
the corners.

947. WILSON. *John Wilson, Barbadoes.*
Armorial. Pictorial. The scene is in the tropics;
a cornucopia pours its riches of fruit upon the
ground, just below the oval shield, which is steadied
by a winged cherub, who gazes off into the clouds;
the background shows trees, an expanse of water,
and either icebergs or snow-capped mountains.

948. WILSON. *John Wilson, Kingston. Jamaica.*
Pictorial. The name is given on an open book,
which is surrounded by a wreath.

949. WINTHROP. *William Winthrop.*
Armorial. Ribbon and Wreath. Motto, *Spes
vincit terrorem.* Signed, *S. Hill.*

950. WINTHROP. *J. W.*
Armorial. (Winthrop arms.) Jacobean. Plate
of John Winthrop; born, Boston, 1681; died in
England, 1747.

951. WISEMAN. *Joseph Wiseman.*
Armorial. Ribbon and Wreath. Motto-ribbon
empty. Signed, *Vallance Sc.* Of Pennsylvania.

x

952. WISNER. *Polydore B. Wisner.*
 Armorial in form. Ribbon and Wreath. Motto,
 Via ad cordem. Signed, *Maverick Sculpt.* Of
 New York.

953. WOLCOTT. *Oliver Wolcott.*
 Armorial. Jacobean. No motto. Of Connecticut.
 Signer of the Declaration.

954. WOOD. *Joseph Wood.*
 Armorial. Chippendale. No motto. Of Pennsylvania. Colonel in Revolutionary Army.

955. WOODBRIDGE. *Wm. Woodbridge.*
 A plain name-label, with the name and the motto,
 Wisely for PLEASURE *and for* PROFIT *read:
 thus hold high* CONVERSE *with the* MIGHTY
 dead, enclosed within a border of ornamental type.
 Of Connecticut. Statesman and jurist.

956. WORCESTER. *The Property of the Worcester Circulating
 Library Company.*
 First Cost. . . . Fine for detention   per day.
 Enclosed in a woodcut border; a coin showing a
 monarch with the wreath of victory on his head,
 above. Very likely to have been printed by Isaiah
 Thomas.

957. WORMELEY. *Ralph Wormeley of Rosegill.*
 Armorial. No crest. Chippendale. Motto, *Nunc
 mihi nunc alii.* Books used in the ornamentation.
 Of Virginia.

958. WORMELEY. *Ralph Wormeley of Rosegill.*
 Armorial. Same arms as above. Chippendale.
 Motto-ribbon empty. No crest. Not the same
 plate as the preceding.

959. WRIGHT. *James Wright Esqr.*
 Armorial. Chippendale. No motto. Last Royal
 Governor of Georgia.

960. WYNKOOP. *Augustus Wynkoop.*
 Armorial. Supporters, bacchantes with bottles in
 hands and wine-cups held aloft, with scant covering
 to their bodies. On the shield, beside a cask, an
 old man holds a glass before a young boy, evidently

in warning ; a grape-vine grows near by. An eagle
for crest spreads his wings over the mantling. The
supporters stand upon the name-frame. Of New
York.

961. WYNKOOP. *C. C. Wynkoop.*
   Same arms as the above. Of New York.

962. WYNKOOP. *Peter Wynkoop.*
   Same arms as the above. Supporters are now
   hideous boys. No motto on the motto-ribbon,
   upon which the boys stand. Of New York. Illustrated in "Curio," page 17.

963. WYTHE. *George Wythe, Virginia.*
   Armorial. Chippendale. Motto, *Secundis dubisque
   rectus.* Of Virginia. Signer of the Declaration.

964. YALE COLLEGE. *The Property of the Brothers in Unity,
   Yale College.*
   Allegorical. Bordered by an oblong frame, the
   name is given in the centre of the design, with this
   verse below,

   > *Friendship and Science thus combine
   > To aid and honour our design :
   > With us unite an equal claim,
   > And share alike the social name.*

   Above, on a ribbon bearing the motto, *E parvis
   oriunter magna,* two grinning females mutually
   support a circular frame, in which the crowd of
   Brothers is seen walking bareheaded under a
   powerful sun. *Omnes in uno concordia* is on the
   frame. The supporters doubtless depict Friendship and Science. A pile of books between them
   completes the inventory. Signed, *Wm. Taylor
   Deln. A. Doolittle Sculpt.*

965. YALE COLLEGE. *Brothers in Unity.*
   Allegorical. Under the name the following lines
   are given : —

   > *Hermes eloquio potens recludit
   > Fontes, ecce, suos : et ampliora
   > Vena Pierii fluunt liquores :
   > Atque arces reserat suas Minerva.*

Above is a delightful engraving. Minerva helmeted and robed but without the spear, attended by Hermes, calls the attention of the approaching group of young men to the pile of books on the ground before them, and also to Demosthenes, who on the near-by sea-shore is declaiming vociferously to the rolling waves. Signed, *E. Tisdale Del. S. S. Jocelyn Sc.*

966. YALE COLLEGE. *Brothers in Unity.*

Allegorical. Beneath the name, which supports itself in mid-air, Minerva (?) is seated, and is directing the efforts of two cherubs who are at work on geographical and architectural problems, as evidenced by the globe and capital before which each bends ; to them comes a third cherub, and, alighting on the capital before one of the cherubs, holds out a scroll on which is written ΑΛΗΘΕΙΑ. The goddess calls the attention of the other cherub to this message. Architectural features abound in the distance. Signed, *O. Pelton. Sc.*

967. YALE COLLEGE. *This book belongs to the Linonian Meeting.*

A view of the college chapel and one of the halls is shown within a loop of a ribbon which runs across the top of the plate ; on the ribbon, *Concordia societatis nostra vinculum est.* Two clasped hands below the name are enclosed by a ribbon, on which is the word, *Amicitia.* Rude quirks and flourishes are introduced, and the whole appearance of the plate is rough.

968. YALE COLLEGE. *Linonian Library, Yale College.*

Allegorical. In the immediate foreground a youth, with some uncertainty in his air, submits to be led by the hand of Minerva, who turns to cheer him, and points to the temple of Fame crowning the summit of the hill, up whose tortuous sides the path they are pursuing leads ; Father Time, with discouraged mien, head resting on his hand, sits upon the globe amid the ruin of architectural fragments, grasping his faithful scythe in the right hand; the temple of Fame is surmounted by an angel, who is blowing mightily on the trumpet of the goddess who presides over the shrine; the word *Immortalitas* is inscribed across the entablature; just over the youth and Minerva, in a cloudy swirl, three cherubs hold aloft a sheepskin, on which is seen *LINONIA Sept. 12. 1753. Quiescit in perfecto.* Above all this a heart-shaped shield is divided into five parts, which hold a pelican in her piety, a book-case, a dove on the olive branch, the phœnix rising from the fire, and a puppy dog, whose meaning is uncertain. Scrolls about the shield bear the motto, *Amicitia concordia soli noscimus.* A cherub's face peers over the shield. Signed, *Doolittle Sc. 1802.*

969. YALE COLLEGE. *Presented to the Linonian Society by . . . .* Allegorical. The name is on a curtain draped beneath the picture of the advancing Minerva, who, helmeted, robed, and with spear in hand, is seen approaching, and apparently speaking as she comes; behind her, seated by a pile of books, an attendant maid reclines against an urn of flowers, and with a sun-glass draws the rays of the sun into strong focus upon a scroll which brings into plain sight the word *Yale.* Signed, *G. Fairman.*

970. YALE COLLEGE. *Moral Library Yale College.* Library interior. The librarian is seated by the desk, on the front panel of which the name is carved; an open book is in his right hand; a large globe before him, and shelves of books behind him; through the open door, which appears to be some distance off, across the tessallated floor, a group of students, headed by a professor in flowing robes, is seen. Over the door the name, *Moral Society*, is placed. Above all, the motto, *Virtus et scientia ad utilitatem dirigunt.*

971. YALE COLLEGE. *Philotechnian Library.* Pictorial. The front of a Greek temple is seen with the space in front of it filled with the emblems

and implements of the arts and sciences. The date, *1795*, is seen on a shield in the centre; probably the date of the founding of the library. Signed, *Jos. Perkins sc N. York.*

972. YATES. *Christr. C. Yates.*

Armorial. Chippendale. Motto, *Ne parcas nec spernas.* Very rough work, and hardly worthy to be classed as Chippendale. Illustrated in " Art Amateur," March, 1894.

973. YATES. *Peter W. Yates. Esqr.*

Armorial. Chippendale. Motto, *Ne parcas nec spernas.* Signed, *H. D. sc.* Of New York.

974. YOUNG. *Alexander Young.*

Plain armorial. Motto, *Robori prudentia praestat.* Unitarian clergyman and historian of Boston.

975. YOUNG. *The Property of Ammi B. Young. Lebanon. N.H.* A small, neatly engraved label.

976. YOUNG. *Thomas J. Young.*

Rector of St. Michael's Church, Charleston, S.C. Born, 1803. Three plates.

977. YOUNG. *William Young.*

Armorial. Ribbon and Wreath. Motto, *Labore.* This plate has very flowing mantling, which terminates at either side in eagles' heads; from their beaks depend the slight festoons which place the plate in the Ribbon and Wreath class.

978. UNIDENTIFIED. (Name defaced.) *Property of . . . . Bookbinder, U. S. A.*

Pictorial. An open book; on the first page, a cradle; on the second, a coffin; behind the book, a sword, quill, and anchor. The following mottoes are used : —

See some strange comfort ev'ry state attend. POPE.
Ah, when the dream of life shall be passed, what will have availed all its agitation, if it leave not one trace of utility behind ? VOLNEY.
Crescit amor nummi.
Stultum est in alieno foro sigitare.

A very rude woodcut.

979. UNIDENTIFIED. (Name defaced.)

Pictorial. An eagle soars aloft, bearing an oval frame with the name of the owner upon it; the broad rays of the sun behind the eagle light up the pine trees on the distant hill-tops. In the lower right-hand corner the smoke rises from the chimney of a house whose roof is just visible, shaded by a peculiar tree.

980. UNIDENTIFIED. (Name defaced.)

Pictorial. An eagle holding a small United States shield in his beak, and a ribbon on which the United States motto is given, *E pluribus unum.* In the oval beneath, *Use this carefully and return it immediately.* A Bible under all. Signed, *W. Barber. Sculpt.*

981. UNIDENTIFIED. Armorial.

Arms, Vert three garbs ppr. Crest, a swarm of bees about a hive. Chippendale. Motto, *Libertas et patria mea.* Signed, *H. Dawkins Sculpt.*

982. UNIDENTIFIED. Pictorial.

Within an oval frame we see the interior of a large room, which might be a library but looks more like a school-room; seated at a desk in the centre of the room is a man in the elaborate costume of the gentleman of the last century; books are before him, and on the floor beside him; a large globe is at hand; the appearance of the seated scholar is that of a professor waiting for his class to file in. The name is given upon a ribbon which is tied above, but it has been cut out of the specimen at hand. Signed, *A. Godwin. Sculp.*

* * *

ADDITIONS WHILE PRINTING.

983. BOSTON. *Boston Architectural Library.*

A large label made up of type ornaments and a woodcut festoon.

984. CHAMPION. *Epaphroditus Champion, Jr.*
Plain armorial. Motto, *Pro rege et patria.* Signed,
P. Maverick, Sc.

985. CHIN. *Henry Chin.*
Armorial. Virginia.

986. EDGAR. *William Edgar.*
Plain armorial. No motto. Of New Jersey.

987. HAVERHILL. *Haverhill Library.* (Mass.)
A small woodcut label; festoons and an ancient
coin.

988. KUNZE. *Johann Christopher Kunze, Prediger in Phila-
delphia.*
Pastor of a Lutheran Church in Philadelphia.
Printed label.

989. MALVIANS. *Malvians.*
Pictorial. A skeleton with the motto, *Ille ego quiad
sanandos vivos seco mortuos,* around it.

990. MUHLENBERG. (Anonymous.)
Armorial. Motto, *Solus minus solus.* This is
probably the plate used by the brother of John
Peter Gabriel Muhlenberg, the "fighting parson"
of the Revolution.

991. OLIVER. *Francis Johonnot Oliver, Boston.*
Armorial. Crest only. Motto, *L'amour et l'am-
itie.* A very graceful design of festoons encloses
the name and motto.

992. SCOTT. *John N. D. S. Scott.*
Armorial. Ribbon and Wreath. Motto, *In God
we trust.* This is the same copper as No. 766.

993. SUMNER. *Geo. Sumner.*
Armorial. Ribbon and Wreath. No motto.

994. WEIBERG. *The Property of Samuel Weiberg : ubi libertas
ibi patria.*
Printed label.

995. WRIGHT. *Joseph Wright.*
Literary. Identical with the George Goodwin.

A CHRONOLOGICAL LIST OF THE DATED PLATES UP TO 1800.

Johannes Williams	1679	Label.
Francis Page	1703	Armorial.
William Penn	1703	Armorial.
Society for Propagating the Gospel	1704	Pictorial.
Thomas Prince	1704	Label.
Samuel Phillips	1707	Label.
William Assheton	1718	Armorial.
William R. Ghiton	1718	Armorial.
The Carpenters' Co. of Philadelphia	1724	Pictorial.
Robert Elliston	1725	Armorial.
John Secombe	1729	Label.
Benjamin Dolbeare	1739	Label.
Jacob Cushing	1746	Label.
Thomas Dering	1749	Armorial.
William Lightfoot	1750	Armorial.
John Burnet	1754	Armorial.
Joseph Dudley	1754	Armorial.
Philemon Robbins	1755	Label.
Benjamin Greene	1757	Armorial.
Albany Society Library	1759	Pictorial.
Jonathan Smith	1760	Label.
East Apthorp	1761	Armorial.
David Routh	1762	Armorial.
American Academy	1770	Pictorial.
John Coffin	1771	Armorial.
Richard Beresford	1772	Armorial.
James Otis	1773	Label.
Gabriel Duvall	1778	Label.
Aaron Putnam	178–	Label.
Thomas Hall	1787	Armorial.
Rev. Joseph Fownes	1790	Label.
I. Walmsey	1792	Armorial.
Sally Richards	1794	Label.
Santa Johannis Ev. Sig. Coll. Latomorum	1794	Pictorial.
William Barroll, Chestertown	1795	Label.
Thomas O. Selfridge	1799	Label.

AN ALPHABETICAL LIST OF THE SIGNED PLATES.

* Plates marked thus have not been seen by the writer, and the exact manner of signing has not been communicated.

NAME.	MANNER OF SIGNING.
Anonymous	{ *Maingot del.* *Maverick Sct.*
Anderson	*A. Anderson. Sculp.*
Andrews	*Callender Sc.*
Henry Andrews	*S. Harris, Sc.*
Apprentices' Library (New York)	*A. Anderson. Sc.*
Theodore Atkinson	*N. Hurd. Scp.*
William King Atkinson	*Callender. Sc.*
Richard Tylden Auchmuty	*A & S.*
*Jonathan Baldwin	Signed by Callender.
*Luke Baldwin	Signed by Callender.
Flamen Ball	*P. R. Maverick Sct.*
The Library Co. of Baltimore	*S. Allardice Phi.*
Abraham Bancker	*Maverick Sculp.*
Charles N. Bancker	*Jones Sc.*
Gerard Bancker	*Dawkins Sculpsit.*
Charles Beck	*N. D. Sc.*
William Betts	*C. P. Harrison. Del. Sct.*
*William Beverly	Signed by J, Kirk.
Absalom Blackley	*Maverick Scp.*
Blakes' Circulating Library	*S. Hill Sc.*
Thomas W. Blatchford	*Wm D. Smith. Sc.*
Bloomfield	*J. Trenchard.*
T. Bond	*W. H.*
Boylston Medical Library	*Annin & Smith.*
Boylston Medical Library	*Callender Sc.*

NAME.	MANNER OF SIGNING.
Philip Brasher	*Maverick Scp.*
Benjamin S. Brooks	*A. D.*
David Paul Brown . . .	*C. P. H. St.*
Jacob Brown	*Engrvd by P. R. Maverick 65 Liberty Street.*
*Thomas Brown	Signed by Hurd.
Peter A. Browne	*Engraved by James Akin.*
John Burnet	*H. Dawkins Sculp. 1754.*
John Callender	*Callender Sc.*
Alpheus Cary, Jr.	*A. Cary del. H. Morse Sc.*
Thomas Cary	*Callender Scp.*
John Chambers	*E. Gallaudet Sculp.*
Epaphroditus Champion, Jr. .	*P. Maverick Sc.*
Gardiner Chandler	*P. Revere Sculp.*
John Chandler, Jr.	*N. Hurd Sculp.*
*Rufus Chandler	Signed by Hurd.
Sl. Chase	*Boyd Sc.*
Francis Child	*H. Dawkins Sculpt.*
Isaac Child	*N. Dearborn and Son.*
George Clark	*J. F. Morin Sc. N.Y.*
C. I. Cleborne, M.D. . . .	*Jarrett. London.*
De Witt Clinton	*P. R. Maverick Sculpt.*
William Cock	*Maverick Sculpt.*
Coffin	*J. Akin Sculp*
Hector Coffin	*J. Akin del. F. Kearny Sc.*
Columbia College Library . .	*Anderson Sculp.*
Charles M. Connolly	*J. G. Bolen. 104 B'way.*
Cushman	*Pulini. Inc.*
James S. Cutting	*Maverick Sct.*
William Cutting	*P. R. Maverick Sct.*
John Cuyler	*Maverick Sculpt.*
Francis Dana	*N. H. Scp.*
Danforth	*N. H. Scp.*
John Day	*J. Smithers Sculp.*
M. W. Day	*W. Chapin del. & Sc.*
Lewis De Blois	*Nathaniel Hurd Sculp.*
Frederick De Peyster . . .	*P. R. Maverick Sct.*
Thomas Dering	*N. Hurd Sculp.*
Doct. I. Dove	*Brooks Sculp.*

NAME.	MANNER OF SIGNING.
James Duane	*H. D. fect.*
Philip Dumaresque	*N. Hurd Sculp.*
Robert Henry Dunkin . . .	*I. H.*
Gabriel Duvall	*T. S.*
Bryan Edwards	{ *Ashby Sculp Russell Court London.*
Barnard Elliott	*P. R. Maverick.*
Erasmus Hall Library	*Maverick Sculpt. New York.*
William Erving	*Callender Sct.*
Farmington Library	*M. Bull's & T. Lee's Sculp*
Fenwick	*J. Smither Sc.*
Eli Forbes	*J. M. Furnass St.*
Ebenezer Foot	*Maverick Set.*
Isaac Foster	*N. Hurd Scpt.*
John Francis	*Callender Sculp.*
John Franklin	*J. Turner Sculp.*
Andrew G. Fraunces	*Maverick Scp.*
John Walter Gibbs	*Abernethie Sculp.*
*James Gibs	Signed by Maverick.
James Giles	*Maverick Sculp.*
Henry D. Gilpin	*C. G. Childs.*
Joseph Gorham	*W. Smith Sculp.*
J. J. J. Gourgas	*P. L.*
Robert Gracie	*Lewis Sculp.*
Henry Hale Graham	*J. Smither Sc.*
Francis Green	*N. Hurd Sculp.*
Benjamin Greene	*N. H. Scp.*
David Greene	*Revere scp.*
Thomas Greene, Jr.	*N. Hurd Scp.*
William Greenleaf	*N. Hurd Scp.*
David Stoddard Greenough .	*William Greenough fecit.*
Robert Hale	*N. Hurd Scp.*
J. W. Hamersley	*Faithorne.*
Rich'd Harrison	*Rollinson Sculpt.*
Harvard College	*N. Hurd Sculp.*
Harvard College	*N. Hurd, Boston.*
Harvard College	*A. Bowen.*

NAME.	MANNER OF SIGNING.
Harvard College	*Andrew Filner.*
Harvard College	*H. Billings del. C. G. Smith*
Hasty Pudding Library . . .	*Callender Sc.*
Barrack Hays	*I. Hutt Sculp*
Elias Hicks	*P. Maverick S.*
Elias Hicks	*Rollinson Sct.*
Whitehead Hicks	*H. Dawkins Sculpt.*
Phillip L. Hoffman	*Maverick Sculpt. New York.*
William Hooper	*N. H. Sep.*
Francis Hopkinson ⎫ one copper	*H. Dawkins Sculp.*
Joseph Hopkinson ⎭	
Horanian Society Library . .	*P. R. Maverick Sct No 3* ⎰
	Crown Street NY. ⎱
*Archibald Hunter	Signed by Dawkins.
William J. Hunter	*Engrd by P. R. Maverick 65*
	Liberty St. New York.
Jonathan Jackson	*N. H. Scp.*
The Bishop of Jamaica . . .	*Griffith & Wiegells 3 St.* ⎰
	James St. London. ⎱
Robert Jenkins	*N. Hurd.*
John I. Johnson	*Maverick St.*
John Johnston	*Maverick Sculpt.*
Thomas Johnston	*Maverick Sculp N.Y.*
Samuel Jones	*Dawkins Sc.*
Benjamin S. Judah	*Maverick Sculpt.*
John Keese	*Maverick Sculpt.*
John Keese	*Maverick Sct.*
Peter Kemble	*J. Lewis.*
Rufus King	*Maverick Sculpt.*
Isaac L. Kip	*Maverick Sculpt.*
Leonard Kip	*B. Brown Sc.*
Benjamin Kissam	*H. Dàwkins Inv. et Sculp.*
Ex Libris L——	*P. Riera.*
Ladd	*S. Felwell Sculpt.*
Edward R. Laurens	*Stout del et Sculpsit.*
John Lee	*S. Mc intire.*
John Lenthel	*Thackara.*

NAME.	MANNER OF SIGNING.
Edward Livingston	*Maverick Sculpt.*
Maturin Livingston	*Maverick Sculpt.*
Peter R. Livingston	*N. Hurd Scp.*
William Smith Livingston . .	*Maverick Sculpt.*
John Lowell	*N. Hurd Scp.*
John Lowell, Jr.	*Annin & Smith Sc.*
John Lowell, Jr.	*A & S.*
Cary Ludlow	*W. Smith sculpt.*
Charles Ludlow	*W. Smith.*
George Ludlow	*Rollinson Sct.*
John Cook Ludlow	*H. D. Sc.*
Gab. W. Ludlow	*H. D. Sc.*
Wm. T. McCoun	*Rollinson, S.*
Bloomfield McIlvaine . . .	{ *I. J. Barralet, Inv.* { *J. H. Seymour Sc.*
Andrew McKelden	*Leonard Sculpt.*
Hugh McLean	*Maverick Sct.*
Henry McMurtrie	*Smither Sculp.*
Henry McMurtrie	*Fairman del. Kearny Sc.*
John Magill	*J. Smither Sct.*
Peter Manigault	*Yates Fecit Royal Exchange*
Henry Marchant	*N. H. Sc.*
John Marston	*N. Hurd Sculp.*
Massachusetts Medical Society	*Callender Sc.*
Peter Masterton	*Maverick Sculpt.*
Maxwell	*Maverick Sculpt.*
Peter Middleton, M.D. . . .	*J. Lewis Sc.*
Horatio Shepheard Moat . .	*Rollinson.*
Nathl. F. Moore	*P. Maverick.*
William Morris	*Shallus. Sculpt.*
Timothy Newell	*I. Thomas print.*
New York College of Pharmacy	*Rollinson Sc. New York.*
New York Society Library . .	*E. Gallaudet Sc.*
New York Society Library . .	{ *Engrd by P. R. Maverick.* { *65 Liberty Street.*
New York Society Library . .	*Maverick Sct Crown Street.*
George W. Norris	*W. G. M.*
Isaac Norris	*Jas. Turner Sc.*

NAME.	MANNER OF SIGNING.
Lewis Morris Ogden	*P. Maverick Sc.*
Orphan Asylum	*L. Simond del — Seney Sc*
Samuel Osborne	*N. Hurd Scp.*
Francis Panton, Jr.	*Maverick Scp.*
John Parke	*I. S. Sculp.*
John Parkman	*Russell and Cutler printers.*
*W. Paulding	Signed by Maverick.
A. L. Pierson	*Annin & Smith Sc.*
Edmd. Penn	*T. Baddick.*
Edward Pennington	*J. J. Plocher Sc*
Library Co. of Philadelphia . .	*Printed by Zachariah Poulson jun. No. 106 Chestnut street.*
Philotechnian Library . . .	*Jos. Perkins sc N. York*
William L. Pierce	*Maverick Sculpt.*
Charles Pierpont	*S. Hill.*
John Pintard	*Maverick Sct.*
John Pintard, LL.D.	*Anderson.*
William Popham	*Maverick Scp.*
Porcellian Library	*F. Mitchell Del.*
John Poulson	*Printed by Zachariah Poulson Junior.*
William H. Prescott	*A & S.*
Halcott B. Pride	*Maverick Sculp.*
By the name of Prince . . .	*Wightman.*
Sam'l Provoost	*Maverick Sculpt.*
Samuel Pruyn	*D. W. Wilson Sc.*
John Randolph of the Middle Temple, Peyton Randolph, } one copper	*BATH, I. Skinner.*
B. J. Raphael, M.D.	*Rohun and Co's Louisville Ky.*
Redwood Library, Newport, R.I.	*Drawn by James Stevens Civil Engr. Engd W. D. Terry, Newport.*
Henry Reverly	*F. Kirk.*
Jacob Roome	*H. Dawkins Sculpsit.*
John L. C. Roome	*H. Dawkins Sculpsit.*

NAME.	MANNER OF SIGNING.
Rosseau	*Karst.*
Thomas Russell	*Callender Sc.*
Rutledge.	{ *S. C. Barnes & Co. Coventry Street.*
Sir John St. Clair	*Ja. Turner Philada Sculpt.*
James Samuels.	*H. Dawkins Philada Fecit.*
Daniel Sargent, Jr. . . .	*Callender Sc.*
Epes Sargent	*P. Revere Sculp.*
William Seton	*Maverick Sculpt.*
Peter Silvester	*Child Sculpt.*
John Sitgreaves	*Maverick Scp New York.*
James Scott Smith . . .	*Maverick Sculp.*
John Adam Smith	*Rollinson Sct.*
Thomas Smith, Jr. . . .	*Maverick Sculpt.*
Thomas J. Smith	Signed by Maverick.
*William Smith	*Maverick Sculpt.*
William P. Smith	*Thomas Johnston Sculp.*
Joshua Spooner	*N. Hurd Scp.*
Richard Sprigg	*T. Sparrow.*
William Spry	*W. Smith's.*
Thomas N. Stanford . . .	*Rollinson.*
John Stewart	*J. Jones Sc. Quebec.*
William L. Stone	*R. Rawdon. Alby.*
Samuel Stringer	*H. D. fecit.*
*John Sturges	Signed by Maverick.
John Sullivan	*J. Callender Scp.*
James Swan	*Callender Sc.*
William Sword	*H. D. Fecit.*
William Taylor	*Maverick Sct.*
Teachers' Union, St. George's Church . . . . . . }	*Rollinson.*
James Thompson	*P. Maverick, Durand & Co.*
Thomas Tillotson	*Maverick Sculpt New York.*
John Tomlinson	*H. D. fecit.*
Nathaniel Tracy	*N. H. Scp.*
Andrew Tyler	*N. H. Sculp.*
Joseph Tyler	*Johnson.*
Dudley Atkins Tyng . . .	*Callender Sp.*
P. I. Van Berkel	*Maverick Scp.*

NAME.	MANNER OF SIGNING.
K. K. Van Rensselaer . . .	*Maverick Scp.*
Richard Varick	*A. Billings Sculpt.*
Josias Short Vavasour . . .	*H. Dawkins Sc.*
Virginia Council Chamber . .	*{ Dent Sculpt Bull Alley Lombard Street London.*
Solomon Vose	*Callender Sc.*
Wall	*J. D. Stout, N.Y.*
John W. Watkins, A.M. . . .	*Rollinson Sct.*
Wentworth	*N. Hurd Scp.*
Stepney Library, Wethersfield .	*Doolittle Sculpt.*
Charles H. Wetmore , . . .	*Doolittle Sculp.*
Prosper Wetmore	*Maverick Sculpt.*
William Wetmore	*Revere Sc.*
W—— Whitebread	*Dawkins Fecit.*
J. B. Whitridge	*{ J. R. Penniman Delt. W. B. Annin Sc.*
Charles Wilkes	*Rollinson Sc.*
—— Williams	*Harris Sc.*
Azarias Williams	*Rollinson Sculpt.*
Gulielmi Williams	*J. Ingram fecit a Paris.*
John C. Williams	*N. H. Scp.*
Samuel Willis	*Thos. Johnston, Sc.*
William Winthrop	*S. Hill.*
Joseph Wiseman	*Vallance Sc.*
Polydore B. Wisner	*Maverick Sculpt.*
Brothers in Unity (Yale College)	*{ Wm. Taylor Deln, A. Doolittle Sculpt.*
Brothers in Unity (Yale College)	*{ E. Tisdale Del. S. S. Jocelyn Sc.*
Brothers in Unity (Yale College)	*{ O. Pelton Sc. P. R. Maverick Sct No. 3 Crown Street, N.Y.*
Linonian Library (Yale College)	*Doolittle Sc.*
Linonian Society (Yale College)	*G. Fairman.*
Peter W. Yates	*H. D. Sc.*
Unidentified	*W. Barber Sculpt.*
Unidentified	*H. Dawkins Sculpt.*
Unidentified	*A. Godwin Sculp.*

Y

A glance at the above list shows that our early engravers had no set rule by which to record their names on plates which they engraved; they used full names or initials as the fancy seized them, or the room on the plate demanded. In the word chosen to denote the fact of engraving a great diversity is seen, though by far the most used *sculpsit* or its abbreviations.

Hurd and Callender seem to have been the most methodical, as they used one form a good deal. Dawkins had several styles, and Maverick had one or two, but was pretty certain to use an abbreviation of *sculpsit*.

FAITHFUL

FRIENDS ARE THEY

MY SILENT BUT

LOUIS · I · HABER

A LIST OF THE MOTTOES FOUND UPON THE EARLY AMERICAN BOOK-PLATES, WITH TRANSLATIONS.

In the Introduction to his " Handbook of Mottoes," Mr. C. N. Elvin separates the mottoes into the following four classes : —

I. Mottoes which have no reference to the name or the armorial bearings of their users.
II. Mottoes which have a direct reference to the bearings.
III. Mottoes which have a punning reference to the name.
IV. Mottoes which have a reference to both name and bearings.

While all these classes are represented in the following list of mottoes and quotations taken from the early American Book-plates, such a classification is hardly adapted to the very limited number of mottoes employed, and we should divide them into but two general classes, under which, however, a number of subdivisions will occur to the reader.

1. The family mottoes : used either as a matter of course or with a reasonable pride in the possession.

2. The mottoes which are the choice or selection of the owner of the plate : in this are included quotations from the classic writers of both poetry and prose, mottoes of a patriotic nature, of a moral and of an educational character, as well as others in lighter vein.

Plates are found, too, that have the family motto and one of private suitability in addition. The expressions against the lending of books and the lines directing the attention to the value of good reading, and kindred sentiments, mentioned in previous chapters, are not included here.

The translations will be found rather " free " in many cases, and it will need but a casual glance at the construction of some of the Latin phrases to see that such a freedom is necessary.

'ΑΚΡΟΓΩΝΙΑΙΟΥ 'ΟΝΤΕΣ 'ΙΗΣΟΥ ΧΡΙΣΤΟΥ. (Eph. ii. 20.) Jesus Christ himself being the chief corner-stone. ANDOVER THEOL. SEM.

'ΑΛΗΘΕΙΑ. Truth. BROTHERS IN UNITY (955).

βελτιῶναι οὐδιδάξαι. Rather virtue than learning. STITH.

ΕΙΣ ΦΑΟΣ. Into the light. BANCROFT.

'Ἐραυνᾶτε τὰς γράφας. (John v. 39.) Search the Scriptures. SMITH (776).

Θήγει φρένα τὸ ἡδὺ τέχνων. Pursuit of pleasure sharpens the wits. PHŒNIX SOCIETY.

Κατὰ σκοπὸν διώκω. (Phil. iii. 14.) I press toward the mark. PINTARD.

ΚΗΡΥΣΣΟΜΕΝ ΧΡΙΣΤΟΝ 'ΕΣΤΑΥΡΩΜΕΝΟΝ. (1 Cor. i. 23.) We preach Christ crucified. CONN. THEO. INST.

Λόγια Ζῶντα. Living oracles. COLUMBIA COLLEGE.

ὁ λόγος ὅσος ἀληθεῖα ἐστι. (John xvii. 17.) Thy word is truth. ANDOVER THEOL. INST.

τοῦ καὶ ἀπὸ γλώσσης μέλιτος γλυκίων ῥέεν ἀυδή. From his lips flowed words sweeter than honey. VIRGINIA COUNCIL CHAMBER.

Ab initio Deus providebit. God will provide from the beginning. DOVE.

Ad astra per aspera. To the stars through difficulties. MINOT.

Adversis major, par secundis. Greater than adversity, a match for prosperity. JARVIS.

Aestate hyeme que idem. In age and winter unchanged. GREEN.

Aliis quod ab aliis. For others because by others. CALLAWAY.

Altera merces. Another reward. McLEAN.

Altius tendo. I reach higher. KINLOCH.

Amicitia. Friendship. LINONIAN SOCIETY LIBRARY.

Amicitia concordia soli noscimus. We alone learn in friendship and harmony. LINONIAN SOCIETY LIBRARY.

Amicitia cum libertate. Friendship with liberty. WILLIAMS.

Amor vincit naturae. The love of nature conquers. GIBBES.

Amore patriae. By the love of country. SCOTT.

Ante victoriam ne cane triumphum. Sing not of triumph before the victory. THOMPSON.

Arcui meo non confido. I trust not to my bow. WILKES.

Ars longa, vita brevis. Art is long and life is fleeting. PRIESTLEY.

At re non impetu. By reason, not by force. HUNTER.

Auctor pretiosa facit. The Giver makes them valuable. LENNOX.

Audacter. Boldly. EWING.

Aude fieri justum. Dare to do the right. PARKER.

Auspice Christo. Under the guidance of Christ. DAVIS.

Aut mors aut vita decora. Either death, or an honorable life. LIVINGSTON.

Aut nunquam tantis aut perfice. Either do not attempt, or complete. HEMING.

Be sure. PASLEY.

Beata Domus, custodita sic cuja Deo Domino est. Blessed the home, so guarded by the Lord God. BRASHER.

Beauty and Grace. SMITH.

Bello virtus. Courageous in war. KEESE.

Beware my edge. GIBBS.

Bona que honesta. Good things and honest. JACKSON.

Bona vince malum. Overcome evil with good. ELLISTON.

Carpe diem. (Hor. *Od.* i. 77.) Seize the present opportunity. HOFFMAN.

Carpe diem: postero ne credo. Seize the present: trust not the future. CUTTING.

Cassis tutissima virtus. Virtue is the safest helmet. KNIGHTS OF THE SQUARE TABLE.

Cave. Beware. PARKER.

Cavendo tutus. Safe by caution. DANA.

Chacun à son goût. Each to his own taste. SMITH.

Cherish virtue. KING.

Christi servitus vera libertas. The service of Christ true liberty. VAUGHAN.

Christo et ecclesia. For Christ and the church. HARVARD COLLEGE LIBRARY.

Cito pede praeterit aetas. With swift foot old age comes on. SARGEANT.

Clarior hinc honos. Hence the brighter honor. BUCHANAN.

Claris dextera factis. (Virg. *Æn.* vii. 474.) A right hand employed in glorious deeds. BYAM.

Clibor ne sceame. CLIBORNE.

Cognoscere occasionem. Recognize the opportunity. NEWTON-WILLIAMS.

Colendo crescent. By cultivating they increase. LIVIUS.

Communiter bona profundere Deorum est. It is the manner of the gods to lavish good upon all. PHILADELPHIA LIBRARY Co.

Concordia societatis nostra vinculum est. Concord is the bond of our society. LINONIAN SOCIETY LIBRARY.

Confido in Domino. I trust in God. SEDGWICK.

Conquer death by virtue. SHERMAN.

Consilio manuque. By counsel, and by the hand. PEIRSON.

Consilio non impetu. By counsel not by force. AGNEW.

Coronat virtus cultores suos. Virtue crowns her worshippers. CLARKE.

Cor unum ira mea. My whole heart in my wrath. TOMLINSON.

Courage sans peur. Courage without fear. LEWIS.

Crescit amor nummi. The desire for riches increases. UN-IDENTIFIED PLATE.

Cui est amiens felix. Happy he who has a friend. WHITRIDGE.

Dabit otia Deus. God will give peace. BRISBANE.

De interiore templo socius. A comrade from within the temple. HORSMANDEN.

Decus virtuti soli. Honor to virtue alone. LUDLOW.

Delectando pariterque monendo. By pleasing while admonishing. MACKAY.

Deo dirigente crescendum est. We must prosper, while God directs. LOWELL.

Deo duce perseverandum. I will persevere under the guidance of God. JAY.

Deo et amicitiae. For God and friendship. FORMAN.

Deo regique debeo. I owe duty to God and the king. JOHNSON.

Deo spes mea. God my hope. THORNTON.

Depressa resurgo. I rise after defeat. PINTARD.

Deus amici et nos. God, our friends, and ourselves. PELL.

Deus dabit. God will grant. FISH.

Deus dux certus. God a safe leader. BRIMAGE.

Deus meumque jus. God and my right. SUPREME COUNCIL, 33d°.

Deus nobis haec otia fecit. (Virg. *Ec.* i. vi.) God hath given us this tranquillity. SMITH.

Deus providebit. God will provide. DOVE.

Dictis factisque simplex. Simple in words and deeds. GILPIN. ROGERS.

Dieu défend de droit. God defends the right. BOUCHER.

Disce pati. Learn to endure. DUNCAN.

Discretio moderatrix virtutum. Discretion mistress of virtues. QUINCY.

Duce natura sequor. I follow the lead of Nature. HOLYOKE.

Ducit amor patriae. Love of country leads me. PHILLIPS.

Dum clarum teneam. While I hold to glory. PENN.

> This is not the complete motto of the family of Penn of Stoke Pogis; it should be, *Dum clarum rectum taneam,* which means, While I hold to glory let me hold to right.

Dum spiro spero. While I breathe I hope. AUCHMUTY. MORRISON. SWAN.

Dum vivimus vivamus. While we live let us live. PORCELLIAN SOCIETY LIBRARY.

E parvis oriuntur magna. From small things great arise. BROTHERS IN UNITY.

E pluribus unum. One from many. GUILFORD LIBRARY. MCKELDEN. U. S. ARMY. UNIDENTIFIED PLATE.

Emollit mores. She civilizes. NEW YORK SOCIETY LIBRARY.

En dat Virginia quartam. Behold Virginia furnishes her fourth. VIRGINIA COUNCIL CHAMBER.

En Dieu est tout. In God is everything. CONNOLLY. WENTWORTH.

En espérance je vie. I live in hope. BROWN.

Ense petit placidam sub libertate quietem. With the sword he strives for calm quiet under the reign of liberty. MASS. LIBRARY OF THE GENERAL COURT.

Esse et videri. To be and to seem to be. DUER.

Esse potius quam habere. To be rather than to have. MINTURN.

Esse quam videri. To be rather than to seem. ARCHDEACON. DUER. FENDALL. TYNG. WHITE.

Et mea messis erit. And mine will be the harvest. DENNY.

Et si ostendo non jacta. Altho' I show, tell it not abroad. OGDEN.

Ex candore decus. Honor from sincerity. MARSHALL.

Ex necessitate. Through necessity. LOW.

Excelsior. Higher. VARICK.

Exemplum adest ipse homo. Man himself furnishes a pattern. FRANKLIN.

Exitus acta probat. The end shows the deed. WASHINGTON.

Exstant recte factus praemia. Rewards await right actions. COFFIN.

Fais bien crains rein. Do well, fear nothing. COLDEN. PINTARD.

Faithful and brave. UNIACKE.

Fama praestante praestantior virtus. Virtue more glorious than glorious fame. MORGAN.

Fama sed virtus non moriatur. Fame, but not virtue, will die. INGERSOLL.

Fare fac. Say and do. FAIRFAX.

Fari aude. Dare to speak. CHILD.

Fari quae sentiat. To speak what he may think. APTHORP. RANDOLPH. TYLER.

Fiat justitia. Let justice be done. BROWNE.

Fide et amicitia. By fidelity and friendship. PORCELLIAN SOCIETY LIBRARY.

Fide, sed cui vide. Trust, but in whom take care. LUDLOW.

Fidelity. PAULDING.

Fidem servabo. I will keep faith. EMERSON.

Fidem servabo genusque. I will be true to my faith and my race. SMITH.

Fidem servat vinculaque solvit. He keeps faith, and breaks his chains. CADENA.

Fides scutum. Faith a shield. BRUEN.

Finis coronat opus. The end crowns the work. SMITH.

Firm. STEARNS.

Floriferis ut apes in saltibus omnia, libant omnia nos. As bees in the flowery meadows taste all, so we taste of all. WILLIAMS.

Flourish in all weathers. ERVING.

Follow reason. SPOONER.

Fors et virtus. Fortune and virtue. DE LOTBINIERE.

Forti non deficit telum. The brave lack not weapons. WATTS.

Fortior quo rectior. He is strongest who is nearest right. SARGENT.

Fortis et fidelis. Brave and faithful. WATKINS.

Fortis et fidus. Brave and trusty. MIDDLETON.

Fortis et veritas. Brave and truthful. MARCH.

Fortiter! Ascende! Courage! Climb! ERASMUS HALL LIBRARY.

Fortiter et fideliter. Boldly and faithfully. COX.

Fortitudo et justitia. Bravery and justice. JUDAH.

Fortuna perit, honestas manet. Fortune perishes, honesty endures. BEETE.

Foy en Dieu. Faith in God. BARTRAM.

Frangas non flectas. You may break, not bend. BLANC.

Freedom and Unity. STEVENS.

Furth — Fortune. MURRAY.

Gaudeo. I rejoice. BROWN.

Gaudia magna nuncio. I bring tidings of great joy. SCOTT.

Gloria. Glory. CHAUNCEY.

God grant grace. GRACIE.

Habeo pro jus fasque. I hold by human and divine right. CUSHMAN.

Haec etiam parentibus. This also for those who obey. HOOPER.

Hazard zit forward. SETON.

Hermes eloquio potens recludit
Fontes, ecce, suos: et ampliora
Vena Pierii fluunt liquores:
Atque arces reserat suas Minerva.

Behold, Hermes, powerful in eloquence, discloses his fountains: and Pierian liquors flow forth from the ample spring. And again Minerva takes her place on her citadel. BROTHERS IN UNITY.

Hinc labor et virtus. Hence labor and virtue. ALLISON.

Hoc age. Do this. IZARD.

Honestum praetulit utili. He has preferred honor to profit. KISSAM.

Honor virtutis praemium. Honor the reward of virtue. BREARLY. PROCTOR.

Honore et amore. With honor and love. HAMERSLEY.

Honore et fide. With honor and trust. SEARS.

Hora è sempre. Now and always. JARVIS.

I pensieri stretti ed il viso sciolto. The thoughts secret and the face open. LUDWELL.

Ignotis errare locis ignota videre,
Flumina gaudebat: studio minuente laborem.

He loved to wander in unknown places, to see unknown rivers: pleasure making the labor light. EUSTACE.

Ille ego qui ad sanandos vivos seco mortuos. I am he who cuts up the dead to heal the living. MALVIANS.

Immortalitas. Immortality. LINONIAN SOCIETY LIBRARY.

Impavide. Fearlessly. POWER.

Improve your hours for they never return. GUILFORD LIBRARY.

In cruce salus. In the cross is salvation. LAWRENCE.

In Deo fides. My trust is in God. GRAY.

In Domino confido. I trust in the Lord. ASSHETON.

In fide et in bello fortis. Strong in faith and war. CARROLL.

In futura spector. I regard the future. PIERCE.

In God we hope. WHITRIDGE.

In God we trust. SCOTT.

In hoc signo vinces. Under this sign thou shalt conquer. EUSTACE.

In lumine tuo videbimus lumen. In thy light shall we see light. COLUMBIA COLLEGE LIBRARY.

In medio tutissimus ibis. Thou wilt go safest in the middle. CARY. SUMNER.

In prudentia et simplicitate. With caution and candor. VAUGHAN.

In silentio et spe. In silence and hope. VAN BERKEL.

In tenebris lucidior. The brighter in darkness. INGLIS.

In reference to the *crest*, — A star surrounded by clouds.

Incorrupta fides nudaque veritas. Uncorrupted faith and naked truth. STEPHENS.

Indefessus vigilando. I will watch unweariedly. READ.

Independence. JACKSON.

Indure but hope. BARRELL.

Initium sapientiae est timor Domini. (Prov. i. 7. Ps. cxi. 10.) The fear of the Lord is the beginning of wisdom. MARTIN.

Innocenter, patienter, constanter. Blamelessly, patiently, constantly. STILLE.

Integra mens augustissima possessio. An honest mind is the most glorious possession. MEREDITH.

Inter feros per crucem ad coronam. Among wild beasts by the cross to the crown. STOWE.

Inter folia fructus. Among the flowers the fruit. HUMPHREY.

J'avance. I advance. BARTRAM.

J'espère en Dieu. I hope in God. RAY.

Je me fie en Dieu. I trust in God. DE BLOIS.

Je recois pour donner. I receive to distribute. INNES.
Jovae praestat fidere quam homine. It is better to trust in God than man. STUYVESANT.
Judicemur agendo. Let us be judged by our deeds. HICKS.
Juncta virtute fides. Fidelity joined to bravery. MURRAY.
Jura sunt mea: vindicabo. These are my rights: I will defend them. TAYLOR.
Juste rem para. Prepare the thing justly. APTHORP.
Justice, Truth. STONE.

Labor omnia vincit. Labor conquers all things. LONGBOTTOM.
Labor to rest. KEMPE.
Labore. By labor. YOUNG.
L'amour et l'amitié. Love and friendship. OLIVER.
Law and Right. ALLEN.
Lectorem delectando partique monendo. To please the reader and partly to admonish. COX.
Lege et intellige. By law and reason. SIMPSON.
Lege et ratione. By law and reason. CROOKSHANK.
Legibus vivo. I live by the law. LISLE.
Lex libertas salusque gentis. Law, liberty and the safety of the race. GEORGETOWN COLLEGE.
Libertas. Liberty. PRIDE.
Libertas et natale solum. Liberty and my native soil. SITGREAVES.
Libertas et patria mea. Liberty and my country. GILES. UNIDENTIFIED PLATE.
Libertatem, amicitiam retenebis et fidem. You will keep liberty, friendship and good faith. ADAMS.
Literatura mentem excandit. Literature brightens the mind. WELCH.
Live to truth. MASTERTON.
Loyal au mort. Loyal to death. BELCHER. KING.
Loyal jusqu'a la Mort. Loyal even unto death. BELCHER.
Loyez ferme. Be steadfast. CLARKE.
Luceo non uro. I shine but do not burn. MCKENZIE.
Lucidior in tenebris. The brighter in darkness. INGLIS.
L'un pour l'autre. For each other. SAMUELS.

Magnanimus esto. Be great-souled. INGRAHAM.
Malo mori quam foedari. I would rather die than be disgraced. BETTS. MURRAY.

Manet amicitia florebit que semper. Friendship endures and is in perpetual bloom. FRANCIS. PIERPONT.

Maximae divitiae sunt prae doctrina et scientia contemnendae : sed virtus omnibus praestat. The greatest riches are to be despised compared with learning and wisdom : but virtue excels all. VINTON.

May concord prevail and the undertaking prosper. ALBANY SOCIETY LIBRARY.

Mediocria firma. The middle course is safe. LARDNER.

Meliora non opto. I desire no better things. JACKSON.

Meliora spero. I hope for better things. PANTON.

Mens sibi conscia recti. A mind conscious of its rectitude. MURRAY.

Mens in arduis aequa. A mind calm in the midst of difficulties. ABERCROMBIE.

Mille malis salutis habeo, species mille. In a thousand evils I have a thousand chances of safety. FOSTER.

Miseris succerrere disco. I learn to succor the unfortunate. LIVERMORE. RUSH.

Modestia victorex. Modesty supreme. SULLIVAN.

Moveo et proficio. I advance and progress. KNOX.

Multum legendum. Much to be read. WHITE.

My hope on high. BEDLOW.

My might makes right. MACKEY.

Natura duces. Nature shall lead. MASS. MEDICAL SOCIETY LIBRARY.

Naturae convenienter vivere. To live conformably to Nature. LUDLOW.

Ne cede malis. Yield not to misfortune. CHASE.

Ne crede colori. Trust not to color. SMITH.

Ne oublie. Do not forget. GRAHAM.

Ne parcas nec spernas. Neither spare nor scorn. YATES.

Ne quid nimis. Not too much of anything. TAZEWELL.

Nec aspera terrent. Difficulties do not daunt. SMITH.

Nec degener. I do not degenerate. SILVESTER.

Nec elatus nec dejectus. Neither overjoyed nor overworried. THOMAS.

Nec gladio nec arcu. Not by sword or bow. DUDLEY.

Nec quaerere honorem nec sperne. Neither to seek nor to despise honor. SARGENT.

Nec sorte nec fato. Neither by chance nor fate. RUTHERORD.

Nec spe nec metu. Neither by hope or dread. READ.

Nec te quaesiveris extra. Seek not beyond yourself. HARISON.

Nec timeo nec sperno. I neither fear nor despise. GREENE.

Nemo nisi Christus. Nothing unless Christ. APTHORP.

Never check. HAWKS.

Never despair. PINTARD.

Nihil me tangere. Nothing smirches me. STEARNS.

Nil conscire sibi. To have a conscience free from guilt. PRES-COTT.

Nil desperandum. Never despair. SHEPHEARD. SHEPPARD. STEWART.

Nil facimus non sponte Dei. We do nothing but by the will of God. ATKINSON.

Nil sine Deo. Nothing without God. WALDO.

Nil sine magno vita labore dedit mortalibus. Life gives nothing to mortals without great labor. EVARTS.

Nil utile quod non honestum. Nothing useful that is not honest. SMITH.

Nobilis ira. Noble in anger. STEWART.

Nocturna versate manu, versate diurna. (Hor.) Ponder night and day. ROBBINS.

Non est vivere sed valere vita. Not living, but health, is life. MOORE.

Non flectere a vero. Not to be moved from the truth. LIVIUS.

Non incautus futuri. Not heedless of the future. LEE.

Non nobis solum. Not for ourselves alone. DRAYTON. ELIOT.

Non oblitus. Not forgotten. MCTAVISH.

Non reverter invitus. Reluctantly I do not return. JENKINS.

Non sibi sed aliis. Not for himself, but for others. OLMSTED.

Non sibi sed patriae. Not for himself, but for his country. HILL.

Non vi sed voluntate. Not by force, but good will. BOUCHER.

Nosce te ipsum. Know thyself. EDWARDS. NEW YORK SOCIETY LIBRARY.

Not always so. BARRELL.

Nulla pallescere culpa. To turn pale from no crime. BYRD.

Nulli praeda. A prey to no one. DEANE.

Nullus in verba. (Hor. *Ep.* Lib. I. i. 14.) At the dictation of no man. MAXEY.

Nunc mihi nunc alii. Now for myself, now for another.
WORMELEY.
Nunquam non paratus. Never unprepared. JOHNSTON.

Occasionem cognoscere. To perceive the opportunity. LOWELL.
Omnes fremant licet dicam quod sentio. Though all rage, I
shall say what I think. SMITH.
Omni fortunae paratus. Ready for any fortune. FORBES.
Omnia Deo pendent. All things depend on God. STOCKTON.
Omnia relinquit servare rempublicam. He leaves all to serve
the state. TUBERVILLE.

Par espérance et activité nous surmontons. By hope and work
we overcome. GORHAM.
Par pari. Equal to my equal. WALL.
Patior ut potior. I endure as I can. SPOTSWOOD.
Patria cara carior libertas. Dear is country, dearer is liberty.
BROWN. CLINTON. MARCHANT.
Patria veritas fides. Country, truth, faith. EVERETT.
Pauper non in spe. Not poor in hope. POOR.
Pax et amor. Peace and love. BACKHOUSE.
Pax et copia. Peace and plenty. JONES.
Pax hospitia ruris. Grateful peace of the country. JONES.
Pax in bello. Peace in war. PRIOLEAU.
Pax quaeritur bello. Peace is secured by war. OLIVER.
Pectore puro. With a pure heart. ROYALL.
Pelle timorem. Drive off fear. WHATLEY.
Peperi. I have brought forth. PEPPERRELL.
Per aspera ad astra. Through trials to glory. JOHNSON.
Per varios casus. By various fortunes. MERCER.
Perge coepisti. Go on as you have begun. TEN BROECK.
Perit ut vivat. He dies that he may live. FENWICK. MAGILL.
Persevere. GALLATIN.
Pia mente studeatur. Study with reverent mind. PHILLIPS
ACADEMY.
Piety is peace. HOPKINS.
Post tenebras speramus lumen de lumine. After the darkness
we hope for the light of the day. COFFIN.
Postero ne credo. Trust not the future. CUTTING.
Praestat opes sapientia. Wisdom excels wealth. LIVINGSTON.
Pro aris et focis. For our altars and our firesides. BLOOMFIELD.

Pro Deo et nobilissima patria Batavorum. For God and my most noble country, Batavia. VAN NESS.

Pro lege et rege. For the law and the king. CHILD. HICKS. WHITEBREAD.

Pro libertate. For liberty. PROVOOST.

Pro patria. For my country. WALLACE.

Pro patria mori. For country, die. GARDINER.

Pro patria semper. Always for my country. FITZHUGH.

Pro rege et patria. For the king and fatherland. CHAMPION.

Probitas laudatur et laget. Honesty is praised and is left to starve. ANTILL.

Probitate et industria. By honesty and industry. BRIDGEN.

Procurator industria. Industry the chief. FRAUNCES.

Progredi non regredi. To advance, not to recede. RUTLEDGE.

Propere et provide. Quickly and carefully. ROBINSON.

Proprium decus et petrum. POWEL.

Prospicere quam ulcisci. Overlook rather than avenge. MAIN-GAULT.

Providentia sumus. We are providence. BLATCHFORD.

Prudenter et simpliciter. Discreetly and simply. VAUGHAN.

Pugna pro patria libertas. I fight for the liberty of my country. MARTIN.

Qui contentus felix. Happy he who is content. SMITH.

Quiescit in perfecto. He rests in labor completed. LINONIAN SOCIETY LIBRARY.

Quo cunque ferar. Whithersoever I may be carried. ST. CLAIR.

Quo fata vocant. Where the fates call. BAY. ERVING. VOSE.

Quo vocat virtus. Where virtue calls. JAUNCEY.

Quod fieri non vis alteri ne fueris. Do not that which you would not wish another to do. COCK.

Recte et suaviter. Justly and mildly. KING.

Recte faciendo securus. Safe in acting justly. INGLIS.

Refero. I bring back. WALL.

Respice finum. Regard the end. McMURTRIE.

Reviresco. I become young again. MAXWELL.

Robori prudentia praestat. Discretion is more than strength. YOUNG.

Rosae inter spinas nascunter. Roses are found among the thorns. THORNDIKE.

Sacra quercus. Holy oak. HOLYOKE.

Saepe pro rege, semper pro republica. Often for the king, always for the commonwealth. VASSALL.

Sans changer. Without changing. MUSGRAVE.

Sans Dieu je ne puis. Without God I cannot do it. SKIPWITH.

Sapienter si sincere. Wisely if sincerely. DAVIDSON.

Secundis dubiisque rectus. Upright both in prosperity and perils. WYTHE.

Seges votis respondet. The crop responds to the prayers. HASTY PUDDING CLUB LIBRARY.

Semper caveto. Be always on guard. BALL.

Semper fidelis. Always faithful. SCHUYLER.

Semper idem. Always the same. CLARK.

Semper paratus. Always prepared. DUNNING. EVERDELL. McCOUN. HOPKINSON.

Serva jugum. Keep the yoke. HAY.

Simplius sicut columbae. More harmless than a dove. THE BISHOP OF JAMAICA.

Sine Deo careo. Without God I want. CARY.

Sine virtute vani sunt honores. Without virtue, honors are vain. BOZMAN.

Sol sapientiae nunquam occidet. The sun of wisdom never shall set. SOCIAL FRIENDS' LIBRARY.

Sola bona quae honesta. Those things only are good which are honest. HUNTER.

Sola salus servire Deo. The only safe course is to serve God. BURKE. JARVIS. MORONG.

Soli Deo gloria et honor. Glory and honor be to God alone. BOUDINOT.

Solus minus solus. Alone yet not alone. MUHLENBERG.

Sperne successus alit. Success nourishes, but to scorn. GURNEY.

Spero meliora. I hope for better things. LIVINGSTON. LUDLOW. PANTON.

Spes mea in Deo. My trust is in God. CABELL.

Spes meliora. The hope of better things. PANTON.

Spes vincit terrorem. Hope conquers all fears. WINTHROP.

Stand sure. GRANT.

Strive for glory. VAVASOUR.

Study to know thyself. GREENE.

Stultum est in foro sigtare. It is foolish to shoot arrows in the forum. UNIDENTIFIED PLATE.

Sublimiora petamus. Let us seek loftier things. BANCKER.
Sublimis per ardua tendo. To the heights through hardships I tend. CHAUNCEY.
Sursum corda. Hearts upward. BANCROFT.
Sustinere. Bear. BROOKS.

Take fast hold of instruction; let her not go, for she is thy life. (Prov. iv. 13.) PHILADELPHIA APPRENTICES' LIBRARY.
Tandem vincitur. At length he is conquered. MORRIS.
Tantes da dir. RUTGERS.
Tentanda via est. The way must be tried. WETMORE.
Terra aut mari. By land or sea. PARKE.
The North against the World. EDWARDS.
This I'll defend. McFARLAN.
Toujours le même. Always the same. GILES.
Toujours fidéle. Always faithful. HORRY.
Toujours prest. Always ready. CARMICHAEL.
Tout en bonne heure. All in good time. HICKS.
To Virtue & Science attend,
And Truth & Justice defend. NEWBERRY.
Transiens adjuvanos. Crossing the sea to help. SOCIETY FOR PROPAGATING THE GOSPEL IN FOREIGN PARTS.
Trust in God. JONES.
Try. BRAZER.
Tutus si fortis. Safe if brave. SMITH.

Ubi libertas ibi patria. Where liberty prevails there is my country. DINWIDDIE. WEIBERG.
Ubi plura nitent paucis non offendar maculis. Where the most is bright, let me not be offended by a few spots. WALKER.
Ubi plura offendar maculis nitent non ego paucis. Where the most is bright, I shall not be offended by a few spots. DANFORTH.
Un loy, un roy, un foy. One law, one king, one faith. HERBERT.
Ut aquila versus coelum. Like the eagle to heaven. BOWDOIN.
Ut quiescas labora. Labor that you may rest. GALLAUDET.
Utere mundo. Use the world. BLACKLEY.
Utraque unum. With either one. GEORGETOWN COLLEGE.

Vera pro gratis. True rather than pleasing. WEBSTER.
Veritas. Truth. HARVARD COLLEGE LIBRARY.

Veritas vincit omnia. Truth conquers all things. WATERHOUSE.

Vérité sans peur. Truth without fear. PETIGRU.

Verum atque decens. The truth and rectitude. WELD.

Verum dicet. He speaks the truth. STANFORD.

Verus in actione consistit. Truth consists in action. CRAVEN.

Vestigia nulla retrorsum. (Hor. *Ep.* i. 1. 73.) No steps backward. KIP.

Vestra cura alitur. Nourished by our care. SOCIAL LAW LIBRARY.

Vi et virtute. By strength and courage. SPAIGHT.

Via ad cordem. The way to the heart. WISNER.

Victoria aut mors. Victory or death. KIP.

Videte et cavete ab avaritia. Recognize and beware of avarice. POWNALL.

Vigila. Watch. ANDERSON.

Vigilemus ut vigilantis. Let us watch as those who are vigilant. U. S. NAVY.

Vincit amor patriae. The love of country surpasses all things. PENNINGTON.

" Vincet amor patriae laudumque immensa cupido." — Virg. *Æn.* vi. 823.

Vincit omnia veritas. Truth conquers all things. HYSLOP.

Vincit veritas. Truth conquers. CHAMBERS.

Virescit vulnere virtus. Her virtue flourishes by her wound. BURNET.

> This is also the motto of the family of Galloway, whose crest is a pelican in her piety.

Virtue, Liberty, and Independence. PENNSYLVANIA HISTORICAL SOCIETY.

Virtus basis vitae. Virtue is the foundation of life. BULL.

Virtus durissima terit. Virtue bears the greatest hardships. McLEAN.

Virtus est natale meum. Virtue is my birthright. TILLOTSON.

Virtus est vera vetustas. Virtue is true old age. VAN RENSSELAER.

Virtus et scientia ad utilitatem dirigunt. Virtue and knowledge direct to usefulness. MORAL LIBRARY.

Virtus interrita pergit. Virtue fearlessly advances. MOORE.

Virtus, libertas et patria. Virtue, liberty, and country. WETMORE.

Virtus sibi munus. Virtue its own reward. VAN CORTLANDT.

Virtus sola nobilitate. Virtue by nobility only. MAYO.

Virtute et fide. By valor and faith. ROOME.
Virtute fideque. By valor and faith. MURRAY.
Virtute invidiam vincas. Conquer envy by virtue. CLEBORNE.
Virtute patria tuemini. By virtue you guard your country.
PEPPERELL.
Virtutem hilaritate colere. Cultivate virtue by mirth. WYN-
KOOP.
Virtutis gloria merces. Glory is the reward of valor. ROBERT-
SON.
Vitanda est improba Siren defidia. The impious Siren, faith-
lessness, must be shunned. WALKER.
Vive ut vivas. Live that you may live. ABERCROMBIE.

Waste not a moment. WETHERSFIELD LIBRARY.
What is, is best. LAURENS.
*Wisely for pleasure and for profit read: thus hold high con-
verse with the mighty dead.* WOODBRIDGE.

Y cadam ae cypwyn. The mighty and cunning. WILLIAMS.

Zyt bestindig. Be constant. DYCKMAN.

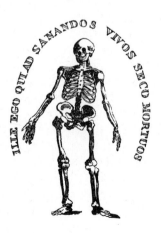

A FEW RECENT EXAMPLES.

ALL book-plates which do not have the flavor of age about them, and which were made quite within the memory of the collector, are classed as recent plates. This is a term of doubtful application; but in a general way it has come to mean all plates made since about 1830. Their number is legion, of course, and no attempt is here made to enumerate them, or even a small part of them, but only to note briefly those of the more recent additions which are especially noteworthy. And now we part with the old styles of plates. The early armorial, with the profuse denticulated mantling, is never used, the pure Jacobean is not seen, the graceful Chippendale has been discarded, and the Ribbon and Wreath, with its fanciful festoons and garlands of roses, is also a thing of the past.

This is of course natural, as the armorial plates, which are the only ones demanding any of these styles of decoration, are very little used now. But we have still the Library Interior, the Literary, the Pictorial, and the Allegorical; but these have changed their appearance so much

MAKE · HASTE · THEREFORE ·
· WHILST · IT · IS · PRIME ·

George H. Ellwanger.

as to be hardly recognizable as the lineal descendants of those of the same type which went
before. Indeed, the recent plates have little in
common with the old, — new motives, new designs, new methods, and new conceptions of what
a book-plate can be have come in, and the change
produced is very marked.

Heraldic plates are still in use, and still being
made, but the number of plain armorials is quite
small. Usually, now, those who wish to show
the family arms on the book-plate do not display
it all by itself, but accompanied by literary
accessories, or pictorial, or with decorative features to relieve what would to-day appear a bare
and unfinished plate, but which in the older days
would have been the pink of perfection.

Among the plain armorial plates of recent
days may be mentioned that of *Henry B. Anthony*, the late senator from Rhode Island, which,
without even a motto, presents the arms of the
family, with the crest, and the name. Another
plain armorial plate is that of *John H. Buck*, of
the Gorham Manufacturing Company, and the
author of " Old Plate." This, too, is perfectly
plain, with no motto. *Frank House Baer* and
Charles W. Burrows, of Cleveland, both use the
plain armorial style, relieved by slight mantling
or scroll work, and with the mottoes on ribbons
beneath the shield. *Mr. Appleton Morgan* has
a plain armorial plate, quartering the Morgan
and Appleton arms. *Mr. Daniel Ravenel*, of
Charleston, also uses a plain armorial shield,
relieved with sprays of marigold (the Huguenot

emblem) and of wall-flower (the French name for which is *Ravenelle*). A plain armorial plate, in colors, is used by the compiler of " America Heraldica." An imposing helmet with blue mantling surmounts the shield, and the motto, *Moins faire mieux faire*, is given on a ribbon which encloses the whole design. *Harry Allen Castle*, of Hartford, uses a design borrowed from the plate of Mr. Thomas Bailey Aldrich. The castle on its wreath is enclosed by a square frame in which the name appears, with the words *His Mark*. In the corners of this frame are the letters *I.H.S.V.*, standing for the motto, *In hoc signo vinces*. A punning friend, upon seeing this plate, remarked to Mr. Castle, that the letters would seem to mean, " I have some volumes." *Dr. J. S. H. Fogg*, the late well-known collector of, and authority on, autographs, used a plain armorial plate, with the motto, *Aut pax aut bellum*. *Prof. J. Max Hark*, of the Moravian Seminary at Bethlehem, Pa., has a plain heraldic plate, with thin mantling about the shield. The motto occupies two lines above and below the shield, and is in imitation of the ancient manner. *What mon aⁿ Honeſtᵉ Nameⁿ doth owᵉn, Toᵒ hyᵐ ryſ ht glaᵉdˡⁱᵉ myⁿ Boᵒkᵉˢ i loᵃn. But ſo toᵒ longᵉⁿ yᵉ Boᵒkᵉˢ be kepⁱt, He ſhal forſoᵒth be a Knavᵉ yclepⁱt.* This is printed with red capitals, on very fine parchment paper with rough edges, and is a very pretty plate. *Dr. Joseph Henry Dubbs*, professor in Franklin and Marshall College, uses a plate which exhibits the arms on a shield which is fastened to a spreading oak-

343

tree. At either side, scrolls are drawn, which
bear the motto, *Ex recto decus*, and the following
dates, which refer to the migrations of the doctor's
ancestors: *Styria, 1446; Helvetia, 1531; America, 1732.* A plate of unique history is that of
The Rawle Law Offices, Established A.D. 1783,
Philadelphia. This inscription is given on a
circular band which encloses the shield of arms,
and the motto, *Morte, Virtute.* Below this, the
name of the successive proprietors of the law-
offices are given, as follows: *William Rawle,*

*1783–1836, William Rawle, 1810–1858, William
Henry Rawle, 1844–1889, William Brooke Rawle,
1867.* *Melvin H. Hapgood,* of Hartford, uses an
oblong plate, which exhibits the shield of arms
at the left of the name space, and which is surrounded by a fine running vine which bears
both fruit and flowers, and among the twistings
of which the motto, *Inter folia fructus*, is woven.
The implements of the architect, and the sec-
ondary motto, *Penna ferro potentior*, are also
cleverly worked into the decorative frame. *Mon-
signor Seton, D.D.,* of Jersey City Heights, uses a

Helvetia · 1551 ·
Suevia · 1446 · · America · 1752
EX
RECTO · DECUS
No:
1880
JOSEPH · HENRY · DUBBS · D·D·
DUBS

C·D·M·N·STAUFFER

small heraldic plate, in which the arms are given in colors, and are surmounted by the clerical hat and tassels. A plain armorial plate is used by *John F. Winslow*, a descendant of Governor Winslow, and one to whose means and energy we owe the building of the first " Monitor." Prof. *Charles Eliot Norton*, of Harvard, uses an heraldic plate, in which the crest only is given. Beneath this, a pile of books is covered by a scroll, which bears upon it the motto, *Amici et amicis.* The *Rev. Morgan Dix*, of Trinity Church, New York City, uses an heraldic plate, in which also the crest only is given. This is surrounded by a circular garter, on which the motto, *Quod dixi factum est*, is printed. This ends our list of plain armorial plates.

Whatever sarcasm and disgust may be stirred up by the assumption of arms by persons not entitled to them, no word can be said against the display of authenticated arms upon the book-plate. Many coats-of-arms run back for several centuries, and an honored ancestry has borne them. A rightful pride in such memorials of past family history induces many who are entitled to them to use their arms thus; and while the plain armorial plate has had its day, and has passed the stage of wide popularity, it is still in use.

Coming, now, to the Library Interior style of book-plates, we mention first the finest example of recent work in this style, — the plate of *Richard C. Lichtenstein*, of Boston. Mr. Lichtenstein is one of the old collectors of plates, a member of

the Council of the Ex Libris Society of London,
and a recognized authority upon American plates.
As we would expect, he has indicated his hobby
in all details of his design. The scene is laid in
the corner of the owner's den, in which are well-
filled shelves, framed prints, photographs, and
the usual accessories. In the immediate foreground, a Cupid is seated at a desk, and in his
outstretched hand holds a plate upon the globe
which stands at hand, while he reads, from an
open book, the description, presumably, of the
treasure lately acquired. Two other Cupids are
at his back: one bearing the *Journal* of the *Ex
Libris Society*, and the other returning from a
successful quest for plates, if we may judge by
the packet under his arm. The presence of the
globe indicates the cosmopolitan character of
the collection the Cupids are examining and adding to. A finely foliated border surrounds the
interior picture; and in a space at the right side
is a package of mounted plates; and on the left,
a tied-up bunch of book-covers, in which Mr.
Lichtenstein keeps his plates. The name appears in white letters upon a black scroll at the
bottom, and behind it is seen a castle of white
stone, — a play on the name of the owner. The
plate is dated 1893, and is signed by the engraver,
George Moore, and the designer, L. Y. Van
Tiffele.

The plate of *James Phinney Baxter* reveals a
most pleasing interior, which is probably from
the actual room. A tall clock is flanked by long
rows of books, a table and easy-chair are in the

No.

Who hears and hears but does not what he hears,
Is one who plows and plows but never sows.

348

foreground, and *bric-à-brac* is disposed upon convenient shelving. At the left of the picture, a portrait of the owner is given, with a fac-simile of his autograph. The following motto, *Who learns and learns but does not what he knows, Is one who plows and plows but never sows*, is also given in fac-simile of handwriting.

The plate of *William Vanamee* shows what is also an actual interior, probably. The stairs enter the room at the left, and the space under them is occupied by books. Pictures adorn the walls, and a cosey bench before the shelves invites the visitor to recline and read. The motto, *Carpe diem*, is given above the picture, and the name below, both in fac-simile of handwriting.

Actual comfort and enjoyment are expressed in the plate of *Louis J. Haber*, of New York City. In this interior, a fire is blazing on the andirons; the drowsy dog lies asleep before it; the hanging lamp sheds a brilliant light over the room, and furnishes the means of reading which the owner is enjoying, as he sits in an easy chair, in lounging-coat and slippers. The rows of books at the far end of the room add to the effect of comfort, and the motto which envelopes the whole design — *My silent but faithful friends are they* — discloses the attitude of the owner towards his volumes.

The plate of *Albert C. Bates*, of the Connecticut Historical Society, at Hartford, is a reproduction of an early woodcut which represents the interior of an old library (University of Leyden, 1614), with long rows of books chained to their desks. Globes are protected by brass covers, the patrons salute each other in apparent silence, and over all there is an air of repression and elevated learning. No seats are provided, and light is admitted through long windows filled with small lozenge-shaped panes of glass.

The beautiful colored plate of *Gerald E. Hart*, of Montreal, represents the interior of a cell in some mediæval monastery; for the tonsured monk is sitting upon his stone bench, illuminating a large volume. The Gothic window admits light through its highly colored design, and rows of vellum lie beside the desk of the old monk.

The plate of *W. E. Baillie*, of Bridgeport, Conn., represents a corner of a modern library, furnished in the Louis XV. style, having some half-dozen frolicsome Cupids, rolling on the rugs, peeking out of the window, reading in arm-chairs, or discussing the volumes taken from the elaborately carved case. This plate is the second one to make use of the half-tone process direct from the pencil sketch.

Continuing with the plates which come properly under the classification " Literary," we find them to be very numerous, very various in design, and very unlike in shape and treatment. A plate which represents the past is used by *Henry M. Brooks*, of Salem, Mass. In this the old ink-pot

and quill, the box of wafers, the wax and seal, and the sand for blotting are disposed about the letter, which, being used before the days of postage stamps and envelopes, bears the amount due and the address upon the back of the sheet. The address seen is that of the owner.

Going still further back in history *E. Irenæus Stevenson* has brought the very serpent of the

Garden of Eden, with the fatal apple of Knowledge in his fangs, into his book-plate. Slipping down between the open pages of a large book, we see this form of his Satanic Majesty, and read upon the apple which he offers *Eritis sicut Deus, Ye shall be as gods.* This, from the Vulgate, is in Latin. Upon the open page we read in Greek, *Be ye wise as serpents.* The Shekinah blazes out all about the book. A very interesting and striking plate.

A very simple but effective reminder of the approach of old age is found in the plate of *George Alexander Macbeth*, of Pittsburgh, Pa. In this, an open book of coarse print lies upon the table, accompanied by a large pair of spectacles. The motto appears in the upper left corner, — *Give me your favor : my dull brain was wrought with things forgotten.*

Very many plates have a shelf of books, or a pile of them, accompanied with a favorite quotation, a bust of some author, the arms of the owner, or possibly his portrait. In the plate of *Clifford Julius King*, we see the row of books, the smoke from the waning cigar, as it rises across the open pages of a book, and the bust of Thackeray, while the motto, *A jollie goode booke, whereon to looke, is better to me than golde*, is suggestive of long evenings by the fireside, with choice editions to read and fondle.

The shelf of books in the plate of *Nathaniel Paine*, of Worcester, Mass., is enclosed within a frame which has suggestions of the heraldic shield. Behind it the palm branches are placed,

NVLLA VESTIGIA RETRORSVM

EX LIBRIS

MARSHALL CLIFFORD LEFFERTS

and the motto is below, on a ribbon, — *Duce natura sequor.* The crest is found in its place above.

"Wrenwood" is the name of the home of *George E. Leighton*, if we may judge by the name which appears on the top of the shield, which rests against his books just inside the library window. The window is open, flowers peek around the mullions, and a wren has hopped upon the sill to examine the surroundings which have borrowed his name for their own.

A pile of three books, labelled *Bacon, Lamb,* and "*Punch,*" is shown in the plate of *David Murray.* The legend, *Some books are to be tasted, some to be swallowed, and some to be chewed and digested,* is given on the back of the books. Above the volumes, the scales carrying the heavy pen on one side, and the lighter sword on the other, is surmounted by a liberty-cap, behind which, in a blaze of glory, appears the motto, *The pen mightier than the sword.*

In the plate of *George Imbrie Sill,* three shelves of books are enclosed within a frame of scrolls which bear the name. A shield is placed across one end of the case, with the arms and crest upon it.

Now we come to a plate which takes us below the surface. A wondrous mermaid, at the very depths, flanked by huge dolphins, is receiving a perfect shower of books, which come tumbling down through the water. This is the plate of *H. W. Bryant,* of Portland, Me.

Marshall C. Lefferts, of New York City, uses small leather labels on which an open book bearing his monogram is stamped in gold. Different colors of leather are provided for different volumes. This is the only instance of the use of leather for a book-plate in this country, if I mistake not: a very handsome material, too, for the purpose, and meriting wider use.

In the plate of *John Herbert Corning*, of Washington, Atlas, with strained muscles, supports the world of letters. *Litterae* is inscribed upon the immense globe which rests upon his shoulders.

Two children of the forest, a boy and a girl, with flowing hair and meagre garments, come towards us in the plate of *A. L. Hollingsworth*, of Boston, bearing between them a panel on which is carved the motto *Un bon livre est un bon ami.* The dense forest is close behind them, and were it not for the reader, one feels as if no person would pass their way to see their lofty

sentiment. So thick, indeed, is the tangle of brush, that the loss of their clothes must be laid to their passage through it.

In the plate of *Dr. George L. Parmelee*, of Hartford, a herald in court costume is proclaiming, through his long trumpet, the loss of a book. The banner hanging from the horn shows the words he uses: *Verloren! Verloren! ein Buch.*

We are again taken far down below the waves, in the plate of *William Ashmead Courtenay*, of Charleston, S.C. Down indeed, to the very bottom of the ocean, where the weeds grow, and the dolphin feeds. Above, the waves are rolling, and a far stretch of water is seen. The view is enclosed within a square frame which bears the name.

The *Rev. Wm. R. Huntington*, rector of Grace Church, New York City, uses a design which is adapted from a frontispiece by Walter Crane for the "Fairy Tales" of the Brothers Grimm, and which represents a youth, with long curls falling from under his cap, opening the door of a house, with a huge key. Upon the roof, two cupids, in imminent danger of sliding off, are making music with lyre and voice. A few stars shine against the night, and the light of the moon falls across the face of the structure, revealing the huge orange-trees in fruit, which flank the doorway. The motto, *In veritate victoria*, is carved upon the steps, and the name *Huntington* is given at the very top of the design.

Other plates whose principal features are "bookish" are those of *Henry A. Morgan*, which has simply a large book, open, with blank leaves: on one is inscribed *The page in waiting;* of *Edward Denham*, which has an owl perched upon an open volume, upon whose pages are the following names, *Bede, Camden, Bradford, Chaucer, Shakspere, Sandys*, with the torch of knowledge and the wreath of victory behind it: the wreath is tied with a ribbon which bears the motto

JOHN E. RUSSELL.

J.E.R.Del. M.T.Callahan.Sculpt.

— *Nulla dies sine linea:* of *Charles F. Jilson*, Chicago, on whose plate simply a closed book is seen, with a palette resting upon it; the brush and the drawing tools reveal the art of the owner, while the half-covered lyre upon the book-cover may be an indication of his hobby; — of *Alfred Trumble*, of New York City, who displays a table whereon the bust of Minerva, the student-lamp, the scroll, ink-stand and quill, and the books jostle each other in delightful literary confusion; — of the *Hon. John E. Russell*, of Boston, who shows the owl of Minerva seated upon the books of the scholar: the globe, materials for writing, and the lamp of knowledge are disposed about, and the whole is encircled by an oval wreath of holly.

The plate of *Thomas J. McKee*, of New York City, represents a volume of Shakespeare's Works, open to the title-page, which is occupied principally by a portrait of the famous author playwright. The arms and name appear upon the fly-leaf of the book, other books are at hand, and the following lines are given at the foot: —

> *Tu mihi currarum requies, tu nocte rel atra*
> *Lumen, et in solis tu mihi turba locis.*

The plate of *Paul Lemperly*, of Cleveland, designed by Garrett, shows the open book, with the serpent circled about it. The stars shine beyond, and the design is enclosed within a rectangular border of holly leaves.

Another class of plates which claim attention to-day is that which is representative of either the hobby or the vocation of the owner. For special collections, for certain kinds of books, plates are designed which express the particular line of reading, or of collecting, which they are to ornament. This style of plate is coming more and more into use, and earnest pleas have been put forth for its wide adoption; notably, one by *Henri Pene Du Bois*, in the " Book Lovers' Almanac," for 1894. In his worthy article on the " Art of the Book-plate," this writer argues forcibly for the expression of a genuine idea in the book-plate. Not mere coats-of-arms, crests, pictorial designs or devices and ornaments which look pretty, seem to him suitable for use as bookplates, but an emphatic representation of an idea, a worthy idea, clad in suitable form. He argues for special plates for special collections, for a specific plate for a specific line of books; not an ornamental label simply, to be placed in each book in one's library, but a different plate, with a reason for its existence, in each different department. Very few, if any, in this country, carry the idea so far; but many plates are now in use which convey at once an idea of the pursuit of the owner, whether it be in literature, art, science, or professional life. The plate of *George Edward Sears*, with its grinning skull, is perhaps at first glance unpleasant in its effect, but when one comes to unravel the plain meaning of the symbolism, the shudder dies away, and we are prepared to regard the plate as one of the very highest types, and most successful in its way. Mr. Sears has gathered a large collection of books relating to the " Dance of Death," and finding in

a 1754 edition of Matthew Merian's work, this plate which seemed no part of the series but an impromptu addition, he adopted it for his book-plate. Mr. W. J. Linton engraved the block, reducing considerably from the original. This plate is used only in the books relating to the topic it suggests. In this plate the skull is placed upon an open book, between a lighted candle and a few flowers in a vase. A wreath encircles the smooth pate, and an hour-glass rests upon it, with the hovering wings of Time, and the scales, just above. The lower half of the plate has a very dark background, while the upper is filled with light.

Henry Blackwell, of New York City, uses a plate in his collection of Welshiana which was designed for the purpose. In this plate we see the sturdy oak raised in the centre of the scene. Upon the right side, the bearded Druid is lopping off the branches of the mistletoe, which seem to be growing with the oak. Opposite to him, the early Briton with his harp makes wild music. A circular medallion upon the tree represents the peak of Snowden, the highest mountain in Wales, and the motto, *Cared doeth yr encilion*, is given upon the frame. This plate, like that of Mr. Sears, was suggested by an illustration in an old book. A second plate is used for the literature upon the famous voyage of Madoc to our shores in A.D. 1170. In this plate we see the old-fashioned, high-sided ship, with its bellying sails, plunging through the rolling waves, as it passes out to sea with the hardy adventurer and his crew.

Dean Sage.

As examples of plates representative of the hobby of their owners, we have the following: *Dean Sage;* an angling plate, very simple in design and very fine in execution, with a large trout, and the rod and the landing net crossed

EX·LIBRIS ·· JOSEPH·H·WHEELER

ARTE·ET·LABORE

1893.

behind it: an enthusiastic fisherman, and the author of a sumptuous volume on salmon-fishing in some of the Canadian rivers, Mr. Sage uses this plate only in the books of his library which relate to the gentle pursuit favored of Walton; — *Howland;* An angling plate of very hand-some design: the shield of arms is surrounded with the implements of the fisherman, with evidences of his success and with the weeds which grow by the water side: the motto *Piscator non solum piscator* floats on a ribbon above; — *Lucius Poole;* the masks of Comedy and of Tragedy are brought together in this plate, as indicative of the books collected by Mr. Poole; — *Arthur Robinson Stone:* a folio volume of music is open to the Largo of· the second part of the " Messiah," by Handel, and is copied from the original score preserved in the British Museum: — in the plate of *Martin Hayden* two Cupids bear a shield on which the name is given: each little Cupid also manages to hold a mask: the motto, *Upward, Onward.*

Fred C. Schlaick: in this we see the uppermost part of a column and its Corinthian capital. A little Cupid flies away from the finished piece of work, carrying the veil which had concealed it from view.   This design hardly needs the word *Architect*, which is added just after the name, to express the profession of the owner.

Edward Stratton Holloway: in this design, the owl is perched upon a limb, with the palette, brushes, sketch-book, and pencils of the illustrator within his clutch.

A most happy plate is that of *Mr. Richard Hoe Lawrence*, which is designed for use only in the library housed at his country seat, " Oscaleta Lodge," and which is mainly botanical.   In this plate the partridge-vine, *Mitchella repens*, is shown in its proper colors, and is surrounded by a double border of red lines, within which the motto, from

FRED. C. SCHLAICH
ARCHITECT

Rabelais, *Fay ce que vouldras*, is given in yellow. The plate was designed by Miss Mary S. Lawrence.

For a Philatelical library, the plate of *Mr. John K. Tiffany* is exceedingly appropriate, the design being enlarged from the old and rare St. Louis Postmaster's stamp of 1845. The book-plate was cut on wood by the same man who designed the original stamp. It is an exact fac-simile of the old stamp, giving the two bears holding between them the circular frame which encloses the arms.

A very good example of the Allegorical book-plate is that of *George H. Ellwanger*, of Rochester. This is designed to illustrate the LXX sonnet of the Amoretti, of Spenser. With all the charming freshness of the early vernal season about her, we see Spring, in graceful drapery, carrying buds and blossoms in her hands, and crowned with a wreath of flowers, approaching us. The garlands, the numerous birds, the new leaves upon the trees, and the sense of warmth in the scene, clearly depict the meaning of the artist.

Turning, now, to the pictorial plates, we find their number rather small. Decorative features, bits of landscape and of interiors are found in many plates; but these little ornamentations do not constitute a real pictorial plate. One of the finest examples is the plate of *E. G. Asay*, of Chicago. In this we find ourselves intruding upon the councils of the Muses; for we see Art seated upon a throne, with the palette and brushes idle in her lap, while about her, in graceful manner, recline History, Music, and Literature.

The lyre of Music is quiet, as, with her hand affectionately placed upon the shoulder of History, she listens to the reading of the just-inscribed

record. Art likewise gives interested attention to the recital; and Literature, with her book closed, leans upon the convenient globe, and listens.

Wholly different is the plate of *Allen Wallace*. In this, one of the Naiadæ reclines upon the over-

Arthur Robinson Stone

turned urn, from which the never-ceasing flow of water falls over the rock, and slips away in a widening stream. With one hand she caresses the limpid flow, as it emerges from the urn. At either side, below her, two dolphins discharge quantities of water from their mouths into an immense shell which receives the stream from the urn as well. Tall sheaves of wheat rise above them, and directly behind the head of the Naiad is the motto, *Nil clarius aquis.*

Mr. H. E. Deats, of Flemington, N.J., has a most beautiful specimen of steel engraving which he uses in his numismatic library. In this, we see a female figure clad in classic costume, with a diadem on her brow, sitting on the clouds, and having at her side an oval shield, on which a very important peacock is depicted as using the globe for his perch. On either side, cornucopiæ of fruit and flowers barely hold their quantities of produce. The motto, *Instauratio saeculi felicis,* is placed upon the edge of the shield.

The plate of *Frances Louise* and *Charles Dexter Allen* represents a female figure in classic robes seated upon a stone bench at the foot of tall trees. It is twilight, and the glint of the weakening light is seen through the leaves. Books, manuscript, and scrolls are strewn around the solitary figure. The motto, *Sapientiam veram petimus,* is carved along the top of the wall behind. One arm of the figure is thrown across the top of an open book, on which the names of the owners are given. This plate was suppressed at the request of the publishers of a magazine in

New York City, as it so closely resembled the design on their cover.

A very effective plate is that of *F. W. Hoyt*, of Albany, N.Y.   In this an Ionic column forms the whole design.   Very beautifully engraved: the lamp of Knowledge is continually burning, and

continually fed on the top of the capital, while the names of the " Immortals " are bound around the shaft on a ribbon, — *Homer, Dante, Cervantes, Shakespeare, Shelley*.   The name of the owner is carved upon the base.

In the plate of *Samuel Wesley Marvin*, is de- picted the sleeping knight, to whom come Pleas-

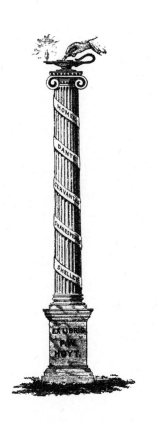

HOMER
DANTE
CERVANTES
SHAKESPEARE
SHELLEY

EX LIBRIS
F. H.
HOYT

ure and Knowledge, each with her offer of satisfaction and reward. The motto, *Courage le diable est mort*, is seen on the broad ribbon which is laid about the picture.

The plate of *Adam Van Allen*, of Albany, is copied from the plate of the brothers Goncourt, and represents the left hand with a pair of dividers

held by the third and fourth fingers, while the first and second are placed upon a sheet of paper bearing the initials *V A*.

Several peculiar plates remain to be mentioned, which belong to no style, but are examples of the individual taste of the owners, which is now so marked a feature of book-plate designing. Not, as formerly, are we controlled as to the style which we shall adopt, but each book-lover can, without appearing eccentric, place whatever design he chooses within his book-covers.

The plate of the well-known *litterateur, W. Irving Way*, of Chicago, is simply a very small bit of paper with his initials in cipher upon it. The plate of *Fred J. Libbie*, of Boston, one of the largest collectors of plates, is a cryptogrammic arrangement of the letters forming his name.

An old plate of *Richard Hoe Lawrence* caricatures each of his three names: the first, by the "dickey bird"; the second, by the agricultural implement suggested by the middle name: and the third, by a picture of the emaciated Saint Lawrence frying over a fire of flaming fagots. As he fries, he reads from a book entitled, *Lawrence on Gridiron*.

The plate of *Marcus Benjamin*, of New York City, is a punning plate, and represents the gentleman himself riding his hobby-horse, which is in the form of a big folio. With a long quill for a lance, and wearing a crucible for a hat, he rides his horse, full merrily. The plate of *J. Hiestand Hartman*, of Lancaster, Pa., is very curious. In this, the shield is borne by a skeleton, who stands erect, with the lance resting in the right arm. A banner floats from the lance-head, ribbons rise in profusion on either side, and the grinning sentinel is enclosed in the fluttering ends. *E. A. Hitchcock*, of the United States Army, has a plate of peculiar and hidden meaning. In this, the prominent feature is a huge dragon, winged, scaly, with forked tail and snakelike head. With the end of his tail in his mouth, he forms a frame of oval form, and repulsive kind, for a picture of a little girl, who seems to be sitting upon a honey-comb, and who holds a necklace in her left hand. The motto, *Non nisi Parvulis*, must contain some reference to the event recorded in the book-plate.

The plate of *George Dudley Seymour* has the unusual feature of a large representation of an

old door, with its carved posts, and pediment of high-boy style. In the centre of the design, above this, at the right, a small view is given of the whole house from which the door is taken, and in the opposite corner a scroll bears the words: *Captain Charles Churchill, hys house at Weathersfield in the Colony of Connecticut in Newe England*, 1754–1885. This plate is by

2 B

W. F. Hopson, of New Haven, Conn., and is very effective. *Mr. Hopson's* own plate is also a very beautiful specimen of his skill. In this, the central panel is filled with three old folios in aged condition, tumbled together upon the table. In the upper corners, a press for plate work and a painting on an easel are seen. Below the central space, a closed portfolio affords space for the record of the number of the volume. About all, are elaborate scrolls of rustic design. Over the space, a small kettle holds a number of fine brushes, and the motto is on a ribbon which is well carried through the scrolled sides. The motto is an adaptation of one of older date, and reads as follows: *Old books to read, old prints to scan, old wood to carve, old friends to greet.*

As yet, we have but one example of the work of C. W. Sherborn, the celebrated engraver, of London, among our American book-plates. This is the beautiful plate of Mr. *S. P. Avery,* of New York City. This is not heraldic, but of a decidedly personal bent, and very indicative of the special lines of collecting to which the owner is devoted. The upper part of the plate is filled with a conventionalized tulip design, which is extremely rich in appearance and graceful in disposition. A ribbon bearing the name, *Samuel Putnam Avery,* flutters in and out among the curves of the tulip stems and leaves. Grouped at the lower edge of the plate are a number of books, in artistic bindings, one being noticeable as having a Grolieresque design. The titles of most of the books can be read, and among them

EX-LIBRIS

GEORGE DUDLEY SEYMOUR.

are De Bury, Shakespeare, Goethe, Emerson, Montaigne, Ruskin, Bewick, and Washington Irving. Rembrandt's " Three Trees," also found among the accessories at the foot, is indicative of the collector of etchings. The graver, eye-piece, cushion, and block on which the portrait of Washington is cut, denote the art of engraving, and the head of Minerva, which rests proudly upon the volume of Ruskin, represents the patron of Art. This plate is a fine example of the peculiar personal flavor which Sherborn has infused into his revival of this particular kind of German work. The grouping of the books at the bottom is excellent, and the graceful sweeps of the tulip pattern, as it fills the upper two-thirds of the plate, are very pleasing. The motto, *Far more seemly were it for thee to have thy Study full of Bookes than thy purse full of money* (Lilly), is placed beneath the design.

Two specimens of the work of Paul Avril, for American owners, are of exceeding daintiness and delicacy in design and execution. The plate of *Clarence H. Clark* represents Venus in gauzy drapery, with a looking-glass in her hand, reclining upon a pile of books, some of which are closed. A fragment of the scroll of a Chippendale frame, with one or two roses about, complete the decoration. The motto, *Amat victoria curam*, is seen upon the open page of a folio volume. The plate is very light and pretty.

In the plate of *George B. De Forest*, by the same artist, we are ushered into the library of the owner. Here a cherub draws back the curtain, and affords a view of the treasures upon the well-filled shelves, not only to the beholder, but also to a scantily clad female who, with one foot upon the step of the shelf-ladder, appears to halt in an ecstasy of delight. An open book on the floor, and a portfolio standing near the shelves, complete the accessories. The whole is surrounded by a frame of foliated scrolls.

In the plates of *Dr. Henry C. Eno* we have examples of the owner's personal skill as an etcher. In one design, a lighted candle is placed upon a closed book, which is labelled *Ex Libris Volume*, and is presumably filled with rare treasures among our very early American plates. The second plate represents a lighthouse, with rolling waves at its foot. The broad bands of light stream from the lighted lantern, across the black night. The scene is enclosed within a circular frame. This is set upon a background, which may represent a fish-net, and is finally enclosed by a border of rope. A bit of rope tied in a sailor's knot lies under the lighthouse picture, and supports the name, *Ex Libris H. C. Eno*.

Among collectors, there has been of recent years a strong desire to secure specimens of the plates of the ladies. In England, where the heraldic features of a lady's plate are required to be in some respects very different from those of the gentleman, they may be said to constitute a class by themselves. But with us, while of equal interest, they do not show any marked difference in their design from the gentlemen's. Indeed, most of them, if not all, would serve just as well for one as for the other. The plate of *Charlotte Cushman*, which is heraldic, is incorrect, if judged by the rules of the art. The arms are not in a lozenge, the crest is given, and the motto is displayed. But the plate has none the less a deep interest to the American collector, who indeed can well afford to overlook any trifling irregularities which may be pointed out by a student of a science not in vogue with us. *Habeo pro jus fasque* is the motto on the plate. Two other heraldic plates are now used by American ladies. The plate of *Mrs. E. H. L. Barker*, of Warren, R.I., is designed by Mr. J. McN. Stauffer, and is heraldically correct, in that no crest is given, and that the frame enclosing the arms is of the required form. However, the motto is given, and the animal of the crest is made to do service as a supporter of the rod on which the shield rests. The plate is small, and very neat in appearance. The plate of *Miss Jessie Brewster*, of Shelton, Conn., is a plain armorial, displaying the arms claimed by the descendants of Elder William Brewster of Massachusetts. Another Rhode Island plate, and one which is representative of the hobbies of the owner, is that of *Mrs. Alonzo Flint*, of Providence. This is a large plate, in the centre of which is an arrow-head of flint, in reference to the name of the owner. In the corners are displayed books, easel and palette, violin, music and 'cello, and two cathedral spires, — all indicative of the likings and pursuits of the user of the plate. A wreath of ragged chrysan-

themums and ivy leaves surrounds the central
design, on which a beehive is placed, among
hollyhocks. This is, as was intended, a plate

EX LIBRIS ~ JULIA DEXTER COFFIN

whose every part is illustrative of the interests of
the owner, who was also its designer.

The plate of *Mrs. Julia Dexter Coffin*, of Windsor Locks, Conn., was designed and is used wholly

for books of music, or in her library of musical literature. The scene is within the choir of some temple. A flood of light enters the lofty apartment from the open door at the far end of the wall, and the small diamond panes of the large window reveal nothing of the outside world. Seated upon the stone bench, in the foreground, clad in classic robes, a member of the chorus, inspired by some longing, has come alone, to pour forth her feelings in song. The lyre in her hands is of old and ornamental design. Behind her, upon the wall, runs a dado on which the sacred dance is pictured; and above this a large mural painting can be seen. In the niche by the door stands a statue of Terpischore. The sound of the music seems to fill the room.

Purely decorative, and having no particular meaning beyond illustrating the motto, is the plate of *Ophelia Fowler Duhme*. The motto, *Inter folia fructas*, is given at the top of the plate, and the strawberry plant, bearing both flower and fruit, fills the whole space below.

Two Cupids disport themselves among sweet roses, in the plate of *Frances Louise Allen*.

In the plate of *Margaret M. Miller*, a cherub, with the hair in a Psyche knot, sits upon a closed book, and inscribes the names of the " Immortals " upon a scroll.

In the plate of *Miss Ada Stewart Shelton*, of Derby, Conn., the motto, *Plus penser que dire*, is given with the name and a single pansy blossom within a rectangular frame which has pansies at each corner.

In the plate of *Mary Bayliss*, we have a frame of Chippendale tendency. The scrolls are edged with shell-work, and the flowers are free and natural.

Very interesting and successful work in designing and engraving book-plates is now being done by Mr. E. D. French, of New York City, Mr. E. H. Garrett, of Winchester, Mass., and by Mr. W. F. Hopson, of New Haven, Conn., all of whom are represented in this volume by prints from the original coppers.

· EX · LIBRIS ·

THE   ORCHARD

FRANCIS · WILSON

AMERICAN COLLECTORS AND COL-LECTIONS.

OLLECTORS of book-plates are not very numerous in the United States; but, small as their number is, it has reached the present figure almost at a bound, for we now count about seventy, who are collecting, while, four years ago, there were scarcely a score.

A survey of our collections shows that all are particularly interested to collect American plates. The early American examples are few, and daily becoming scarcer, as the search for them grows hotter, and the competition between prospective owners increases.

The scarcity and value of our early specimens are not appreciated fully by our brother-collectors over the sea, nor is our national pride in keeping them within our borders realized. Having so few, we cannot be lavish with the rare examples we are able to find; and so it comes about that the demand for our plates is not met as it once was. The book-plates of our ancestors are not so easily found as are those of the past generation in the older countries. Books were fewer here, devastation by fire and pillage has ruined much that we lament over, and the good old plates turn up but rarely now.

Our collections are not large as compared with the gigantic aggregations which we hear of as being made in England. Think of one collector having one hundred thousand specimens! The largest collection here will not exceed six thousand, and those next nearest to that fall some two thousand behind it. Our collections are good, representative of the best foreign styles and dates, and do not include much that is valueless. "Small, if need be, in numbers, but excellent in quality," would seem to be the maxim of those who collect over here. German plates, particularly of the oldest engravers, French plates, and the English plates of men of prominence, are well represented. Plain heraldic plates are not held in high esteem, while the Pictorial, Literary, Library Interior, and Ladies' plates are all sought for.

Among the very first to enter the field as a collector of book-plates in the United States was the late James Eddy Mauran, of Newport, R.I.

Mr. Mauran was a New Yorker by birth, the son of a West India merchant. He was a painstaking collector, a close student, and a man fully acquainted with the foreign languages, and the literature of the times he felt an especial interest in. While deeply interested in other lines of research and collecting, he found time to gather a good collection of American and foreign book-plates, which were mounted with the nicety and taste shown in all branches of his collecting.

At the time of his death, in 1888, he had about 3500 plates in all, and they were appraised by Mr. Hewins, a friend of Mr. Mauran, at three hundred dollars, and were sold to a Philadelphia gentleman. Mr. Mauran had a way of mounting his plates which was original and unique. He pasted them down on pieces of marbled paper, and other kinds of paper used in the ornamental binding of books. He was at pains to obtain from binders, stationers, and booksellers all the pieces of paper of this kind that could be found, in order to have as many different mounts as possible. These papers were all mounted on stiffer white paper, and formed a good substantial ground for the final mounting.

His titled plates were mounted on gold and silver paper; and the ladies' plates on bits of silk, damask, satin, or old pieces of brocade and other things pertaining to ladies' wear. The American plates were mounted on the older styles of marbled papers, and on fancy patterns and colors in use years ago. They were numbered on the back, and were kept in alphabetical order. Very often the back of the mount was covered with notes about the owner of the plate. Portraits, autographs, views of houses, and sketches of the owners from newspapers, were also mounted and placed with the plate they were identified with. The plates were kept in old book-covers of fine, polished calf, beautifully tooled on the back and edges. An interesting history is connected with these covers. Mr. John Austin Stevens, of New York, had made a fine collection of the poetry, ballads, and romances of the mediæval ages, which was bound in the sumptuous style mentioned. Upon the occasion of a visit to Europe, Mr. Mauran, who was a friend of Mr. Stevens, saw them carefully packed in boxes, which were deposited in the vaults of the Chamber of Commerce building in New York, and insured for ten thousand dollars. During the absence of the owner, the negro janitor of the building broke open the boxes, and, tearing out the insides of the treasured volumes, sold them for waste paper! Portions were recovered; but the covers were of no further use as originally intended, and they fell to Mr. Mauran, who used them to hold his book-plates. This collection was quite rich in the early plates of America; for Mr. Mauran, being well-nigh the first in the field, had the cream of collecting for some time, and was able to secure plates which now are not to be had.

Not very long ago, this collection changed hands again, as the first purchaser, having no time to make use of the plates, was willing to sell them to some collector who could make them of greater use among others interested in the same topic. In some way the collection became disrupted, and parts of it are owned by different collectors.

Mr. E. N. Hewins is one of the older collectors among us. Mr. Hewins has a very interesting album of American plates, in which a goodly number of the rarer specimens find a resting-place. Other albums are used for the foreign examples, and the number of plates in the collection places it well up towards the head of the

list of large and valuable collections. The plates
are classified by styles.

Mr. Richard C. Lichtenstein, of Boston, has a
large collection of book-plates. A part of his
collection is arranged alphabetically in a large
quarto bound in brown morocco, with gold tool-
ing, and made especially for the purpose with
leaves of very thin tinted paper. Individual
mounts are also used. This collection is one of
the largest and probably the best, as regards
Americana, of all in the United States.

Another Boston collector who has been collecting for some time, and who has a valuable
collection, is Mr. Fred J. Libbie. Mr. Libbie
has a copy of *Warren*, most beautifully bound in
crushed levant, which is extra-illustrated by the
insertion of rare original plates, autograph letters,
portraits, and views. The volume is extended to
fully three times its original thickness, and is an
elegant specimen of the book-binders' art, as well
as a most valuable storehouse of fine book-plates.
Other works on the subject of book-plates are in
process of extra-illustration by Mr. Libbie, who
is an enthusiastic collector, confining himself to
no specialties, but making an excellent collection
in all lines.

The largest collection of plates is that belonging to Mr. H. E. Deats, of Flemington, N.J.
This industrious collector, while a rather new
comer, has distanced all the older men, and, being
the owner of the bulk of the Mauran collection,
has some very fine examples, as well as large
numbers, to boast of.

Dr. Henry C. Eno, of Saugatuck, Conn., has a large and valuable collection mounted in volumes bound in full levant.

We number among our collectors several ladies, and it is earnestly to be hoped that here, as in England, we may have plates designed by lady artists. Probably the earliest lady collector is Mrs. Richard J. Barker, of Warren, R.I., who has several albums filled with good plates, and who has contributed an interesting article on the subject of early American plates to the literature of our topic. Other ladies who are collecting are Miss Helen E. Brainerd, of Columbia College Library; Mrs. C. H. Duhme, of Cincinnati; Mrs. E. M. Gallaudet, of Washington; and Miss Louise Fitz, of Newton Centre, Mass.

The mounting and arrangement of plates are vexed questions among collectors. The really satisfactory method has not yet been discovered. Many ways are tried; and experience shows that while one may at different times think he has found the very best way, its disadvantages are sure to appear, and a new method will be looked for.

Mr. E. H. Bierstadt, of New York, keeps his collection in large albums constructed for the purpose. The leaves are of double thicknesses of heavy calendered manilla paper. The plates are pasted down on mounts of a stiff white ledger paper, and are then placed in the book, four to the page, by slipping the corners of the mounts into slits cut for the purpose in the page. This allows the easy readjustment, the easy exchange of a poor specimen for a better one, the re-placing of a plate wrongly classed, and the extension of alphabetical arrangement *ad infinitum.* The appearance of the volume is handsome.

Mr. Henry Blackwell, of New York, is mounting all his plates on rather large sheets of a stiff paper, of a dark tint, which shows off the plates to good advantage. They are arranged in alphabetical order, and are kept in neat wooden boxes.

The plates of Mr. Pickering Dodge, of Washington, D.C., are mounted on a dove-colored mount, which is an advantageous tint. The plates are arranged according to styles. This collector, however, is about to change to albums.

Mr. Nathaniel Paine, of Worcester, Mass., has his plates mounted directly upon the pages of an album made for them. Portraits, views, etc., are also interspersed.

The present writer used originally the individual mount; but becoming dissatisfied with that method, because of injury by careless handling, adopted the albums, using in both instances the " hinges " of the stamp collector to fasten the plates down with. He is now changing back to the individual-mount plan, as it admits of more freedom in comparison, easy changes, and the better display of the collection, either to a few, or to an audience.

The larger part of our collectors do not mount their plates at all, or have any system of arranging them. They are kept in odd envelopes, boxes, between the leaves of books, or in a desk-drawer, and there await the new arrival, or the shaking up incident to the search for a particular specimen. This is ruinous.

The larger part of our collectors are members of the Ex Libris Society, of England, while many have also joined the societies in France and Germany. No American Society has as yet been seriously proposed.

A LIST OF AMERICAN MEMBERS OF THE EX LIBRIS SOCIETY.

Charles Dexter Allen	Hartford, Conn.
G. A. Armour	Chicago, Ill.
S. P. Avery	New York City.
William E. Baillie	Bridgeport, Conn.
Mrs. Richard J. Barker	Warren, R.I.
Walter R. Benjamin	New York City.
E. H. Bierstadt	New York City.
Henry Blackwell	New York City.
E. W. Blatchford	Chicago, Ill.
Boston Athenæum	Boston, Mass.
Boston Public Library	Boston, Mass.
Helen E. Brainerd	New York City.
William George Brown	Lexington, Va.
J. H. Buck	New York City.
William A. Butterfield	Boston, Mass.
Dr. Charles E. Clark	Lynn, Mass.
J. H. Corning	Washington, D.C.
Hon. W. A. Courtenay	Charleston, S.C.
Dr. R. B. Coutant	Tarrytown, N.Y.
George W. Cram	Norwalk, Conn.
H. E. Deats	Flemington, N.J.
Pickering Dodge	Washington, D.C.
Dr. J. H. Dubbs	Lancaster, Pa.
Mrs. E. H. Duhme	Cincinnati, Ohio.
George Wharton Edwards	New York City.
Dr. Henry C. Eno	Saugatuck, Conn.
F. W. French	Boston, Mass.

E. H. Frost . . . . Charleston, S.C.
Mrs. E. M. Gallaudet . . . . Washington, D.C.
Christian Gerhardt . . . . New York City.
Grolier Club . . . . New York City.
E. N. Hewins . . . . Boston, Mass.
A. L. Hollingsworth . . . . Boston, Mass.
W. F. Hopson . . . . New Haven, Conn.
Paul Lemperly . . . . Cleveland, Ohio.
Fred J. Libbie . . . . Boston, Mass.
Richard C. Lichtenstein . . . . . . Boston, Mass.
George A. Macbeth . . . . Pittsburg, Pa.
Montague Marks . . . . New York City.
Charles T. Martin . . . . Hartford, Conn.
Thomas L. Montgomery . . . . . . Philadelphia, Pa.
Newberry Library . . . . Chicago, Ill.
New York State Library . . . . . . Albany, N.Y.
Nathaniel L. Paine . . . . Worcester, Mass.
George B. Perry . . . . Boston, Mass.
Daniel Ravenel . . . . Charleston, S.C.
Henry S. Rowe . . . . Boston, Mass.
Rowfant Club . . . . Cleveland, Ohio.
J. Douglas Scott . . . . Hyde Park, Mass.
Heromich Shugio . . . . Washington, D.C.
Howard Sill . . . . Glendale, Mass.
Fred Webber . . . . Washington, D.C.
Horace W. Whayman . . . . Newport, Ky.
John P. Woodbury . . . . Boston, Mass.
Worcester Public Library . . . . . . Worcester, Mass.

Others who have collections, or who are interested in book-plates, but are not members of the societies, are : —

Samuel Auxer . . . . Lancaster, Pa.
Albert C. Bates . . . . Hartford, Conn.
Arlo Bates . . . . Boston, Mass.
Robert A. Brock . . . . Richmond, Va.
Henry M. Brooks . . . . Salem, Mass.
Henry B. Bult . . . . New York City.
H. B. Bryant . . . . Portland, Me.

Dr. Swan M. Burnett . . . . Washington, D.C.
William J. Campbell . . . . Philadelphia, Pa.
Beverly Chew . . . . New York City.
Dartmouth College Library . . . . . Hanover, N.H.
Henri Pene Du Bois . . . . New York City.
Howard Edwards . . . . Philadelphia, Pa.
Paul Leicester Ford . . . . Brooklyn, N.Y.
Frank B. Gay . . . . Hartford, Conn.
Edward D. Harris . . . . New York City.
Laurence Hutton . . . . New York City.
Charles C. Moreau . . . . New York City.
Edward W. Nash . . . . New York City.
New York Historical Society . . . . New York City.
Henry Thorpe . . . . Brooklyn, N.Y.
Lyon G. Tyler . . . . Williamsburg, Pa.
William H. Whitmore . . . . Boston, Mass.

Jeremiah Evarts.

Nil sine magno vita labore dedit mortalibus.

No. 806.

THE EX LIBRIS SOCIETIES.

HE Ex Libris Society, of London, was organized in 1891, and now has four hundred members, of whom about fifty are residents of the United States. The Society publishes a handsomely illustrated Monthly Journal, which is free to members. The Annual Dues are ten shillings, sixpence. The Entrance Fee is two shillings, sixpence. This Society will probably limit its membership and raise its dues before long. All persons interested in the collecting of book-plates, except dealers in plates, are eligible to membership. The prepayment of the Entrance Fee and the Annual Dues constitutes one a member.

The Honorable Secretary of the Society is Mr. W. H. K. Wright, of Plymouth, England. The Corresponding Secretary for the United States is Mr. Charles Dexter Allen, Hartford, Conn.

DES EX–LIBRIS–VEREINS ZU BERLIN.

The German Society published the first number of its Quarterly in October, 1891. This is beautifully illustrated with many plates in colors, and is free to all members. The Annual Dues are twelve marks. The address of the Secretary is, Friedrich Warnecke, Friedrich-Wilhelmsstrasse, 4. Berlin, W., Germany.

SOCIETE FRANÇAISE DES COLLECTIONNEURS D'EX LIBRIS.

The French Society was organized in 1893, and published the first number of its Archives in January, 1894. This monthly is free to all members. The Annual Dues are nineteen francs and fifty centimes. The address of the Secretary is, 3 Foubourg Saint-Jacques, Paris.

BIBLIOGRAPHY.

AMERICAN, ENGLISH, AND FRENCH.

THE AMERICAN BIBLIOGRAPHY.

By Eben Newell Hewins.

BOOK-PLATE collecting in the United States is of such recent growth that the literature on the subject is naturally limited, consisting of only a few scattered magazine and newspaper articles.

The following list is believed to be nearly, if not quite, complete.

The compiler desires his thanks to all who have assisted him in his work; and especially would he thank Mr. H. W. Fincham and Mr. James Roberts Brown, for kind permission to use their exhaustive English Bibliography, which is here reprinted from the journal of the Ex Libris Society; and also Mr. Walter Hamilton, for permission to use his Bibliography, prepared for his " Hand-Book of French Book-Plates."

Additions to this list are desired, and correspondents having knowledge of articles not noted here will confer a favor by communicating with either the author or compiler.

1. **The Heraldic Journal.** Vol. I., American book-plate engravers; Thomas Johnson, p. 6; Nat. Hurd, p. 19; John Cole, Jun., pp. 95–108. Vol. II., American book-plate engravers; Thomas Turner, p. 94. Vol. III., The Harris collection of book-plates, pp. 21–24; Thomas Child's book-plate, p. 190. Vol. IV., The Spooner book-plate, p. 45; the William King Atkinson book-plate, p. 119; Heraldic Painters and Engravers, p. 192.

J. K. Wiggin, Boston, 8vo, 1865–1868.

2. **Whitmore (William H.).** Elements of Heraldry.

Boston, 1866.

Contains copies of book-plates and notices of early American book-plate engravers.

3. **Winsor (Justin).** A catalogue of the collection of books and manuscripts formerly belonging to the Rev. Thomas Prince, . . . now deposited in the public library of the city of Boston, v., viii., illustrated.

Boston, U.S.A., 4to, 1870.

Describes the various book-plates of the Rev. Thomas Prince, 1687–1758.

4. **Brown (John Coffin Jones).** The Coffin family, its armorial bearings, and origin of the name, illustrated.

Boston, 8vo, 1881.

5. **Literary World.** A Library Pest, July 2, 1881. The Study of Book-plates. A review of Warren, Aug. 13, 1881. (By Rev. Dr. Joseph Henry Dubbs.)

Boston, U.S.A., 1881.

6. **Leach (Frank Willing).** The Right to bear Arms, illustrated. *The Continent*, Vol. III., pp. 513–523.

Philadelphia, Penn., U.S.A., April 25, 1883.

Many of the illustrations given are copies of book-plates.

7. **Lichtenstein (Richard C.).** Early Book-plates. *The Boston Daily Globe*, April 22, 1885.

8. **Book-Mart.** Original stanzas for insertion on the fly-leaves of lent books, III., 27.

Pittsburgh, Penn., U.S.A., 8vo, 1885.

9. **The Book Buyer.** A List of American Book-plate Collectors, III., 165. The Original and Imitation Washington Book-plate, illustrated, III., 234. Practical Suggestions for Book-plates, illustrated, III., 377.

New York, Scribner, 4to, 1886.

10. **Hutton (Laurence).** Some American Book-plates, illustrated. *The Book Buyer*, Vol. III., 7–9, 63–65, 112–114, 159–161. New York, Scribner, 4to, 1886.

These articles were reprinted in the *Ex Libris Journal*, Vol. II., pp. 42, 52, 69.

11. **New York Genealogical and Biographical Record,** Vol. XVIII., No. 1. Samuel Provoost, First Bishop of New York. An address to the Genealogical and Biographical Society. Illustrated with portrait and book-plate of Bishop Provoost. New York, January, 1887.

12. **Lichtenstein (Richard C.)**. Early New England and New York Heraldic Book-plates. *New England Historical and Genealogical Register*, XL., 295–299. Published under the direction of the New England Historic Genealogical Society. Boston, 8vo, 1886.
Also privately printed with additions.

13. **Lichtenstein (Richard C.)**. Early Southern Heraldic Book-plates. *New England Historical and Genealogical Register*, XLI., 296. Published under the direction of the New England Historic Genealogical Society.
Boston, 8vo, 1887.
Also privately printed.

14. **Lichtenstein (Richard C.)**. American Book-plates and their Engravers, illustrated. *The Curio*, 11–17, 61–66, 110–114 ; Washington's Library, illustrated, 246–252.
New York, U.S.A., R. W. Wright, folio, 1887.
The Curio was discontinued after the sixth number.

15. **Martin (Charles Towneley)**. Book-plates and their Early Engravers. *City Mission Record.*
Hartford, Conn., 1888.

16. **Dubbs (Rev. Dr. Joseph Henry)**. Peter Miller's Book-plate. *Reformed Church Messenger* (Whitehall Papers, second series, No. V.).
Philadelphia, Penn., U.S.A., June 19, 1889.

17. **The Century Magazine**, Vol. XXXIX. The Grolier Club, 87. New York and London, 8vo, 1889.
Contains the book-plate of the Grolier Club.

18. **The American Book Maker**. Book-plates, illustrated. Vol. XI., No. 2, 8vo, August, 1890 ; Vol. XIII., No. 3, 8vo, September, 1891. New York, U.S.A.

19. **The Book Lover**. Edited by Ingersoll Lockwood, Phil. Bibl. Book-plate, A Classical, by Rhead, 60; An American, 35 ; An Artistic, by Rhead, 79 ; Book-plates, by Rhead, 53, 91 ; Centennial, by A. B. Bogart, 69 ; Design for, 23 ; for Cultured Collectors, 115 ; Book-plates, 13. All the above articles are illustrated.
New York, William Evarts Benjamin, 8vo, 1890.
Publication discontinued after twelfth number.

20. **The Sunday Sun.** South Carolina Book-plates.
Charleston, S.C., January 4, 1891.

21. **Dubbs (Rev. Dr. Joseph Henry).** Hobbies and How to
Ride them. *The Interior*, June 11, 18, 1891.
Chicago, Ill., 1891.
These articles do not directly refer to book-plates, but contain inci-
dental allusions.

22. **Providence Sunday Journal.** Collecting Book-plates, Mrs.
E. H. L. Barker.
Providence, R.I., U.S.A., November 15, 1891.

23. **The News and Courier.** A Bibliographical Hint. Something about Book-plates.
Charleston, S.C., U.S.A., March 1, 1892.

24. **Stevenson (E. Ireneus).** The Book-plate and How to
Make it. *The Christian Union.*
New York, U.S.A., April 30, 1892.

25. **The Collector.** Some Historic Book-plates (Rev. Dr. J. H.
Dubbs), V., 151–152, 164–165, 176–177; German
Book-plates of Pennsylvania (Rev. Dr. J. H. Dubbs),
VI., 3–5; The Book-plate of Jacob Sargeant, illustrated
(Charles Dexter Allen); Collection of Book-plates, VI.,
29. New York, Walter Romeyn Benjamin, 4to, 1892.

26. **Hutton (Laurence).** From the Books of Laurence
Hutton. On Some American Book-plates, chapter i.,
3–29. New York, Harper & Bros., 12mo, 1892.
A reprint of the articles which appeared in the *Book Buyer*, 1886,
and also in the *Ex Libris Journal*, Vol. II.

27. **American Dictionary of Printing and Book-making,** Part
iv., 180, 181. Ex Libris, illustrated.
New York, Howard Lockwood & Co., 4to, 1892.

28. **The Book Buyer.** Some English Book-plates. A review
of Mr. Castle's book, illustrated, V., pp. 19–22. Some
French Book-plates. A review of Mr. Hamilton's book,
illustrated, V., pp. 65–67.
New York, Charles Scribner's Sons, 4to, 1893.

29. **The Library Journal.** Note of the Ex Libris Society of
London. New York, May, 1893.

30. **Jamaica Plain News**. Book-plates. A review of Mr. Castle's book, illustrated.
Jamaica Plain, Mass., U.S.A., July 8, 1893.

31. **The Critic**. Book-plates of New England Authors. A review of Mr. Castle's book, illustrated, Vol. XIX., pp. 82, 83. Some American Book-plates, illustrated, Vol. XX., pp. 88, 89.
The Critic Company, New York, folio, 1893.

32. **The Hartford Post**. Hundreds of Book-plates in the Collection of a Hartford Gentleman, illustrated.
Hartford, Conn., U.S.A., August 19, 1893.

33. **The Richmond Despatch**. Arms of the Virginia Company. An interesting historical book-plate. R. A. Brock, Secretary Southern Historical Society, September 17, 1893. That old Book-plate. Note on the Arms of the Virginia Company, October 15, 1893.
Richmond, Va., U.S.A., 1893.

34. **The Richmond Despatch**. Note on the *Ex Libris Journal*.
Richmond, Va., December 3, 1893.

35. **The Albany Argus**. Note on Book-plate of the Albany Library Society.
Albany, N.Y., U.S.A., November, 1893.

36. **Magazine of Art**. "Ex Libris." A review of Mr. Castle's book.
New York, folio, December, 1893.

37. **The Book-Lover's Almanac**. The Art of the Book-plate, by Henri Pene DuBois, with seven caricature designs by Henriot. The Carroll Book-plate, by Charles Dexter Allen, illustrated.
New York, Duprat & Co., 1893.

38. **The Art Amateur**. Ex-Libris Notes, illustrated, Vol. XXX., pp. 92, 121, 148, 173.
New York, Montague Marks, Publisher, 25 Union Square, folio, 1894.

39. **The Dial**. Private Book-marks. A note of Mr. Hardy's book, p. 88.
Chicago, Ill., February 1, 1894.

40. **The Collector.** A Current Record of Art, Bibliography, Antiquarianism, etc. Published semi-monthly.
> Alfred Trumble, 454 West 24th Street, New York.

The following numbers contain brief articles on book-plates: Vol. IV., Nos. 13, 14, 20; Vol. V., No. 1, 1893; Vol. V., Nos. 8, 9, 1894. This is not to be confounded with *The Collector*, published by Walter R. Benjamin.

41. **The Inland Printer.** The Book-plate, its Literature, etc., by W. Irving Way, illustrated, Vol. XII., No. 6, pp. 460–461.
> The Inland Printer Co., Chicago, Ill., March, 1894.

42. **Book Reviews.** American Book-plates, by Charles Dexter Allen.
> New York, Macmillan & Co., Vol. II., No. 1, May, 1894.

* * *

Allusions to book-plates, or reproductions of interesting plates, are found in the following works : —

Bridgman (**Thomas**). The Pilgrims of Boston and their Descendants. Book-plate of Peter Kemble, Esq.
> Boston, Phillips, Sampson & Co., 8vo, 1856.

Magazine of American History. November, 1880, Kissam book-plate, p. 376 ; February, 1881, Washington's book-plate, p. 88 ; March, 1881, Kissam book-plate, pp. 225, 302 ; April, 1881, W. Smith's book-plate, p. 274 ; August, 1884, Roger Morris ; book-plate of Henry Clinton, grandson of Sir H. Clinton.

Ralph Waldo Emerson. His Maternal Ancestors. With some Reminiscences of Him. By David Greene Haskins, D.D. Boston, Cupples, Upham & Co., 12mo, 1886.
Book-plate of Rev. William Emerson, father of Ralph Waldo.

Lion Gardiner and his Descendants, by Curtis E. Gardiner.
> St. Louis, 1890.

Book-plates of John Gardiner, Fifth Proprietor of Gardiner's Island, and John Lyon Gardiner, Seventh Proprietor.

History of the Centennial Celebration of the Inauguration of George Washington as First President of the United States. New York, Appleton & Co., 1892.

Book-plate of George Washington.

Pene DuBois (Henri). Four Private Libraries of New York. New York, Duprat & Co., 8vo, 1892.

Book-plates of C. Jolly-Bavoillet and George B. DeForest.

Customs and Fashions in Old New England. Book-plates, p. 286. Alice Morse Earle.

New York, Charles Scribner's Sons, 1893.

Jamaica Plain News. Sketch of a " talk " on Book-plates, by Mr. E. N. Hewins.

Jamaica Plain, Mass. U.S.A., March 3, 1894.

Origin and Growth of the Library of the Massachusetts Historical Society. A paper presented at a Meeting of the Society, November 9, 1893, by Samuel Abbott Green, M.D. Pamphlet.

John Wilson & Son, University Press, Cambridge, Mass., 1893.

Describes the various book-plates used by the Society, and is illustrated with several fac-similes.

The Jaunceys of New York. Pamphlet, 24 pp.

New York, 1876.

William Jauncey's book-plate for frontispiece.

Annals of the Van Rennselaers in the United States, by Rev. Maunsell Van Rennselaer, D.D., LL.D.

Albany, 8vo., pp. 241. 1888.

Book-plate of K. K. Van Rennselaer, to face page 214.

Pennsylvania Magazine of History and Biography, Vol. IX., page 14.

Book-plate of Sir John St. Clair. Notices on him by Charles R. Hildeburn. 1885.

THE ENGLISH BIBLIOGRAPHY.

By H. W. Fincham, Esq., and James Roberts Brown, F.R.G.S.

[Reprinted by their kind permission.]

1. **Bartsch (Adam).** Le Peintre Graveur, Vol. VII., for plates by Dürer and others.
   Vienna, 21 vols., 8vo, 1803–1821.

2. **Moule (Thomas).** Bibliotheca Heraldica Magnæ Britanniæ, pp. 367–388. London, royal 8vo, 1822.
   Moule used the cut on the title-page as his book-plate.

3. **The Gentleman's Magazine.** Remarks on the invention of book-plates, Part ii., 613. London, 8vo, 1822.

4. **The Gentleman's Magazine.** Book-plates (C. S. B.), Part i., 198–199. London, 8vo, 1823.

5. **Wadd (William).** Mems., Maxims, and Memoirs, pp. 146–147. London, Callow & Wilson, 8vo, 1827.

6. **Parsons (Rev. Daniel).** On Book-plates. Third Annual Report of the Oxford University Archæological and Heraldic Society, pp. 17–25.
   Oxford, J. Vincent, royal 8vo, 1837.

7. **Notes and Queries,** 1st Series. Book-plates, whimsical one, vi., 32 ; motto, i., 212 ; early, iii., 495 ; iv., 46, 93, 354 ; vii., 26 ; xi., 265, 351, 471 ; xii., 35, 114.
   London, 1849–1855.

8. **Dennistoun (James).** Memoirs of Sir Robert Strange . . . and Andrew Lumisden, ii., 283–284.
   London, Longman, 2 vols., 8vo, 1855.
   Gives the dates of three book-plates engraved by Strange.

9. **Notes and Queries,** 2d Series. Book-stamps, armorial, x., 409. London, 1856–1861.

10. **Notes and Queries,** 3d Series. Book-plates, armorial, vi., 306 ; their heraldic authority, xii., 117, 218. ; by R. A., wood engraver, viii., 308. London, 1862–1867.

11. **Beaupré (M.).** Notice sur quelques Graveurs Nancéiens du XVIII Siècle. Nancy, Lucien Wiener, 8vo, 1862.

Contains description of a number of book-plates engraved by Dominique Collin.

12. See American Bibliography, No. 1.

13. See American Bibliography, No. 1.

14. See American Bibliography, No. 2.

15. **Leighton, F.S.A. (John).** Book-plates, Ancient and Modern, with examples, illustrated. *Gentleman's Magazine*, 4th Series, Vol. I., pp. 798–804.
London, 8vo, June, 1866.

Reprinted in the *Ex Libris Journal*, July, 1891; also reprinted in the *British and Colonial Printer and Stationer*, August 6, 1891.

16. **Hugo, M.A. (Thos.).** The Bewick Collector, illustrated, pp. 303–322. London, Reeve & Co., 8vo, 1866.

17. **Larousse (Pierre).** Ex Libris, mots latins qui signifient littéralement des livres, d'entre des livres, faissant partie des livres, avec le nom du propriétaire. Ces mots s'inscrivent ordinairement en tête de chaque volume d'une bibliothèque avec la signature du propriétaire. On connait ce trait d'ignorance d'un financier, homme d'ordre avant tout, qui avait ordonné à son chapelier de coller soigneusement au fond de son chapeau, " Ex Libris Vaudore." Grand Dictionnaire Universel du XIX Siècle, Vol. 7. Paris, 16 vols., 4to, 1866–1877.

18. See American Bibliography, No. 1.

19. See American Bibliography, No. 1.

20. **Notes and Queries,** 4th series. Book-plates, armorial, iv., 409, 518; v., 65, 210, 286; ix., 160; exchanged, x., 519. London, 1868–1873.

21. **Hugo, M.A. (Thos.).** The Bewick Collector Supplement, illustrated, pp. xxiii., 152–155.
London, Reeve & Co., 8vo, 1868.

22. **Howard, LL.D., F.S.A. (Joseph Jackson).** *Miscellanea Genealogica et Heraldica*, illustrated, Vol. I. Examples of Armorial Book-plates: Hooke, 1703; Rogers, 1700; Rogers, Gage, 1805; Dallaway, 284; Billingsley, Egerton, 1707; Snell, 299. London, royal 8vo, 1868.

23. **Bibliophile Français.** Gazette illustrée des amateurs, de livre d'estampes, et des hautes curiosités.

Paris, 7 vols., royal 8vo, 1868–1873.

This work incorporates the "Armorial du Bibliophile" of Guigard.

24. **Bachelin-Deflorenne,** bookseller, of Garrick Street, Covent Garden, London, December, 1869. Catalogue of, describes two book-plates dated respectively 1279 and 1314. *Vide The Book Fancier,* P. Fitzgerald, p. 129.

25. **Guigard (Joannis).** Armorial du bibliophile, avec illustrations dans le texte.

Paris, Bachelin-Deflorenne, 2 vols., 8vo, 1870–1872.

Contains about 1400 cuts of super-libris.

26. **Tourneaux (Maurice).** Ex Libris. Amateur d'autographes. April, 1872. An article on the collection of ex libris in the possession of M. Aglaüs Bouvenne.

27. **Notes and Queries,** 5th Series. Book-plate, R. T. Pritchett's, ix., 29, 75 ; query, x., 428 ; armorial, i., 386 ; exchanged, i., 60, 199 ; ii., 159 ; punning, iv., 464 ; v., 35 ; handbook of, vi., 465 ; vii., 36, 76 ; heraldic, vi., 369, 543 ; vii., 28, 36, 76, 233, 435, 515 ; earliest known, vii., 76, 235 ; mottoes on, vii., 427 ; viii., 111, 258 ; collections, vii., 435, 515 ; viii., 38, 79, 118, 158, 178, 360 ; xi., 260 ; dated, viii., 200, 298, 397, 517 ; ix., 198 ; xi., 446 ; xii., 33 ; how to arrange collections, ix., 20 ; papers on, ix., 360. London, 1874–1879.

28. **Poulet-Malassis (A.).** Les Ex Libris Français, depuis leur origine jusqu'à nos jours. Plates.

Paris, P. Rouquette, royal 8vo, 1874.

29. **De Rieffenberg.** De Marques et devises mises à leur livres par un grande nombre d'amateurs. Paris, 1874.

30. **Athenæum.** "Les Ex libris Français." Review of Poulet-Malassis' book "Les Ex Libris Français."

London, p. 469, October 9, 1875.

31. **Longpérier-Grimoard (Comte de).** Etude sur les Ex Libris. Senlis, 8vo, 8 pp., 1875.

A paper read before the Comité-Archéologique de Senlis, December 11, 1874.

32. **Longpérier-Grimoard (Comte de)**. Letter to Monsieur Aubry on a Super-Libris of Crozat. *Bulletin de Bouquiniste*, No. 416. Paris, Aubry, April 15, 1875.

33. **Poulet-Malassis (A.)**. Les Ex Libris Français. Nouvelle edition, revue, très-augmentée et ornée de vingt-quatre planches. Paris, P. Rouquette, royal 8vo, 1875.

34. **Tooke (M. A.)**. Notes on Book-plates, illustrated. *The Art Journal*, new series, XV., 267–270.
London, Vèrtue, folio, September, 1876.

35. **Longpérier-Grimoard (Comte de)**. Une marque inconnue (College du cardinal le Moine). Paris, Aubry, 1876.

Reprinted from the *Bulletin de Bouquiniste*, December 1 and 15, 1876.

36. **Van de Haeghen**. Dictionnaire des devises des hommes des lettres, imprimeurs, libraires, bibliophiles, etc.
1876–1879.

37. **Howard, LL.D., F.S.A. (Joseph Jackson)**. *Miscellanea Genealogica et Heraldica*, Vol. II., illustrated. Examples of Armorial Book-plates : Barker, 505 ; Beddington, 244 ; Bowdon, 525 ; De Burgo, 1720, 287 ; Cary-Elwes, 556 ; Furneaux, 170 ; Gomm, 184 ; Haslewood, 128 ; Hilliard, 87 ; Lorimer, 421 ; Palmer, 487 ; Potter, 570 ; Waldy, 583. London, royal 8vo, 1877.

38. **Pall Mall Gazette**. Occasional Notes, "Old Bookworm," p. 4, November 19 ; p. 5, December 18.
London, 1877.

39. **The Genealogist**, Vol. II. Book-plate of Anthony Stewart, illustrated, 192.
London, Golding & Lawrence, 8vo, 1878.

40. **Warren, M.A. (The Hon. J. Leicester)**. Guide to the Study of Book-plates. Plates.
London, John Pearson, 8vo, 1880.

41. **The Bookseller**. A Guide to the Study of Book-plates. Review of Warren's book, "A Guide to the Study of Book-plates." London, October 6, 1880.

42. **The Graphic.** The Reader. Review of Warren's book, " A Guide to the Study of Book-plates."

London, October 16, 1880.

43. **Saturday Review.** Book-plates. A review of Warren's book, " A Guide to the Study of Book-plates."

London, October 20, 1880.

44. **The Academy.** Art Books. Review of Warren's book, " A Guide to the Study of Book-plates."

London, November 13, 1880.

45. **The Antiquary,** edited by E. Walford, M.A., Vol. I. Notes on Book-plates, 75–77 ; Book-plates (W. Hamilton), 117–118 ; Book-plates, 189 ; Notes on Curious Book-plates, 236–237 ; Another Chapter on Book-plates (Alfred Wallis), 256–259.

London, Elliot Stock, 4to, 1880.

46. **The Antiquary,** edited by E. Walford, M.A., Vol. II. A Supplementary Chapter on Book-plates, 6–10 ; An Essay on Book-plates (E. P. Shirley), 115–118 ; Book-plates, 133, 272.   London, Elliot Stock, 4to, 1880.

47. **Howard, LL.D., F.S.A. (Joseph Jackson).** *Miscellanea Genealogica et Heraldica,* Vol. III., illustrated. Examples of Armorial Book-plates : Andrews, 171 ; Bedford, 189 ; Carson, 156 ; Burr, 156 ; Courthope, 327 ; Dalton, 438 ; Fenwick, Note respecting Bewick, 433 ; Gregory, 290 ; Harrington, 1706, 195 ; Hoblyn, 353 ; Hyett, 95 ; Jackson, 402 ; Millard, 445 ; Mitchell, 101, 143 ; Nott, 1763, 233 ; Ridgway, 1871, 47 ; St. George, 82 ; Strangways, 22 ; Tomes, 273 ; Waggett, 182 ; Walters, 226, 252 ; White, 1878, 206 ; Woodroffe, 65.

London, royal 8vo, 1880.

48. **Notes and Queries,** 6th Series. Book-plates, collections of, i., 2, 178, 197, 266, 386 ; ii., 272, 302 ; vi., 161, 298 ; x., 24 ; of Lord Keane and others, i., 336 ; ii., 34, 94, 255 ; " As " on, i., 516 ; armorial, ii., 367, 396, 427 ; iii., 73, 126, 278, 298 ; xi., 267, 410 ; their removal, ii., 445, 491 ; iii., 31 ; their arrangement, iii., 28, 130, 195 ; dated, iii., 204, 302 ; iv., 206, 247, 466, 486 ; v., 9, 78, 151 ; vi., 357 ; vii., 146, 166 ; ix., 480 ; x., 34 ; accu-

mulated, iii., 289, 473 ; iv., 16 ; Burton, iii., 386 ; their collection, 402 ; cryptographic, 403 ; with astronomical symbols, 429 ; something new in, 506 : Austro-Hungarian, 508 ; with Greek mottoes, iv., 266, 414, 497 ; v., 296, 457 ; vi., 136, 218, 398 ; vii., 295, 304, 336 ; viii., 278 ; their mounting, iv., 305 ; their exchange, v., 46 ; curious, v., 226, 305, 374, 457 ; vi., 15, 76 ; Bishop of Clonfert's, 1698, v., 346 ; portrait, v., 407 ; vi., 14, 157 ; Joseph Ignace's, vi., 68, 237 ; Rev. Adam Clarke's, vii., 304 ; foreign, viii., 268, 298 ; John Collet's, 1633, ix., 308, 437 ; Boteler, x., 27 ; unidentified, 129 ; German, 269, 373 ; Arthur Charlett's, xi., 267, 411, 433, 451 ; ancient, xii., 8, 78 ; heraldic, 10, 429 ; parochial, 69, 152 ; typographical, 288, 352, 415 ; their antiquity, 512.   London, 1880–1885.

49. **Stoeber (Auguste)**. Petit Revue d'ex libris Alsaciens.
                                    Mulhouse, 12mo, 1880.

50. Nouvelle etude sur l'unversité de Pont-à-mousson.
                                    Nancy, 1880.

51. **The Antiquary**, Vol. III. Reviews. A Guide to the Study of Book-plates, 77.
                        London, Elliot Stock, 4to, 1881.

52. **The Antiquary**, Vol. IV. Last Words on Book-plates, 106–111.   London, Elliot Stock, 4to, 1881.

53. **Dobson (Austin)**. The Book-plate's Petition : a poem.
                        Notes and Queries, Jan. 8, 1881.

54. **Hamilton, F.R.G.S. (Walter)**. Leaves from a Library, on Book-plates. *West Middlesex Advertiser*, March 26 ; April 2, 9, 16, 23, 30 ; May 7, 14.
                    London, Shields, Sloane Square, 1881.

55. **The Genealogist**, Vol. V. "A Guide to the Study of Book-plates" (a review of Warren), illustrated, 74–77. Grant of Arms to John Leyland, illustrated with book-plate, 184.   London, George Bell & Sons, 8vo, 1881.

56. **Palatine Note Book**, Vol. I. Book-plates, 15, 16, 30, 52, 53, 69, 114, 195 ; illustrated, 217 ; of Jesus Coll., Camb., 128 ; Walpole's, 209.   Manchester, 4to, 1881.

57. **Paper and Printing Trades Journal.** Ex Libris, illustrated. March, p. 48 ; September, p. 19.
London, 4to, 1881.

58. **Western Antiquary,** Vol. I., edited by W. H. K. Wright, F.R.H.S. Book-plates, Francis Drake's, 32, illustrated ; proposed work on, by Walter Hamilton, 174.
Plymouth, 4to, 1881.

59. **Daily News.** A leader on book-borrowers, book-plates, and mottoes. London, April 29, 1881.

60. **Lang (Andrew).** *The Library*, pp. 42–59.
London, Macmillan, 8vo, 1881.

61. See American Bibliography, No. 5.

62. **Hardy (W. J.).** Book-plates. The *Globe*, November 3.
London, 1881.

Reprinted in Turnovers from the *Globe.*
London, The *Globe* office, 8vo, n.d.

63. **The Antiquary,** Vol. V. Book-plates, 85, 86.
London, Elliot Stock, 4to, 1882.

64. **Antiquarian Magazine and Bibliographer,** edited by E. Walford, M.A., Vol. I. Notes on English Book-plates, No. 1 (W. J. Hardy), illustrated, 173–177.
London, Reeves, royal 8vo, 1882.

65. **Antiquarian Magazine and Bibliographer,** edited by E. Walford, M.A., Vol. II. Notes on English Book-plates, No. 2 (J. Harrop), 53–55, illustrated ; on Book-plates (F. J. Thairlwall), 277–280, illustrated ; Book-plates, 48, 106, 161, 322.
London, Reeves, royal 8vo, 1882.

66. **Palatine Note Book,** Vol. II. Book-plates, 18, illustrated.
Manchester, 4to, 1882.

67. **Printing Times and Lithographer.** Curiosities of Book-plates, viii., 265–268, 290–292.
London, Wyman & Sons, 4to, 1882.

68. **Western Antiquary,** edited by W. H. K. Wright, F.R.H.S., Vol. II. Book-plates, local, 197 ; Armorial, 211, 212, illustrated. Plymouth, 4to, 1882.

69. **Paper and Printing Trades Journal.** A Curious Book-plate, illustrated, No. 40, p. 45.
London, 4to, September, 1882.

70. **The Antiquary,** Vol. VII. Book-plates, early reference to, 231. London, Elliot Stock, 4to, 1883.

71. **Antiquarian Magazine and Bibliographer,** edited by E. Walford, M.A., Vol. III. Book-plates (D. P.[arsons]), 2–7, 53–56, illustrated (R. Day), 272–273; Book-plates, 104, 161, 274.
London, Reeves, royal 8vo, 1883.

72. **Antiquarian Magazine and Bibliographer,** edited by E. Walford, M.A., Vol. IV. Book-plates (W. Hamilton), 110, 111. London, Reeves, royal 8vo, 1883.

73. **Palatine Note Book,** Vol. III. Book-plates, 51, 97, 191, 233, illustrated. Manchester, 4to, 1883.

74. **Benoit (Arthur).** Les Ex Libris de Schœpflin, illustrated.
Paris, 8vo, 1883.

An extract from " Le Bulletin de la Société pour la conservation des monuments historiques d'Alsace," 2d Series, xii., 30–33.

75. **Benoit (Arthur).** Les Ex Libris dans les trois évêches, Toul, Metz, Verdun, 1552–1790. Paris, 8vo, 1883.

76. **Antiquarian Magazine and Bibliographer,** edited by E. Walford, M.A., Vol. V. A Bibliography of Book-plates (W. Hamilton), 78–80; Book-plates, 106, 107, 162, 217.
London, royal 8vo, 1884.

77. **Griggs (W.).** Eighty-three examples of Book-plates from Various Collections. Plates. Privately printed.
W. Griggs, Hanover Street, Peckham, London, 4to, 1884.

78. **Howard, LL.D., F.S.A. (Joseph Jackson).** *Miscellanea Genealogica et Heraldica,* Vol. IV., illustrated. Examples of Armorial Book-plates: Carew, 154; Clutton, 300; Collins, 274; Fletcher, 214; Gidley, 19; Hayman, 54; Heysham, 375; Heywood, 202; Humphry, 314; Littleton, 166; Lynch, 387; Meade, 6; Pole, 131; Pringle, 190; Symons, 250; Soltau, 250; Traherne, 102; Underhill, 78; Wickham, 67; Wilmer, 238; Wilmer Ex Dono, 1599, 238.
London, royal 8vo, 1884.

79. **Benoit (Arthur).** Les bibliophiles, les collectioneurs, et les bibliothèques des monasteres des trois évêches, 1552- 1790. Paris, royal 8vo, 1884.

80. See American Bibliography, No. 8.

81. **Day, F.S.A., M.R.I.A. (Robert).** Notice of book-plates engraved by Cork artists. Journal of the Royal Histori- cal and Archæological Association of Ireland, illustrated, No. 61, Vol. VII., January, 1885.

Privately reprinted, 7 pp., 8vo. Reprinted in the *Ex Libris Journal,* August, 1891.

82. **Day, F.S.A., M.R.I.A. (Robert).** "Ex Libris." Journal of the Birmingham Central Literary Association, illus- trated.

Privately reprinted, 7 pp., 8vo, 1885.

83. See American Bibliography, No. 7.

84. **Western Antiquary,** edited by W. H. K. Wright, F.R.H.S., Vol. IV. Book-plate of J. O. H. Glynn, 38, illustrated. Plymouth, 4to, 1885.

85. **The Antiquary,** Vol. XIII. Book-plate, 231, 278. London, Elliot Stock, 4to, 1886.

86. See American Bibliography, No. 9.

87. See American Bibliography, No. 9.

88. See American Bibliography, No. 9.

89. **East Anglian,** edited by the Rev. C. H. Evelyn White, F.S.A. Pretyman's Book-plate, New Series, i., 246. Ipswich, 8vo, 1886.

90. **Fitzgerald (Percy).** *The Book Fancier,* 128–131. London, Sampson Low, 8vo, 1886.

91. **Howard, LL.D., F.S.A. (Joseph Jackson).** *Miscellanea Genealogica et Heraldica,* 2d Series, Vol. I., illustrated. Examples of Armorial Book-plates: Brownlowe, 1698, 221; Chauncy, 28; Chetwode, 85; Lady Mary Booth, Chetwood, 122; Conder, 61; Dade, 311; Dering, 1630, 285; Elizabeth, Countess of Exeter, 268; Murray, 347; Shank, 235; Smith, 347; Walpole, 364. London, royal 8vo, 1886.

113. **Carlander (C. M.).** Svenska Bibliotek och Ex Libris auteckningar, med 84 illustrationer.
Stockholm, Adolf Johnson, 8vo, n.d. (1889).

114. **Aveling (S. T.).** Heraldry: Ancient and Modern Book-plates, 370–371, illustrated.
London, F. Warne & Co., 8vo, 1890.

115. **The Book-Plate Collector's Miscellany,** a monthly supplement to the *Western Antiquary*, illustrated. Edited by W. H. K. Wright, F. R. Hist. Soc.
Plymouth, W. H. Luke, 4to, 1890–1891.

116. **Howard, LL.D., F.S.A. (Joseph Jackson).** *Miscellanea Genealogica et Heraldica*, 2d Series, Vol. IV., illustrated. Examples of Armorial Book-plates : N. D'Eye, 25 ; Ball, R. Ball Dodson, 41 ; Paul Jodrell, 89 ; Vassall, 120; Cooke, 1712, 136; Sr. G. Cooke, 1727, 152; Harrison, 1698, 168; Langley, 184; Wyndham, 201; Prentice, 216; Yardley, 1721, Yardley, 1739, 232.
London, royal 8vo, 1890.

117. **Demmin (A.).** Papier u. andere Beschreibstoffe Schreibgeräth, Handschrift, Buch, Buchandel, u. Zeitungswesen, Buchdruck — u. Buchbinderkunst, Buchdrucker — u. Bucherzeichen (Ex Libris), Initialen, Zieleisten. With 46 illustrations. Wiesbaden, 8vo, 1890.

118. **Guigard (Joannis).** Nouvelle Armorial du Bibliophile, Guide de l'Amateur des Livres Armoriés. Contenant la Reproduction de 2500 Armoiries et Riches Reliures Armoiriées. Paris, Emile Rondeau, 2 vols., 8vo, 1890.

119. **Warnecke (F.).** Die Deutschen Bücherzeichen (Ex Libris). Von ihrem Ursprunge bis zur Gegenwort. Twenty-one illustrations in the text, and 26 plates.
Berlin, T. U. Stargardt, royal 8vo, 1890.

120. **Rogers (Walter Thomas).** A Manual of Bibliography, 103–105, with diagrams.
London, H. Grevel & Co., 8vo (1890), 1891.

121. **Bouchot (Henri).** Les Ex Libris et Les Marques de Possession du Livre. Fifteen plates.
Paris, Edouard Rouveyre, 8vo (1890), 1891.

122. **The Antiquary,** Vol. XXIII. A notice of the Ex Libris Society, 142. London, Elliot Stock, 4to, 1891.

123. **The British Bookmaker.** Book Notes, a review of " Les Ex Libris " (Bouchot), illustrated, Vol. IV., No. 47, p. 5. " Ex Libris," illustrated, Vol. IV., No. 48, p. 4. Book-plates, Vol. V., No. 49, p. 8.
London, Raithby, Lawrence & Co., 4to, 1891.

124. **Hardy, F.S.A.** (**W. J.**). Book-plates. *The Library,* iii., 47–53, 93–98. London, Elliot Stock, 8vo, 1891.

125. **The Library.** Record of Bibliography. Reviews of " Die deutschen Bücherzeichen " (Warnecke) and " Les Ex Libris " (Bouchot), iii., 17–19.
London, Elliot Stock, 8vo, 1891.

126. **The Daily Chronicle.** Book-plates, April 1. A note of the Ex Libris Society, July 22. London, 1891.

127. **Oxford University Herald.** The Ex Libris Society.
Oxford, May 23, 1891.

128. See American Bibliography, No. 20.

129. **Journal of the Ex Libris Society,** illustrated.
London, A. & C. Black, for the Society, 4to, 1891.

130. **British and Colonial Printer and Stationer.** The Ex Libris Society, July 16. Book-plates, Ancient and Modern, with illustrations (a reprint of No. 15), August 6. Book-plates, October 15. London, 1891.

131. **The Daily Free Press.** A leading article upon collecting Book-plates and the Ex Libris Society.
Aberdeen, July 17, 1891.

132. **The Globe.** Book-plates. London, July 25, 1891.

133. **The Saturday Review.** Book-plates, a review of the *Ex Libris Journal.* London, July 25, 1891.

134. **The Daily News.** A note of the Ex Libris Society.
London, August 3, 1891.

135. **The Publishers' Circular.** Book-plates.
London, August 8, 1891.

136. **Answers.** The Collecting Fad.
London, 4to, December 12, 1891.

137. **Griggs (W.).** Examples of Armorial Book-plates, Second Series. Plates.
London, W. Griggs & Sons, Ld., 4to (1891), 1892.

138. **Carlander (C. M.).** Svenska Bibliotek och Ex Libris anteckningar II., med 22 illustrationer.
Stockholm, Gernandts Boktoyckeri-Aktiebolag, 8vo, 1891.

139. **Le Livre Moderne,** Vol. IV. Remarques sur Quelques Ex Libris Contemporains, illustrated, 1–18; Quelques Nouveaux Ex Libris, illustrated, 323–330.
Paris, Maison Quantin, small 4to, 1891.

140. **La Curiosite Universelle.** À propos d'Ex Libris, No. 228. Le Plus Grand Ex Libris, Nos. 248, 250, 251, 252, et 254. Review of the German Ex Libris Society's *Journal,* No. 258. Paris, 4to, 1891.

141. **Ex Libris.** Zeitschrift für Bücherzeichen Bibliotheken-kunde und Gelehrtengeschichte. Organ des Ex Libris zu Berlin, illustrated.
Berlin, C. A. Starke, 4to, No. 1, October, 1891.

142. **Benoit (Arthur).** Le Serpent Emblème des Chirurgiens et des Medecins. 6 pp., n.d.
Treats of serpents appearing on book-plates. An extract from *Revue Nouvelle d'Alsace-Lorraine.*

* * *

Illustrations of Book-plates are to be found in the following works, apart from the bibliography of the subject : —

143. **Grace, F.S.A. (Sheffield).** Memoirs of the Family of Grace. London, royal 8vo, 1823.
Illustrated with above a dozen book-plates of Grace family, some dated.

144. **Dibdin, D.D. (Thomas Frognall).** A Bibliographical Tour in the Northern Counties of England and Scotland. Trotter Brockett's book-plate by Bewick, illustrated, i., 392. London, 8vo, 1838.

145. **Eyton, F.S.A.** (**Joseph Walton King**). Catalogue of the Library of. London, large paper, royal 8vo, 1848.

Illustrated with three examples of J. W. King Eyton's book-plates, one of which is in colors.

146. **Palmer, F.S.A.** (**Charles John**). The Perlustration of Great Yarmouth.
Great Yarmouth, 3 vols., 4to, 1872–1875.

A number of book-plates are used here to illustrate the arms of the families mentioned.

147. **Siennicki** (**S. J.**). Les Elzévirs de la Bibliothèque de l'Université Imperiale de Varsovie. 1874.

Contains eighteen fac-similes of remarkable book-plates in Warsaw University Library.

148. **Warnecke** (**F.**). Heraldische Kunstblätter.
Görlitz, C. A. Starke, 3 vols., folio, 1876.

Contains many fac-similes of German book-plates.

149. **Siennicki** (**S. J.**). Recueil des éditions des imprimeurs célèbre de l'Italie, de la France, et de la Belgique conservées dans la Bibliothèque de l'Université Imperiale de Varsovie. 1878.

Contains fac-similes of remarkable book-plates in Warsaw University Library.

150. **Leighton, F.S.A.** (**John**). Suggestions in design, . . . with descriptive and historical letter-press, by J. K. Collings, F.R.I.B.A. Blazon, Heraldry, Rebuses, &c., plates, 50, 51, 52, 53, 54.
London, Blackie & Son, 4to, 1880.

151. See American Bibliography, No. 6.

152. **Asta Libraria Antiquaria Catalogo**, N. 42.
Florence, Franchi & Co., February, 1886.

The catalogue contains fac-similes of a Medicean Super Libros, and of another not identified.

153. **Griggs** (**W.**). Illustrations of Armorial China. Plates.
Privately printed, folio, 1887.

Contains a number of fac-similes of book-plates.

154. See American Bibliography, No. 17.

155. **The Strand Magazine**, Vol. II. London, 4to, 1891.
Page 120, the book-plate of H. Stacy Marks, R.A.

156. **Blackburn (Henry).**   Randolph Caldecott, a personal reminiscence, 194–196.
> London, Sampson Low, Marston & Co., 8vo, 1891.

Contains a description of the "Seaman" book-plate by R. Caldecott, with illustration.

157. **Theydon Mount**: its Lords and Rectors.   Edited by J. J. Howard, Farnham Burke, and the Rev. L. N. Prance.
> Privately printed, 4to, n.d. (1891).

Contains a fac-simile of the book-plate of "Sir Edward Smith, of Hill Hall, Co. Essex, Bart.," and another.

158. See American Bibliography, supplementary list.

* * *

The following articles having appeared since the English list was prepared, are here inserted : —

The Yellow Book.   An Illustrated Quarterly.   Cuts of book-plates by Aubrey Beardsley and R. Auning Bell, p. 251.
> London, Elkin Mathews and John Lane.
> Boston, U.S.A., Copeland & Day, Vol. I., 8vo, April, 1894.

The Strand Magazine.   The handwriting of Mr. Gladstone, with fac-similes.   Vol. VIII., No. 43.
> London, 8vo, July, 1894.

Fac-simile of early book-plate of Mr. Gladstone.

Daily News.   Book-plate collecting.   A review of Mr. Hamilton's "Dated Book-plates, Part I."
> London, July 17, 1894.

Quakerana, No. 5, July, 1894, page 77.   Note of Ex Libris Society's exhibition in July, 1894, with special reference to book-plate of William Penn.
> London, Edward Hicks, Jun., 14 Bishopsgate Street Without, E.C.

The Studio, edited by Gleeson White, has contained several articles on book-plates.   Vol. III., No. 16, July 16, 1894 : result of a prize competition for a book-plate design, with 22 designs reproduced ; Vol. III., No. 17, August 15, 1894 : cuts of three book-plates and review of Hamilton's "Dated Plates."
> London, 1894.

ADDITIONAL BIBLIOGRAPHY OF BOOK–PLATES.

By H. W. Fincham and James Robert Brown, F.R.G.S.

[Reprinted from the Journal of the Ex Libris Society.]

1. **Historic Society of Lancashire and Cheshire.** Proceedings and Papers. Description of a Warrington Book-plate (Dr. J. Kendrick), illustrated, 134–135.

   Liverpool, 8vo, 1854.

2. See American Bibliography, No. 3.

3. **Portalis (Le Baron Roger) et Beraldi (Henri).** Les Graveurs du Dix-Huitième Siècle, illustrated, 3 vols. in 6.

   Paris, Morgand et Fatout, 8vo, 1880–1882.

   Contains lists of book-plates by many French engravers.

4. **Spectator.** "A Guide to the Study of Book-plates." (A review of Warren.)   London, October 13, 1880.

5. **St. James Gazette.** "A Guide to the Study of Book-plates." (A review of Warren.)

   London, October 14, 1880.

6. **The Athenæum.** Mr. Thorn's book-plate.

   London, May 21, 1881.

7. See American Bibliography, No. 4.

8. **Beraldi (Henri).** Les Graveurs de XIX Siècle, illustrated, 12 vols.

   Paris, L. Conquet, 8vo, 1885–1892.

   Contains lists of book-plates by many French engravers.

9. **Forening for Boghaandvaerk.** Aarsskrift 1890 und 1891. Mit einer Buchdruckfarbentafel, zalreichen Autotypien und Holzschnitten, Schriften, Druckerzeichen, Ex Libris und Einbände reproducirend.

   Kopenhagen, 2 vols., 4to, 1891.

10. **Ledien (Alcius).** Les Reliures Artistiques et Armoriées de la Bibliothèque Communale d'Abbeville, illustrated.

    Paris, Gruel-Engelmann, 4to, 1883.

11. See American Bibliography, No. 18.

12. See American Bibliography, No. 27.

13. **The Antiquary.** Unique Book-plates. Erasmus and Dr. Hector Pomer (H. W. Pereira). Illustrated, xxv., 242–244.   London, Elliot Stock, 8vo, 1892.

14. **The Bookworm.** A Hunt for Book-plates in Paris (W. Hamilton), 171–173 ; the Avery Book-plate, 202.
London, Elliot Stock, 8vo, 1892.

15. **Castle (Egerton), M.A., F.S.A.** English Book-plates, an illustrated handbook for students of Ex Libris.
London, George Bell and Sons, imp. 16mo, 1892.
Second and enlarged edition, 1892.

16. See American Bibliography, No. 25.

17. **La Curiosité Universelle.** Un souvenir de la Terreur, illustrated ; Franc-Maçonnerie ; Le plus grand Ex Libris, No. 262 ; Publication sur les Ex Libris, Nos. 265, 266, 267, 268, and 269 ; Ex Libris d'Auvergne (Ambroise Tardien), illustrated ; Appel aux Collectionneurs d'Ex Libris, No. 269 ; Ex Libris Rares et Inedits (Ferd. Reiber) ; Un grand Ex Libris (Fr. Perot) ; Un autre souvenir de la Terreur (L. B.) ; Ex Libris Alsaciens; Sociétés des Collectionneurs d'Ex Libris, No. 288 ; Les Ex Libris Oratoriens (P. Ingold), illustrated, No. 299.   Paris, 4to, 1892.

18. **Dictionary of English Book Collectors.** Billibald Pirkheimer (M. Kerney), illustrated, Part i.
London, Bernard, Quaritch, 8vo, 1892.

19. **Fincham (H. W.) & Brown (James Roberts) F.R.G.S.** A bibliography of book-plates.
Plymouth, printed for private distribution, 8vo, 24 pp., 1892.

20. **Griggs (W.).** One hundred and forty-seven Examples of Armorial Book-plates from various collections (second series). Plates.
London, W. Griggs & Sons, 4to, 1892.

21. **Hamilton (Walter).** French Book-plates. A handbook for Ex Libris Collectors, illustrated.
London, George Bell & Sons, imp. 16mo, 1892.

22. **Hildetrandt (Professor Ad. M.).** Heraldic Book-plates. Twenty-five Ex Libris invented and drawn by.
Berlin, J. A. Stargardt, 8vo, 1892.

23. See American Bibliography, No. 26.

24. **Incunabula, geographica et chalcographica,** illustrated.
Munich, Ludwig Rosenthal's Antiquariat, folio, 1892.

   A catalogue of early woodcuts, containing a number of very early German Ex Libris, among them being that of Hildebrand Brandenburg, and the hedge-hog of Johannes Knabensperg, called Igler, circa 1450.

25. **Ingold (C. P.).** Les Ex Libris Oratoriens, illustrated.
Paris, C. Poussielque, 15 Rue Cassette, 8vo, 16 pp., 1892.

26. **The Library.** Record of Bibliography. Review of Fincham and Brown's Bibliography of Book-plates, iv., 262.
London, Simpkin, Marshall, Hamilton, Kent & Co., 8vo, 1892.

27. **The Morning Post.** Book-plates, June 14; Literary Notes, August 25.   London, 1892.

28. See American Bibliography, No. 23.

29. **Notes and Queries,** 8th Series.   Book-plates : Boyer, i., 7 ; royal, i., 126, 175 ; Rabelais's, ii., 147; armorial, ii., 188, 274, 490 ; iii., 97 ; iv., 168 ; Mountaine and Burden, engravers of, i., 247, 324 ; book-lending and book-losing, i., 322 ; Ex Libris Society, ii., 500 ; English Book-plates, a review, iii., 79 ; portraits as book-plates, iii., 81, 129, 210 ; French Book-plates, a review, iii., 160 ; Book-plates, a review, iii., 419.   London, 4to, 1892.

30. **Ris-Paquot,** Dictionnaire Encyclopédique des Marques et Monogrammes, Chiffes, Lettres, Initials, Signs, Figuratifs, etc., etc., contenant 1200 Marques.
Paris, R. H. Laurens, 6 Rue de Tournon, 2 vols., 4to, 1892.

31. **Archives de la Société Française des Collectionneurs d'Ex Libris,** illustrated.
Paris, 3 Faubourg Saint-Jacques, 4to, No. 1, December, 1893.

32. **The Athenæum.** The Laws of Book-borrowing (G. H. Powell).   London, December 23, 1893.

33. **The Bookman.** Wm. Cowper's copy of Robert Burns' Poems, containing his book-plate, illustrated, September, October. London, folio, 1893.

34. See American Bibliography, No. 40.

35. **El Coleccionista Argentina.** Ex Libris, January; Ex Libris y Eliquetas de libreros, March; The Journal of the Ex Libris Society, April; Ex Libris, illustrated, June; Ex Libris, illustrated, September.
Buenos Ayres, 8vo, 1893.

36. **Ex Libris Imaginaires et supposés de personnages célèbres anciens et modernes.** Plates.
Paris, L. Joly, 8vo, 1893.

37. **The Globe.** The Latest Hobby.
London, March 29, 1893.

38. **Hardy (W. J.), F.S.A.** Book-plates. Plates.
London, Kegan Paul, Trench, Trübner & Co., 8vo, 1893.

39. See American Bibliography, No. 32.

40. **Kissel (Clemens).** Symbolical Book-plates. Twenty-five Ex Libris designed and drawn by.
London, H. Grevel & Co., 8vo (1893), 1894.

41. **Miscellanea Genealogica et Heraldica** (Dr. J. J. Howard, LL.D., F.S.A.), Vol. V., illustrated. Examples of Armorial Book-plates : Richard Pritchett, 89 ; John Bennett, 104 ; (Phillipps, 1892), 136 ; (Thomas Carter), 166 ; Sir John Collum and Dame Susanna, 1760 ; John Cullum, Rev. Sir John Cullum, Richard Merry, Thomas Gery Cullum, Sir Thomas Gery Cullum, Mary Hanson, 1773 ; Thomas Gery Cullum, Rev. Sir Thomas Gery Cullum, Mary Anne Cullum, S. A. Milner Gibson Cullum, Gery Milner Gibson Cullum, Reginald Gurney, Arethusa Robertson, Gery Milner Gibson Cullum, 193. Irish Book-plates : Thomas Ridgate Mannsell, Sisson Darling, 264 ; Richard Baldwin, John Butler, 281.
London, royal 8vo, 1893.

42. **The Portfolio.** A description of the Burlington Fine Arts Club Book-plate, by Mr. C. W. Sherborn, xxi.
London, Seeley & Co., folio, 1893.

43. **The Scottish Review**.   Book-plates, xxi., 315–329.
    London, 8vo, April, 1893.

44. **The Studio**.   Designing for book-plates, with some recent
    example (G.[leeson] W.[hite]), illustrated, 24–28;
    some recent book-plates, with seven examples, illustrated,
    148–150, 253.   London, 4to, 1893.

45. **Teske (Charles)**.   The Book-plates of Ulrick, Duke of
    Mecklenburgh.   Plates.
    Berlin, J. A. Stargardt, 4to (1893), 1894.

46. **Tit-Bits**.   Who has the finest collection of book-plates in
    this country?   London, October 21, 1893.

47. **Vicars (Arthur), F.S.A.**   *Ulster King of Arms*.   Book-
    plates (Ex Libris), Series I., Library Interior Book-
    plates ; Series II., Literary Book-plates ; Series III.,
    Book-piles, illustrated.   Plymouth, 4to, 1893.
    For private circulation.   Reprinted, with additions and corrections,
    from *The Journal of the Ex Libris Society*.

48. **Wheatley (H. B.)**.   Diary of Samuel Pepys.   Pepys' book-
    plates, i., xv., lv.
    London, George Bell & Sons, 8vo, 1893.

49. **The Muses**.   The Study of Ex Libris and Book-plate col-
    lecting, illustrated, 17–20 (H. Berkeley Score, F.R.G.S.).
    Ormskirk, William Leak Hutton, 4to, 1894.

*   *   *

Illustrations of book-plates, apart from the bibliography of
the subject, are contained in the following articles : —

50. Lines written in Jerpoint Abbey.
    London, 8vo, 1820.
    One of Sheffield Grace's book-plates.

51. **Benson (Robert), M.A.**   Memoirs of the Life and Writings
    of the Rev. Arthur Collier, from 1704 to 1732.
    London, 8vo, 1837.
    Collier book-plate.

52. See American Bibliography, No. 11.

53. **Fragmenta Genealogica**, Vol. I., 58.
   Private press of Frederic Arthur Crisp, 4to, 1889.
   Book-plate of " William Cowper, Esqr., Clerk of the Parliaments."

54. **The Bookman.** London, May, 1892.
   Mr. Gladstone's book-plate.

55. See American Bibliography, supplementary list.

56. See American Bibliography, supplementary list.

57. **Revue Encyclopédique.** Les livres en vente publique,
   14–18. Paris, 4to, 1892.
   Several modern French book-plates.

58. **The Christian Pictorial.** Cowper's Retreat.
   London, April 6, 1893.
   William Cowper's book-plate.

59. **Dictionary of English Book Collectors.**
   London, Quaritch, 8vo, Part ii., 1893.
   The book-plate of the Huth Library.

60. **Leslie (G. D.), R.A.** Letters to Marco.
   London, Macmillan, 8vo, 1893.
   Mr. Leslie's book-plate.

61. **The Sketch.** Mr. W. Herrics Pollock.
   London, folio, July 7, 1893.
   Mr. Pollock's book-plate.

62. **The Sketch.** Mr. Clement K. Shorter.
   London, folio, July 18, 1893.
   Mr. C. K. Shorter's book-plate.

63. **Visitation of England and Wales.** Edited by Joseph
   Jackson Howard, LL.D. (Maltravers Herald Extraor-
   dinary), and Frederic Arthur Crisp. Vol. I.
   London, Mitchell & Hughes, 4to, 1893.

64. **Warren (John Leicester), Lord de Tabley, M.A., F.S.A.**
   Poems, Dramatic and Lyrical.
   London, Elkin Mathews & Lane, 8vo, 1893.
   Mr. J. L. Warren's book-plate.

THE FRENCH BIBLIOGRAPHY.

BEING A LIST OF THE PRINCIPAL WORKS REFERRING TO FRENCH
EX LIBRIS.

[Reprinted by kind permission of Walter Hamilton, Esq.]

A Guide to the Study of Book-plates (Ex Libris).   By the
Hon. J. Leicester Warren, M.A., London.
John Pearson, 1880.

Although not dealing especially with *French* ex libris, this guide is an
almost indispensable book of reference to every collector of book-
plates.

L'Amateur d'Autographes, April, 1872.

This contains an article by M. Maurice Tourneux, on the collection of
book-plates in the possession of M. Aglaüx Bouvenne, a well-known
artist and designer of book-plates.

Armorial du Bibliophile. Avec illustrations dans le texte.   Par
Joannis Guigard.
Paris, Bachelin-Deflorenne, 2 vols., royal 8vo, 1870–1873.

Contains many illustrations of super libris, which are frequently
useful in assisting to discover the owners of anonymous French
armorial book-plates.   (See also "Nouvel Armorial du Bibliophile.")

Bibliophile Français.   Gazette illustrée des amateurs de livres,
d'estampes, et de hautes curiosités.
Paris, 7 vols., royal 8vo, 1868–1873.

This work incorporates the "Armorial du Bibliophile" of Joannis
Guigard.

Les Bibliophiles, les Collectionneurs, et les Bibliothèques des
trois évêchés, 1552–1790.   Par Arthur Benoit (illustrated).   Paris, royal 8vo, 1884.

The Book-plate Collector's Miscellany.   Edited by Mr. W. H.
K. Wright, Borough Librarian, Plymouth.   Quarto, illustrated, 1890–1891.   Plymouth, W. H. Luke.

The Bookworm.   May, 1892.   A Hunt for Book-plates in
Paris.   By Walter Hamilton.
London, Elliot Stock.

Bulletin du Bouquiniste. Paris, No. 416, April 15, 1875.

Letter from the Comte de Longpérier-Grimoard on a Super Libris of Crozat, December 1 and 15, 1876. A letter from the Comte de Longpérier-Grimoard, " Une Marque inconnue."

La Curiosité Universelle.

A small weekly newspaper published at 1 Rue Rameau, Paris. This has contained several articles and letters on the topic of French ex libris, and advocates the formation of an Ex Libris Society in Paris. No. 228, June 1, 1891, À propos d'Ex Libris; No. 262, January 25, 1892, illustrated; No. 268, March 7, 1892, Article on ex libris; No. 269, March 14, 1892, illustrated.

Dictionnaire des devises des hommes de lettres, imprimeurs, libraires, bibliophiles, etc. Par Van de Haeghen, 1876–1879.

Étude sur les Ex Libris. Par le Comte de Longpérier-Grimoard. Seulis, 8vo, 8 pp., 1875.

A paper read before the Comité Archéologique de Senlis, December 11, 1874.

Les Ex Libris Français, depuis leur origine jusqu'à nos jours. Par A. Poulet-Malassis. Nouvelle édition, revue, très augmentée, et ornée de vingt-quatre planches.

Paris, P. Rouquette, royal 8vo, 1875.

Les Ex Libris, et les Marques de Possession du Livre. Par Henri Bouchot, du Cabinet des Estampes. Paris, Edouard Rouveyre. With numerous illustrations, 104 pp., 8vo, 1891.

Only 750 printed.

Les Ex Libris dans les trois Évêchés, Toul, Metz, Verdun, 1552–1790. Par Arthur Benoit. Paris, 8vo, 1883.

Les Ex Libris Oratoriens. Par le P. Ingold. Paris, Libraire Charles Poussielgue, Rue Cassette, 15, 1892.
Crown 8vo, 16 pp. With thirteen illustrations.

Les Ex Libris de Schoepflin. Par Arthur Benoit.
Paris, 8vo, 1883.

Reprinted, with illustrations, from " Le Bulletin de la Société pour la conservation des Monuments historiques d'Alsace." Second series.

Les Femmes Bibliophiles de la France. Avec 43 Planches d'Armoiries. Par E. Quentin-Bauchart.

Paris, 8vo, 1886.

The Journal of the Ex Libris Society. A. and C. Black, Soho Square, London. Quarto, illustrated, 1891–1892. (In progress.)

A monthly journal containing numerous articles on French book-plates.

Le Livre Moderne, Revue du Monde Littéraire.

Paris, Maison Quantin, 1891.

No. 19 (July, 1891) contains an article by M. Octave Uzanne, entitled, "Remarques sur quelques Ex Libris contemporains," with fac-similes of 36 interesting examples. No. 24 (December, 1891) contains an article in continuation of the above, entitled, "Quelques Nouveaux Ex Libris," also by M. Octave Uzanne, with many illustrations.

Des Marques et devises mises a leur livres par un grand nombre d'Amateurs.   Paris, De Rieffenberg, 1874.

Notice sur quelques Graveurs Nancedins, du XVIII siecle. Par M. Beaupré.   Nancy, Lucien Wiener, 8vo, 1862.

This work contains descriptions of a number of book-plates engraved by Dominique Collin.

Nouvelles Etudes sur l'Université de Pont-à-Mousson. Par M. Favier (illustrated).   Nancy, 1880.

Nouvel Armorial du Bibliophile, Guide de l'Amateur des Livres Armoriés.   Contenant la Reproduction de 2500 Armoiries et riches Reliures armoiriées.   Par Joannis Guigard. Paris, Emile Roudeau, 2 vols., 8vo. 1890.

Petite Revue d'Ex Libris Alsaciens. Par Auguste Stoeber. Avec un fac-simile d'un ancien Ex Libris (C. Wolf-hardt).   Millhouse, Veuve Bader, 12mo, 1881.

The author of this charming little pamphlet died a few years ago.

Le Serpent Embleme des Chirurgiens, et des Médecins.   Par Arthur Benoit.   6 pp. n.d.

An extract from "La Revue Nouvelle d'Alsace-Lorraine," which treats of serpents shown on book-plates.

CONCLUSION.

THE end of our pleasant task is reached; and it only remains to thank the gentle reader who has kindly followed us, and to re-assert as a parting word, that this work does not aspire to cover every point which collectors may wish to have decided. Its modest purpose will be served if any reader is led to take an interest in the subject, if collectors find it useful as an assistant in intelligent collecting, or an instigation to further and more careful research.

Undoubtedly, there lie in old garrets, bookcases, and forgotten cupboards, dust-covered books, in which some fortunate searcher will one day discover plates as yet unknown. It is hoped that any such will publish their success for the benefit of the steadily increasing number who find something interesting in these memorials of the past, and who take pleasure in their preservation and pride in their possession.

INDEX.

423

Malvians, 312, 339.
Manigault, Peter, 52.
Mann, John Preston, 59, 245.
Mann, Timothy, 27.
Martin, Luther, 155.
Marvin, Samuel Wesley, 366.
Maryland plates :

	LIST NUMBER.
Baltimore Liby. Co.,	50
Bonaparte,	89
Bozman,	101
Calvert,	133
Carmichael,	135
Carroll,	138
Chalmers,	144
Chase,	150
Duvall,	243
Forman,	280
Georgetown College,	299, 300
Guinaud,	337
Johnston,	436
Kerr,	452
Key,	453
McTavish,	544
Maxcy,	569
Read,	722
Roberts,	733
Sprigg,	816
Stewart,	824
Tayloe,	845

Massachusetts Historical Society, 78.
Massachusetts plates :

	LIST NUMBER.
Adams, J.,	3
Adams. J. Q.,	4, 5, 6, 7
Agar,	8
Allen,	13
American Academy,	17
Andover Theol. Inst.,	19
Andrew,	20
Andrews,	22, 23, 24
Apthorp,	26, 27, 28, 29
Atkinson,	38, 39
Auchmuty,	42
Baldwin,	46, 47
Barrell,	58
Barroll,	59
Beck,	68
Belcher,	71, 72
Blake,	82
Boston Architectural Library,	983

	LIST NUMBER
Boston Shakespeare Circulating Library,	93
Boston Social Law Libr'y,	94
Bowdoin,	97
Bowdoin College,	98
Boylston Med. Libr'y,	99, 100
Brazer,	103
Brown,	112
Cabot,	126
Callender,	132
Cary, Alpheus,	140
Cary, Thomas,	142
Chandler, Gardiner,	147
Chandler, John, Junr.,	148
Chandler, Rufus,	149
Chauncey,	151, 152, 153
Child, Isaac,	158, 159
Child, Thomas,	160
Cleveland,	170
Coffin,	173
Coffin, Hector,	174
Coffin, John,	175
Cooley,	182
Courtenay,	184
Cranch,	187
Curwen,	192
Cushing,	193
Dana, E. T.,	200
Dana, Francis,	201
Dana, R. H.,	202
Danforth,	203
Dartmouth College,	204
Dartmouth College, Social Friends,	205
De Blois, L.,	212
Dedham : Scripture Study Society,	214
Dering, N.H.,	218
Dering, T.,	219, 220
Dexter,	222
Dill,	223
Dolbeare,	225
Duane,	232
Dudley,	233
Dumaresque,	236
Dummer,	237
Emerson,	256
Erving,	258, 259
Evarts,	261
Everett,	263
Forbes,	279
Foster,	281
Foster, I,	282
Fownes,	284
Foxcroft,	285
Francis,	286

Matthews, Brander, 99.
Mauran, James Eddy, 16, 98; his collection, 378.
Maverick, Peter, 142.
  Peter Rushton, 6, 56, 140.
McGinley, Mary, 19.
McIlvaine, Bloomfield, 57, 157.
McKee, Thomas J., 357.
McMurtrie, 59.
Member of the Ex Libris Society, 384.
Middleton, Peter, 10.
Miller, Margaret M., 375.
Minot, 40.
Moat, Horatio Shepherd, 56.
Moral Library, 6, 7.
Morgan, Appleton, 341.
Morgan, Henry A., 356.
Mottoes, use of, 16, 17.
  different kinds, 21.
  languages used on, 21.
  against book-borrowing,21–27.
  from the Bible, 21, 22.
  school-boy, 23.
  care of books, 25–27.
  poetical, 24–26, 28.
  generous, 27.
  in praise of books and reading, 28.
  quotations used, 28.

Mounting plates, ways of, 382.
Murray, David, 353.
  John, Rev., 252, 253.

Name-labels, 16, 18, 19.
New England book-plates, 4, 87.
New Hampshire plates:

New Jersey plates:

New London Public Library, 73.
New York plates:

Volapük motto, 34.

Wadsworth, Jeremiah, iv.

Wallace, Allen, 364.

Waller, 8.

Warren, John C., 299, 300.
W., 300, 301.

Washington, Bushrod, 95, 96, 300.

Washington, George, his plate, 90; his motto, 30, 79; fraudulent, 91; genuine, 94.

Washington, D.C., plates:

LIST NUMBER.

Lenthall, 481
Ruff, 744

Watkinson Library, Hartford, 75.

Way, W. Irving, 368.

Webster, Daniel, 97.

Welsh mottoes, 33.

Weld, John (of Pomfret, Conn.), 18.

Wentworth, 53, 107.